# SYNTHESIZING RESEARCH

## Third Edition

D1459692

Applied Social Research Methods Series
Volume 2

# APPLIED SOCIAL RESEARCH
# METHODS SERIES

*Series Editors*
**LEONARD BICKMAN,** Peabody College, Vanderbilt University, Nashville
**DEBRA J. ROG,** Vanderbilt University, Washington, DC

Other volumes in this series are listed at the back of the book

# SYNTHESIZING RESEARCH

## Third Edition

## A Guide for Literature Reviews

## Harris Cooper

**Applied Social Research Methods Series**
**Volume 2**

SAGE Publications
*International Educational and Professional Publisher*
Thousand Oaks   London   New Delhi

*For information:*

SAGE Publications, Inc.
2455 Teller Road
Thousand Oaks, California 91320
E-mail: order@sagepub.com

SAGE Publications Ltd.
6 Bonhill Street
London EC2A 4PU
United Kingdom

SAGE Publications India Pvt. Ltd.
M-32 Market
Greater Kailash I
New Delhi 110 048 India

Printed in the United States of America

*Library of Congress Cataloging-in-Publication Data*
    Cooper, Harris
        Synthesizing research: A guide for literature reviews / by Harris
        Cooper. — 3rd ed.
            p.   cm. — (Applied social research methods ; v. 2)
        Rev. ed. of: Integrating research. 2nd ed. c1989.
        Includes bibliographical references and index.
        ISBN 0-7619-1347-5 (acid-free paper). — ISBN 0-7619-1348-3 (pbk.:
        acid-free paper)
            1. Social sciences—Research. I. Cooper, Harris    Integrating
        research. II. Title. III. Series: Applied social research methods
        series ; v. 2.
        H62.C5859 1998
        300'.72—dc21                                    97-33792

This book is printed on acid-free paper.

        00   01   02   03   10   9   8   7   6   5   4

| | |
|---|---|
| *Acquiring Editor:* | C. Deborah Laughton |
| *Editorial Assistant:* | Eileen Carr |
| *Production Editor:* | Astrid Virding |
| *Production Assistant:* | Lynn Miyata |
| *Typesetter/Designer:* | Danielle Dillahunt |
| *Cover Designer:* | Candice Harman |
| *Print Buyer:* | Anna Chin |

*To Elizabeth*

# CONTENTS

# PREFACE TO THE
# THIRD EDITION

Every scientific study begins with the researcher examining reports of previous studies related to the topic of interest. Without this step, researchers cannot expect to construct an integrated, comprehensive picture of the world. They cannot achieve the progress that comes from building on the efforts of others. Also, investigators working in isolation are doomed to repeat the mistakes made by their predecessors.

Until recently, little guidance was available for how to conduct a research synthesis—how to find, evaluate, and integrate previous studies. This book helps fill that void. It is intended for use by social, behavioral, and medical scientists who already possess a background in basic research methods and statistics.

The approach to research synthesis presented in this book represents a significant departure from how reviews had been conducted just 20 years ago. Instead of a subjective, narrative approach, this book presents an objective, systematic approach. Here, the reader will learn how to carry out an integration of research according to scientific principles and rules. The intended result is a research synthesis that can be replicated by others, can create consensus among scholars, and can focus debate in a constructive fashion. Most important, users of this approach should complete their research synthesis feeling knowledgeable and confident that their future primary research can make a contribution to the field.

The scientific approach to research synthesis has rapidly gained acceptance. In the years between the three editions, the procedures outlined in this book have changed from controversial practices to accepted ones. Indeed, in many fields this approach is now obligatory. The years have also brought improvements in synthesis techniques. The technology surrounding literature searching has changed dramatically. The theoretical underpinnings of meta-analysis—the statistical combination of studies—have been developed, and the application of these procedures has become more accessible. Many novel techniques have been applied to help present results. Methodologists have proposed ways to make syntheses more resistant to criticism. This third edition incorporates these changes.

Several institutions and individuals have been instrumental in the preparation of all three editions of this book. First, the United States Department of Education provided research support while the first and third editions of the manuscript were prepared. Special thanks go to seven former graduate students: Kathryn Anderson, Brad Bushman, Maureen Findley, Ken Ottenbacher, Pamela Hazelrigg, David Tom, and Julie Yu. Each performed a research review in their own area of interest under my supervision. Each has had their work serve as an example in the book and three of their efforts are used in the current edition to illustrate the abstract points. Three reference librarians, Jeanmarie Fraser, Kathleen Connors, and Judy Pallardy, helped with the sections on literature searching. Larry Hedges has examined my expositions of statistical techniques. Three more graduate students, Cyndi Kernahan, Laura Muhlenbruck, and Jeff Valentine, read and reacted to this third edition. Cathy Luebbering and Pat Shanks have typed, retyped, and proofread my manuscripts. My thanks to these friends and colleagues.

—Harris Cooper

# 1

# *Introduction*

This chapter presents a definition of the term *research synthesis,* a justification for why attention to research syntheses is important, and a five-stage model for the synthesis process. The chapter also introduces four research syntheses that serve as practical examples in the chapters that follow.

The pursuit of knowledge with the tools of science is a cooperative, interdependent enterprise. The hundreds of hours spent conducting a scientific study ultimately contribute just one piece to an enormous puzzle. The value of any single study is derived as much from how it fits with previous work as from the study's intrinsic properties. Although it is true that some studies receive more attention than others, this is typically because the piece of the puzzle they solve (or the puzzle they introduce) is extremely important, not because they are solutions in and of themselves.

## THE NEED FOR ATTENTION
## TO RESEARCH SYNTHESIS

Given the cumulative nature of science, trustworthy accounts of past research are a necessary condition for orderly knowledge building. Until recently, however, social science methodologists paid little attention to how investigators ought to find, evaluate, and integrate past research. This omission in methods became especially glaring when huge increases in the amount of social science research put the lack of synthesis procedures in bold relief. As the amount of research grew, so did the need for trustworthy research syntheses.

The ability to gain access to social science information also changed dramatically. In particular, retrieval of past work has been facilitated by the computer and the on-line literature search. The computer's ability to rapidly scan research abstracts has improved scientists' access to evidence, if they know how to use the technology.

Finally, the need for trustworthy accounts of past research was also heightened by growing specialization within the social sciences. Today, time constraints make it impossible for most social scientists to keep up with primary research except within a few topic areas of special interest to them. Three decades ago, Garvey and Griffith (1971) wrote about this situation in psychology:

> The individual scientist is being overloaded with scientific information. Perhaps the alarm over an "information crisis" arose because sometime in the last information doubling period, the individual psychologist became overburdened and could no longer keep up with and assimilate all the information being produced that was related to his primary specialty. (p. 350)

What was true three decades ago is still true today.


## GOALS AND PREMISES OF THE BOOK


The goal of this book is to serve as an introductory methods text on how to conduct a research synthesis in the social, behavioral, or medical sciences. It will apply the basic tenets of sound data gathering to the task of producing a comprehensive integration of past research on a topic. The rules of rigorous, systematic inquiry are the same whether the inquirer is conducting a primary study or a research synthesis. The two types of inquiry, however, require techniques specific to their purpose.

There is one critical premise underlying the methods described in this text: Integrating separate research projects into a coherent whole involves inferences as central to the validity of knowledge as the inferences involved in drawing conclusions from primary data analysis. The validity of conclusions based on research integrations cannot be taken for granted; validity must be evaluated against scientific standards. A social scientist performing a research synthesis makes numerous decisions that affect the outcomes of his or her work. Each choice may create threats to the outcome's trustworthiness. Therefore, if social science knowledge contained in research syntheses is to be believable, research synthesists must be required to meet the same rigorous methodological standards that are applied to primary researchers.

Substantial attention has been paid to validity issues in primary research (Bracht & Glass, 1968; Campbell, 1969; Campbell & Stanley, 1963; Cook & Campbell, 1979). Until recently, however, the social sciences lacked a conceptualization of the research integration process that provided systematic guidelines for evaluating the validity of synthesis outcomes. This book describes the organizing scheme that has emerged in recent years.

## DEFINITIONS OF LITERATURE REVIEWS

There are many terms that sometimes are used interchangeably to label the activities described in this book. These terms include *literature review, research review, integrative research review, research synthesis,* and *meta-analysis.* In fact, some of these terms are interchangeable, whereas some are broader or narrower in meaning than others.

The broadest term is literature review. Literature reviews typically appear as detailed independent works or as brief introductions to reports of new primary data. When a literature review appears independent of new data, it can serve many different purposes. It can have numerous different focuses, goals, perspectives, coverage strategies, organizations, and audiences (Cooper, 1988). For instance, literature reviews can focus on research outcomes, research methods, theories, applications, or all these. Literature reviews can attempt to integrate what others have done and said, to criticize previous scholarly works, to build bridges between related topic areas, to identify the central issues in a field, or all these.

The scope of a literature review that introduces a new primary study is typically quite narrow. It will be restricted to those theoretical works and empirical studies pertinent to the specific issue addressed by the new study.

Literature reviews combining two specific sets of focuses and goals appear most frequently in the scientific literature. The first type of literature review has been alternately called a research synthesis, integrative research review, or research review. Research syntheses focus on empirical studies and seek to summarize past research by drawing overall conclusions from many separate investigations that address related or identical hypotheses. The research synthesist hopes to present the state of knowledge concerning the relation(s) of interest and to highlight important issues that research has left unresolved. From the reader's viewpoint, a research synthesis is intended to "replace those earlier papers that have been lost from sight behind the research front" (Price, 1965, p. 513) and to direct future research so that it yields a maximum amount of new information.

The second kind of literature review is a theoretical review. Here, the reviewer hopes to present the theories offered to explain a particular phenomenon and to compare them in breadth, internal consistency, and the nature of their predictions. Theoretical reviews will typically contain descriptions of critical experiments already conducted or suggested, assessments of which theory is most powerful and consistent with known relations, and sometimes reformulations or integrations or both of abstract notions from different theories.

Often, a comprehensive literature review will address several of these sets of issues. Research syntheses are most common, however, and theoretical reviews will typically contain some synthesis of research. It is also not unusual for research syntheses to address multiple, related hypotheses. A synthesis might examine the relation between several different independent or predictor variables and a single dependent or criterion variable. For example, Brown (1996) summarized research on several types of antecedents to job involvement, including personality variables, job characteristics, supervisory variables, and role perceptions. Also, a synthesis might try to summarize research related to a series of temporally linked hypotheses. Harris and Rosenthal (1985) studied the mediation of interpersonal expectancy effects by first synthesizing research on how expectations affect the behavior of the person who holds the expectation and then synthesizing research on how this behavior influenced the behavior of the target.

The major emphasis of this book will be on research synthesis. Not only is this the most frequent kind of literature review in the social sciences but also it contains all the decision points present in other reviews—and some unique ones as well. I have chosen to favor the label "research synthesis" for these types of reviews because it is the label used by *The Handbook of Research Synthesis* (Cooper & Hedges, 1994), a text that describes approaches consistent with those presented here but in a more advanced manner. The term meta-analysis, often used as a synonym for research synthesis or research review, will be used in this book specifically to describe the quantitative procedures that a research synthesist uses to statistically combine the results of studies (these procedures are described in Chapter 5).

## STAGES OF RESEARCH SYNTHESIS

Textbooks on social science methodology present research projects as a sequenced set of activities. Although methodologists differ somewhat in their definitions of research stages, the most important distinctions in stages can be identified with a gratifying degree of consensus. Methodologists also agree that the sequencing of stages is not fixed: Practicing researchers often skip over one or more stages and sometimes move backward as well as forward (Judd, Smith, & Kidder, 1991).

In this book, the process of research synthesis will be conceptualized as containing five stages: (a) problem formulation; (b) data collection or the literature search; (c) data evaluation, in this case assessing the quality of studies; (d) analysis and interpretation; and (e) presentation of results. Each stage of the synthesis serves a function similar to the one it serves in primary research. For example, in both primary research and research synthesis the problem formulation stage involves defining the variables of interest, and the analysis and interpretation stage involves making a choice about what results are significant. Synthesists, like primary data collectors, can make different choices about how to carry out their inquiries. Differences in methodologies will create differences in conclusions. Most important, each methodological decision at each stage of a synthesis may enhance or undermine the trustworthiness of its conclusion or, in more scientific terms, create a threat to its validity. (A more formal definition of validity appears in Chapter 4).

The functions, sources of variance, and potential threats to validity associated with each stage of the synthesis process are summarized in Table 1.1. In the chapters that follow, each stage will be examined in greater detail.

*Problem Formulation Stage.* The first step in any research endeavor is to formulate the problem. During problem formulation, the variables involved in the inquiry are given both abstract and concrete definitions. At this stage, the researcher asks "What are the concepts I want to study?" and "What operations are expressions of these concepts?" The researcher must decide what distinguishes relevant from irrelevant material.

In Chapter 2, I examine the decision points encountered by a synthesist during the problem formulation stage. Included in this discussion will be answers to the following questions:

1. What affects a synthesist's decisions about the conceptual relevance of particular studies?
2. How should a synthesist handle hypotheses that involve the interaction of two or more independent variables?
3. What role should past reviews play in formulating a problem?

Chapter 2 will also present some concrete recommendations about what information a synthesist should collect from empirical studies that have been judged relevant to a problem area.

**TABLE 1.1**

Research Synthesis Conceptualized as a Research Project

Stage of Research

| Stage Characteristics | Problem Formulation | Data Collection | Data Evaluation | Analysis and Interpretation | Public Presentation |
|---|---|---|---|---|---|
| Research question asked | What evidence should be included in the review? | What procedures should be used to find relevant evidence? | What retrieved evidence should be included in the review? | What procedures should be used to make inferences about the literature as a whole? | What information should be included in the review report? |
| Primary function in review | Constructing definitions that distinguish relevant from irrelevant studies | Determining which sources of potentially relevant studies to examine | Applying criteria to separate "valid" from "invalid" studies | Synthesizing valid retrieved studies | Applying editorial criteria to separate important from unimportant information |
| Procedural differences that create variation in review conclusions | 1. Differences in included operational definitions<br>2. Differences in operational detail | Differences in the research contained in sources of information | 1. Differences in quality criteria<br>2. Differences in the influence of nonquality criteria | Differences in rules of inference | Differences in guidelines for editorial judgment |

| Sources of potential invalidity in review conclusions | 1. Narrow concepts might make review conclusions less definitive and robust | 1. Accessed studies might be qualitatively different from the target population of studies | 1. Nonquality factors might cause improper weighting of study information | 1. Rules for distinguishing patterns from noise might be inappropriate | 1. Omission of review procedures might make conclusions irreproducible |
| | 2. Superficial operational detail might obscure interacting variables | 2. People sampled in accessible studies might be different from target population of people | 2. Omissions in study reports might make conclusions unreliable | 2. Synthesis-based evidence might be used to infer causality | 2. Omission of review findings and study procedures might make conclusions obsolete |

SOURCE: Cooper (1982). Copyright 1982 by the American Educational Research Association, Washington, DC. Reprinted by permission.

7

*The Literature Search.* The data collection stage of research involves making a choice about the population of elements that will be the target of the study. In primary social science research, the target will typically include individuals or groups. In research synthesis, identifying target populations is complicated by the fact that synthesists want to make inferences about two targets. First, they want the cumulative result to reflect the results of all previous research on the problem. Second, they hope that the included studies will allow generalizations to the individuals or groups that are the focus of the topic area.

In Chapter 3, I present a detailed discussion of methods for locating studies. The discussion includes a listing of the sources of studies available to social scientists, how to access and use the most important sources, and what biases may be present in the information contained in each source.

*Data Evaluation Stage.* After data are collected, the researcher makes critical judgments about the quality of data. Each data point is examined in light of surrounding evidence to determine whether it is too contaminated by factors irrelevant to the problem under consideration to be of value. If it is, the bad data must be discarded or given little credibility. For example, primary researchers examine how closely the research protocol was followed when each participant took part in the study. Research synthesists evaluate the methodology of studies to determine if they were carried out properly.

In Chapter 4, I discuss how to evaluate the quality of research. I also look at biases in quality judgments and make some suggestions concerning the assessment of interjudge reliability. Also, Chapter 4 contains some recommendations concerning what synthesists can do when research reports are unavailable or when obtained reports do not have the needed information.

*Analysis and Interpretation Stage.* During analysis and interpretation, the separate data points collected by the researcher are synthesized into a unified statement about the problem. Interpretation demands that the researcher distinguish systematic data patterns from "noise" or chance fluctuation. In both primary research and research synthesis, this process involves the application of statistical procedures.

In Chapter 5, I explain some methods for combining the results of separate studies. I also show how to estimate the size or magnitude of a relation. Finally, I illustrate some techniques for analyzing why different studies find different relationship strengths.

*Public Presentation Stage.* Creating a public document that describes the investigation is the task that completes a research endeavor. In Chapter 6, I offer some concrete guidelines on how to report research syntheses.

## FOUR EXAMPLES OF
## RESEARCH SYNTHESIS

I have chosen four research syntheses to illustrate the practical aspects of conducting rigorous summaries of research. The topics of the four reviews represent a broad spectrum of social science research, encompassing qualitatively different kinds of research. They involve diverse conceptual and operational variables. Even though the topics are diverse, they are also general enough that readers in any discipline should find all four topics instructive and easy to follow without a large amount of background in the separate research areas. A brief introduction to each topic will be helpful, however.

*The Effect of Homework on Academic Achievement (Cooper, 1989).* Requiring students to carry out academic tasks during nonschool hours is a practice as old as formal schooling itself. The effectiveness of homework, however, is still a source of controversy. Public opinion about homework has fluctuated throughout the twentieth century. Past summaries of the homework research concluded that homework had positive effects or no effects, that the research was inconclusive, or that the effects of homework were mediated by too many circumstantial variables for any general conclusion to be drawn.

In examining the literature, this illustrative synthesis uncovered 10 different questions motivating homework research. Three dealt with the general issue of whether homework is effective and 7 with variations in homework procedures (e.g., the effects of grading homework assignments). Two questions relating to homework's overall utility asked whether students doing homework outperformed students doing no homework or doing in-class supervised study. The third question asked whether the amount of homework students do correlates with their achievement. The results of research examining only the first question will be used here as an example: Do students doing homework achieve better than students receiving no homework and no alternative compensatory treatment?

*Personality Moderators of Interpersonal Expectancy Effects in Labora-*
*tory Experiments (Cooper & Hazelrigg, 1988)*. One of the best established
findings in social psychology is that the expectations one person holds for
another can affect the other person's behavior. Empirical tests of interpersonal expectancy effects were first carried out in laboratory settings. Naive
experimenters were led to believe photos of faces would receive either
success or failure ratings from subjects. In fact, identical photos were used
in both conditions. Results revealed experimenters expecting more successful ratings obtained more successful ratings from their subjects.

Realizing that not all people are equally susceptible to interpersonal
expectancy effects, efforts were then undertaken to identify personality
variables that might moderate the degree to which expectancies influenced
behavior. When the literature was searched, it was found that five general
hypotheses guided this research. Three hypotheses related to the experimenter. These proposed that experimenters who had a greater need to
influence others, who were better encoders of nonverbal messages, and
who made a more favorable impression on their subjects should produce
more dramatic interpersonal expectancy effects. Two hypotheses related to
the subject. These proposed that subjects who were more acquiescent and
who were better decoders of nonverbal messages ought to be more prone
to behave in the way the experimenter expected. Cooper and Hazelrigg
(1988) undertook collecting and summarizing research testing these five
hypotheses.

*The Effects of Alcohol on Human Aggression (Bushman & Cooper,*
*1990)*. People have long assumed that humans behave more aggressively
when they are under the influence of alcohol. The purpose of this research
synthesis was to summarize studies meant to determine if a causal relationship exists between alcohol consumption and aggressive interpersonal
behavior. To accomplish this goal, the authors collected experimental
research in which participants were randomly assigned either to consume
or not consume alcohol and were then placed in a situation that afforded
an opportunity to aggress or not aggress against another person.

The research literature contained many variations on this simple para-
digm. Most important, some researchers were interested in whether it is the
physiological effects of alcohol or the social expectancies surrounding
alcohol consumption that influence aggression. These researchers manipulated how participants were treated in the "no alcohol" condition. Some
studies included a placebo condition in which participants not receiving
alcohol were told a beverage they consumed contained alcohol. Other
studies included an "antiplacebo" condition in which participants were told

they would not receive alcohol, but they actually did receive alcohol. These manipulations helped researchers compare the accuracy of prediction made by different theories of how alcohol influences human aggression. Bushman and Cooper's (1990) research synthesis also examined a host of potential influences on the size of the alcohol-aggression relationship. These included the type and quantity of alcohol consumed, whether a nonaggressive alternative behavior was available to the participant, and whether the experimenter was unaware of the condition of the participant.

*Individual Differences in Attitudes Toward Rape (Anderson, Cooper, & Okamura, 1997).* Rape is a serious social problem. Every day, hundreds of woman without their consent are forced by men to have sex. This research synthesis examined the demographic, cognitive, experiential, affective, and personality correlates of attitudes toward rape. Demographic correlates of attitudes toward rape included age, ethnicity, and socioeconomic status. Experiential correlates included involvement in previous rapes, knowing others who had been in a rape, and use of violent pornography. Personality correlates included the need for power and dominance and self-esteem. The authors found research that examined the attitudes of both men and women.

What value is there in summarizing research on rape attitudes? Anderson et al. (1997) hoped to improve programs meant to prevent rape by helping identify people who would benefit most from rape interventions. The synthesis might also uncover what correlates of rape attitudes—for example, a person's acceptance of interpersonal violence—might also be the target of rape interventions.

## EXERCISE

The best exercise to carry out while reading this book is to conduct a research synthesis in an area of interest to you. The synthesis should attempt to apply the guidelines outlined in the chapters that follow. If this is not possible, try to conduct the more discrete exercises that appear at the end of each chapter. Often, these exercises can be further simplified by dividing the work among members of your class.

# 2

# *The Problem*
# *Formulation Stage*

**This chapter describes the process of formulating a hypothesis for guiding a research synthesis. Topics include the consideration of concepts and operations, the distinction between study-generated and synthesis-generated evidence, the treatment of main effects and interactions, the role of previous syntheses in new synthesis efforts, the development of coding sheets to gather information from primary research reports, and the threats to validity that arise during problem formulation.**

All empirical work must begin with a careful consideration of the research problem. In its most basic form, the research problem includes the definition of variables and the rationale for relating the variables to one another. The rationale can be that a theory predicts a particular association between the variables (as in confirmatory research) or that some practical or intuitive consideration suggests that a discovered relation might be important (as in exploratory research). Either rationale can be used for undertaking primary research or research synthesis.

The choice of a problem to study in primary research is influenced by the interests of researchers and the social conditions that surround them. This holds true as well for the choice of topics in research synthesis, with an important difference. Primary researchers are limited in their topic choice only by their imaginations. Research synthesists must study topics that already appear in the literature. In fact, a topic is probably not suitable for research synthesis unless it already has created sufficient interest within a discipline or disciplines to have inspired enough research to merit an effort at bringing it all together.

The fact that syntheses are tied to only those problems that have generated previous research does not mean research synthesis is less creative than primary data collection. Rather, creativity is used in different ways in research synthesis. Creativity enters when the investigator must propose overarching schemes that help make sense of many related but not identical studies. Also, more often than not, the cumulative results of studies are much more complex than the results of any single study. The synthesist's capacity for uncovering variables that explain why results differ in different studies and the ability to generate notions that explain these higher-order relations are the most creative and challenging aspects of the research synthesis process.


## DEFINITION OF VARIABLES
## IN SOCIAL SCIENCE RESEARCH


### Similarities Between Primary
### Research and Research Synthesis

The variables involved in any social science study must be defined in two ways. First, the variables must be given conceptual definitions. These describe qualities of the variable that are independent of time and space but that can be used to distinguish events that are and are not relevant to the concept. For instance, a conceptual definition of *achievement* might be "a person's level of knowledge in academic domains." *Aggression* might be defined as "behavior meant to harm another living being."

Conceptual definitions can differ in breadth—that is, in the number of events to which they refer. Thus, if achievement is defined as "something gained through effort or exertion," the concept is broader than it is using the first definition. The second definition would consider as achievement goals reached in social, physical, and political spheres, as well as academic ones. When concepts are broader, we can also say they are more abstract.

Both primary researchers and research synthesists must choose a conceptual definition and a degree of breadth for their problem variables. Both must decide how likely it is that an event represents an instance of the variable of interest.

To relate concepts to concrete events, a variable must also be operationally defined. An operational definition is a description of the observable events that determine if a concept is present in a particular situation. In other words, a concept is operationally defined when "the conditions that produce the concept are carefully specified" (Elmes, Kantowitz, & Roediger, 1995, p. 50). An operational definition of the concept *interpersonal expectancy effect* might include "the difference between subjects' responses when the experimenter is expecting a certain behavior (e.g., success) versus when the experimenter is expecting the opposite behavior (e.g., failure)." Again, both primary researchers and research synthesists must specify the operations included in their conceptual definitions.

## Differences Between Primary
## Research and Research Synthesis

Some differences in the defining of variables can also be found between the two types of research. Primary researchers have little choice but to define their concepts operationally before they begin their studies. They cannot start data collection until variables have been given an empirical reality. A primary researcher studying aggression must define how aggression will be measured before running the first subject.

Synthesists, however, need not be quite so conceptually precise, at least not initially. For them, the literature search can begin with only a conceptual definition and a few known operations that measure it. Then, the concept and associated operations can grow more precise as they become more familiar with the research. Synthesists have the comparative luxury of being able to evaluate the conceptual relevance of different operations as they appear in the literature. For example, a synthesist interested in homework can decide after the literature search has begun whether after-school tutoring is "within" the conceptual definition.

Of course, some a priori specification of operations is necessary and most synthesists begin with empirical realizations in mind. During a literature search, however, it is not unusual for synthesists to come across operations that they did not know existed but are relevant to the construct being studied. In summary, a primary researcher usually knows exactly what events constitute the domain to be sampled before beginning data collection. A research synthesist may discover unanticipated elements of the domain along the way.

Another distinction between the two types of inquiry is that a primary study typically involves only one, and sometimes two, operational definitions of the same construct. In contrast, research syntheses usually involve many empirical realizations. Although no two participants are treated exactly alike in any single study, this variation will ordinarily be small compared to variation introduced by the differences in laboratories, sampled populations, treatments, measurements, and analysis techniques used in separate studies (Light & Pillemer, 1984). The multiple operations contained in research syntheses introduce a set of unique issues that must be examined carefully.

## MULTIPLE OPERATIONS
## IN RESEARCH SYNTHESIS

*The "Fit" Between Concepts and Operations.* Research synthesists must be aware of two potential incongruities that may arise because of the variety of operations in the literature. First, synthesists expecting to find many operations may begin a literature search with broad conceptual definitions. They may discover, however, that the operations used in previous relevant research have been quite narrow. For instance, the synthesis of research on rape attitudes might have begun with a broad definition of rape, including instances of women forcing sex on men. If this were the case, the literature search would have led to disappointment because the vast majority of past research dealt only with men as the perpetrators of rape. When such a circumstance arises, the synthesist must narrow the conceptual underpinnings of the effort to be more congruent with existing operations. Otherwise, the conclusions will appear more general than warranted by the data.

The opposite problem, using narrow concepts defined by multiple broad measures, can also confront a synthesist. This might have occurred if the aggression and alcohol synthesis had initially sought only physical measures of aggression, but the literature search revealed that many other types of aggressive behavior, such as verbal insults, were used as dependent variables. The synthesists would then have faced the choice of either broadening the concept or excluding many studies.

As the literature search proceeds, it is extremely important that synthesists take care to reevaluate the correspondence between the breadth or abstractness of their concepts and the variation in operations that primary researchers have used to define them. In primary research, this redefinition of a problem as a study proceeds is frowned on. In research synthesis, it appears that some flexibility may be necessary and may indeed be beneficial.

*Multiple Operationism and Concept-to-Operation Correspondence.* Webb, Campbell, Schwartz, Sechrest, and Grove (1981) presented strong arguments for the value of multiple operationism. They define *multiple operationism* as the use of many measures that share a conceptual definition "but have different patterns of irrelevant components" (p. 35). Multiple operationism has positive consequences because

> once a proposition has been confirmed by two or more independent measurement processes, the uncertainty of its interpretation is greatly reduced. . . . If a proposition can survive the onslaught of a series of

> imperfect measures, with all their irrelevant error, confidence should be placed in it. Of course, this confidence is increased by minimizing error in each instrument and by a reasonable belief in the different and divergent effects of the sources of error. (p. 35)

Although Webb and colleagues hold out the potential for strengthened inferences when a variety of operations exists, their qualification must also be underscored. Multiple operations can enhance concept-to-operation correspondence if all or most of the measures encompassed in the research synthesis are at least minimally valid. This reasoning is akin to the reasoning applied in classical measurement theory. Small correlations between individual items on a test or questionnaire and a "true" score can add up to a reliable indicator if a sufficient number of minimally valid items are present. The test (in this case, conclusion of the synthesis) will be invalid, however, if the majority of items (in this case, operations) bear no correspondence to the underlying concept or the items (operations) share a different concept to a greater degree than they share the intended one. This is true regardless of how many items (or operations) are involved.

The research synthesist must examine research designs for threats to the correspondence of operations and concepts. If the research designs uncovered by a literature search contain the same invalidating procedures, then the correspondence between operations and concepts is threatened. The synthesis of research concerning homework and achievement provided a good example. All the homework studies were conducted in naturally occurring classrooms. These studies often involved only a small sample of classrooms, with only one or two classrooms in the homework and no-homework conditions. Furthermore, many were conducted as theses or dissertations by teachers using their own students as participants. Therefore, knowingly or unknowingly, the teacher can treat the students in the classes differently in ways other than whether or not he or she assigned homework. If all the studies uncovered by the literature search were conducted by teachers teaching both homework conditions, then the rival hypothesis that "differences in how students were treated other than homework might account for achievement differences" could not be ruled out, no matter how many studies had been conducted. Luckily, studies were also conducted in which different teachers were randomly assigned to either homework or no-homework conditions or in which homework was manipulated within the same class.

Investigations of alcohol effects on aggression provide a similar example. In some studies, the experimenter was kept unaware of the subjects' alcohol and alcohol-expectancy conditions, whereas in other studies the experimenter was aware of the subjects' status on the two manipulations. The synthesists found that the effects of alcohol were larger in the "aware" studies. Thus, had all studies been conducted with aware experimenters, the effect of alcohol would have been overestimated—it would have confounded alcohol effects with experimenter expectancy effects. In other words, the operationalization of "under the influence of alcohol" would have included other systematic but unrelated operations—in this case, differences in treatment by the experimenter based on the subjects' expected behavior.

In summary, the existence of a variety of operations in research literatures presents the potential benefit of stronger inferences if it allows the synthesist to rule out irrelevant sources of influence. Multiple operations, however, do not ensure concept-to-operation correspondence if all or most of the operations lack minimal correspondence to the concept or if research designs all share a similar confounding of unintended influences with intended ones.

*Substituting New Concepts for Old Ones.* Perhaps the most challenging circumstance in the social sciences occurs when a new concept is introduced to explain old findings. For example, in a classic social psychology experiment the notion of cognitive dissonance was used to explain why an individual who is paid $1 to voice a counterattitudinal argument subsequently experiences greater attitude change than another person paid $25 to perform the same activity (Festinger & Carlsmith, 1959). Dissonance theory suggests that because the amount of money is not sufficient to justify the espousal of the counterattitudinal argument, the person feels discomfort that can be reduced only through a shift in attitude. Bem (1967), however, recast the results of this experiment by proposing a self-perception theory. Briefly, he speculated that participants who observed themselves espousing counterattitudinal arguments inferred their opinions the same way as an observer: Participants who observe themselves making an argument for $1 assume that because they are performing the behavior with little justification they must feel positive toward the attitude in question.

No matter how many replications of the $1/$25 experiment were uncovered, a research synthesist could not use the results to evaluate the correctness of the two theories. The research synthesist must take care to differentiate concepts and theories that predict similar and different results for the same set of operations. If predictions are different, the accumulated evidence can be used to evaluate the correctness of one theory or another or the different circumstances in which each theory is correct. If the theories make identical predictions, however, no comparative judgment based on research outcomes is possible.

*The Use of Operations Not Originally Related to the Concept.* Literature searches often uncover research that has been cast in a conceptual framework different from the synthesist's but that includes measures or manipulations relevant to the concepts the synthesist had in mind. For instance, there are several concepts similar to interpersonal expectancy effects that appear in the research literature (e.g., behavior confirmation). When relevant operations associated with different abstract constructs are identified, they most certainly should be considered for inclusion in the synthesis. In fact, different concepts and theories behind similar operations can often be used to demonstrate the robustness of results. There probably is no better way to ensure that operations contain different patterns of irrelevant components than to have different researchers with different theoretical backgrounds perform related experiments.

*The Effects of Multiple Operations on Synthesis Outcomes.* Multiple operations do more than introduce the potential for clearer inferences about conceptual variables. They are also the most important source of variance in the conclusions of different syntheses meant to address the same topic. A variety of operations can affect synthesis outcomes in the following two ways:

1. *Variance in operational definitions:* The operational definitions used in two research syntheses on the same topic can be different from one another. As noted earlier, two synthesists using an identical label for an abstract concept can employ very different operational definitions. Each definition may contain some operations excluded by the other, or one definition may completely contain the other.

2. *Variance in operational detail:* Multiple operations also affect outcomes by leading to variation in the attention synthesists pay to methodological distinctions in the literature. This effect is attributable to differences in the way study operations are treated after the literature has been searched. At this point, research synthesists become detectives who search for "distinctive clues about why two variables are related differently under different conditions" (Cook et al., 1992, p. 22). They use the observed data patterns as clues for generating explanations that specify the conditions under which a positive, null, or negative relationship will be found between two variables.

Synthesists differ in how much detective work they undertake. Some pay careful attention to study operations. They decide to identify meticulously the operational and sample distinctions among retrieved studies. Other synthesists feel that method- or participant-dependent relations are unlikely or may simply use less care.

## Synthesis Examples

Two of the four research synthesis examples provide good illustrations of differences in breadth of definitions and fit between concepts and operations. The search for personality moderators of interpersonal expectancy effects uncovered 32 different scales used to measure experimenter personality and 27 scales used for subjects' personality. Eight different scales were used to measure the experimenter's need for social influence, 9 to measure expressiveness, and 11 to measure likability (4 measured constructs unrelated to the hypotheses). For subjects, 11 different scales were used to measure influenceability. Clearly, multiple operations have been used in this area. Thus, because multiple operations were used, we can be fairly certain that other personality variables confounded with any single scale had little effect on conclusions regarding these four hypotheses. Although the broad hypotheses may appear to be covered by the multiple scales, however, nearly all the measures were of the paper-and-pencil variety. Therefore, we must still entertain the possibility that confounds associated with paper-and-pencil tests (such as the social desirability of answers and evaluation apprehension) may still be confounded with personality in the synthesis' results.

Four different operationalizations were used to measure interpersonal expectancy effects. The simplest operation used raw score ratings and entered the different expectancy condition (e.g., the success or failure of the person in a photo) into an analysis of variance along with the personality dimension. Other procedures defined expectancy effects by looking at the discrepancy between the expected and obtained ratings. These measures differ not only in how they were calculated but also in whether they defined an expectancy effect by the extremity of the obtained rating or by the accuracy with which the obtained rating reflected the expectation—two very different ways of viewing the phenomenon.

Whereas "personality" is a broad construct that could encompass many dimensions and measures, "attitudes toward rape" is a much narrower idea. Once the term *rape* was defined as "sexual intercourse between a man and a woman without the woman's consent," the literature search uncovered 17 different measures of rape attitudes but only 5 that were used with much frequency. These measures varied somewhat in how attitudes were defined. Two focused on general belief statements about rape, 1 on the acceptance of myths surrounding rape, 1 on attributions of blame for rape, and 1 on the degree of empathy for the rapist and rape victim.

The concept used to define predictors of rape attitudes, "individual differences," however, was extremely broad and diffuse. Seventy-four distinct individual difference variables were identified that could be clustered into broad groups consisting of demographic, cognitive, experiential, affective, and personality measures. Much of the creative challenge and reward in doing research synthesis lies in identifying groupings such as these and making sense of their different relationships.

## JUDGING THE CONCEPTUAL
## RELEVANCE OF STUDIES

So far, I have left a fundamental question unanswered: How were studies judged to be conceptually relevant in the first place? The rules synthesists use to distinguish relevant from irrelevant studies determine the degree of fit between concepts and operations.

Information scientists have examined what makes a study relevant to a research problem. Regrettably, the degree of concept abstractness that a literature searcher employs has not been examined as an influence on the relevance judgment. It has been shown, however, that judgments about the relevance of studies to a literature search are related to open-mindedness and expertise in the area (Davidson, 1977), whether the decision is based on titles or abstracts (Cooper & Ribble, 1989), and even the amount of time the searcher has for making relevance decisions (Cuadra & Katter, 1967). Thus, although the conceptual definition and level of abstractness that a synthesist chooses for a problem are certainly two influences on which studies are deemed relevant, a multitude of other factors also affect this screening of information.

The only general recommendation that can be made with regard to conceptual relevance is that the synthesist should begin the literature search with the broadest conceptual definition in mind. In determining the acceptability of operations for inclusion within the broad concept, the synthesist again should remain as open-minded as possible. At later stages—notably, during data evaluation—it is possible to exclude particular operations due to their lack of relevance. In the problem formulation and search stages, however, the synthesist should err on the overly inclusive side, just as a primary researcher collects some data that might not later be used in analyses. It is very distressing to find out after studies have been retrieved and cataloged that available pieces of the puzzle were passed over and a new search must be conducted.

A broad conceptual search also allows the synthesis to be done with greater operational detail. The benefits of broad conceptualizations are underscored many times in the chapters that follow.

## Synthesis Examples

The synthesis of the effectiveness of homework faced several problems concerning whether to include certain kinds of operations. Behavior therapists often assign their clients "homework," or exercises meant to help them overcome phobias. A broad conceptualization might include this type of homework. Closer to the usual school-related meaning, some students receive tutoring after school hours. Others take study-at-home television or videocassette courses. Some ways to define the concept of homework might include all or any of these activities. Ultimately, the decision was made to exclude these types of homework by defining it as "tasks assigned to students by school teachers that are meant to be carried out during nonschool hours."

The alcohol and rape attitude syntheses presented fewer cases in which studies were difficult to classify as relevant or irrelevant. The manipulation of alcohol in an aggression study was always clear-cut, as was whether or not a researcher measured participants' attitudes toward rape. What constituted an act of aggression or how to define an individual difference, however, was more problematic. Decisions about how to handle operations at the boundaries of these definitions (e.g., Is verbal taunting aggression? Are attitudes toward dating a stable individual difference?) would likely lead to some disagreement among different social scientists.

## RELATIONS BETWEEN DIFFERENT
## CONCEPTS IN RESEARCH SYNTHESIS

The problems that motivate most research syntheses initially involve relations between two variables. There is a simple explanation for this: Bivariate relationships have typically been tested more often than any given interaction involving three variables. Two of the four synthesis examples—homework and achievement and alcohol and aggression—took a bivariate relation as the initial focus. The synthesis on rape attitudes and individual differences related a single conceptual variable to a host of other conceptual variables but still did so one variable at a time. All these syntheses, however, also examined potential influences on the bivariate relationship. The synthesis examining personality moderators of interpersonal expectancy effects began by examining a three-variable relationship. The bivariate relationship involved the impact of interpersonal expectancies on behavior, but the relation of interest involved how this association was influenced by the personality of the expecter and target.

Although some specific interactional hypotheses in the social sciences have generated enough interest to require independent research synthesis, for the vast majority of topics the initial problem formulation will involve a two-variable question. Again, however, the initial undertaking of the synthesis to establish the existence of a bivariate relationship should in no way diminish the attention paid to discovering interactive or moderating influences. Indeed, discovering that a two-variable relationship exists quite often would be viewed as a trivial contribution by the research community. If bivariate relationships are found to also be moderated by third variables, however, these findings are viewed as a step forward in understanding and are given inferential priority. Even when an interaction is the primary focus of a synthesis, the search for higher-order interactions should continue. Thus, the synthesis of personality moderators examined whether these interaction effects were more or less likely to appear under different circumstances, including the presence of incentives for the experimenter to obtain expectancy effects and the degree of ambiguity in the expectancy task. More will be said on the relations between variables in Chapter 5, which discusses how main effects and interactions are interpreted in research synthesis.

## STUDY-GENERATED AND SYNTHESIS-GENERATED EVIDENCE

There are two different sources of evidence about relations contained in research syntheses. The first type is called *study-generated evidence.* Study-generated evidence is present when a single study contains results that directly test the relation being considered. Research syntheses also contain evidence that does not come from individual studies but rather from the variations in procedures across studies. This type of evidence, called *synthesis-generated evidence,* is present when the results of studies using different procedures to test the same hypothesis are compared to one another.

Any relation, either causal or simple association, can be examined through either study- or synthesis-generated evidence. Only study-generated evidence based on experimental research, however, allows the synthesist to make statements concerning causality. An example will clarify the point. With regard to alcohol and aggression studies, suppose we are interested in whether distilled alcoholic beverages (e.g., vodka) and brewed alcoholic beverages (e.g., beer) have different effects on aggression. Suppose also that 16 studies were found that randomly assigned participants to alcohol and no-alcohol experimental conditions. The accumulated results of these studies could then be interpreted as supporting or not supporting the idea that alcohol causes aggressive behavior. Now assume that we uncovered 8 studies that compared only distilled alcohol to a no-alcohol control group and 8 other studies that compared only brewed alcohol to no-alcohol controls. If this synthesis-generated evidence revealed more aggressive behavior when participants had distilled alcohol than brewed alcohol, then we could infer an association but not a causal relation between type of alcohol and aggression.

Why is this the case? Causal direction is not the problem with synthesis-generated evidence. It would be foolish to argue that the amount of aggression by participants caused the experimenters' choice of alcoholic beverage. Still problematic, however, is another ingredient of causality—the absence of potential third variables causing the relation, or nonspuriousness. A multitude of third variables are potentially confounded with the original experimenters' choices of alcoholic beverage. For instance, the experimenters who used distilled alcohol may also have employed more sensitive measures for assessing aggression or greater blood alcohol levels than experimenters who used brewed beverages.

Synthesis-generated evidence cannot legitimately rule out other variables confounded with the study characteristic of interest as possible true causes. Spuriousness cannot be eliminated because the synthesist did not randomly assign alcohol types to experiments. It is the ability to employ random assignment of participants that allows primary researchers to assume third variables are represented equally in the experimental conditions.

*Studying Descriptive Statistics or Bivariate Relationships Using Synthesis-Generated Evidence.* The distilled versus brewed alcohol example illustrates how synthesis-generated evidence is used to examine a third variable's influence on the strength or direction of a two-variable relationship. As in this example, most synthesis-generated evidence examines some type of interactional hypothesis.

It is also possible to integrate descriptive evidence across studies, or what Rosenthal (1991) calls "aggregate analysis." For example, the homework synthesis might have asked the question, "On average, how much homework do students report doing?" This question would have led me to collect from each study the average amount of time students reported spending on homework. Then, I would have averaged these averages.

This descriptive evidence could have been used to look at bivariate associations. For example, I might have examined whether the average amounts of homework were different when studies that sampled elementary school students were compared with studies that sampled high school students.

It is often difficult to aggregate descriptive statistics or to test bivariate relationships with this type of synthesis-generated evidence. This is because social scientists often use different scales to measure their variables. Suppose I wanted to aggregate across studies descriptive levels of achievement. This would be very difficult, if not impossible, if some studies were found that measured achievement using teacher-made tests and others standardized tests and if, among standardized tests, some reported raw scores and others reported grade-level equivalent scores. The time-on-homework example produces much less difficulty. Metrics for measuring time should be consistent across studies or easily convertible, one to another (e.g., hours to minutes).

The problem of nonstandard measurements is lessened when study characteristics are tested as third variables because the bivariate relationships within the studies can be transformed into standardized effect size estimates, thus controlling for different scales (see Chapter 5). The problem of incommensurable scales, however, remains when third variables are examined across studies.

It is important for synthesists to keep the distinction between study-generated and synthesis-generated evidence in mind. Only evidence coming from experimental manipulations within a single study can support assertions concerning causality. The occasional lesser strength of synthesis-generated evidence with regard to causal inferences, however, does not mean this evidential base should be ignored. The use of synthesis-generated evidence allows testing of relations that may have never been examined by primary researchers. For example, it may be the case that no previous primary study has examined whether the relation between homework and achievement is different at different grade levels or whether different types of alcoholic beverages differ in whether they cause aggression. By searching across studies for variations in grade level or alcohol type, synthesists can produce the first evidence on these potentially critical moderating variables. Even though this evidence is equivocal, it is a major benefit of research synthesis and a source of potential hypotheses for future primary research.

## THE ROLE OF PAST SYNTHESES

If a topic has a long history of research, it is likely that a synthesist will find that previous attempts at integration already exist. Obviously, these efforts need to be scrutinized carefully before the new synthesis is undertaken. Past syntheses can help establish the necessity for a new one. This assessment process is much like that used in primary research before undertaking a new study.

There are several things a new synthesist can look for in past syntheses. First, previous syntheses can be examined to identify the positions of other scholars in the field. In particular, they can be used to determine whether conflicting conclusions exist about the evidence and, if they do, what has caused the conflict.

Second, an examination of past syntheses can assess the earlier efforts' completeness and validity. For example, Cooper and Dorr (1995) compared a statistical synthesis of research on race differences in need for achievement to a nonquantitative synthesis on the same topic (Graham, 1994). Using the same studies, Cooper and Dorr demonstrated that the nonquantitative conclusions missed some important relationships and used different criteria for "significance" in different research domains.

Past syntheses can also be an important aid in identifying interacting variables that the new synthesists might wish to examine. Rather than restart the compilation of potential moderating variables, previous synthesists will undoubtedly offer many suggestions based on their own intellect and reading of the literature. If more than one synthesis of an area has been conducted, the new effort will be able to incorporate all the suggestions.

Finally, past syntheses allow the new one to begin the compilation of a relevant bibliography. Most syntheses will have fairly lengthy bibliographies. If more than one exists, their citations will overlap somewhat but may also be quite distinct. Along with other techniques described in Chapter 3, the research cited in past syntheses provides an excellent place for the new synthesist to start the literature search.

**Synthesis Examples**

Of the four synthesis examples, homework and achievement is the one that best demonstrates the use of past syntheses. Nine previous independent efforts to integrate the literature were found that made statements about whether homework affected academic achievement. Given that so many past syntheses existed, it was necessary to justify the need for yet a tenth review. First, I showed that the nine older syntheses differed dramatically in their general conclusions concerning homework's effectiveness. Second, different syntheses examined different sets of variables posited as modera- tors of homework's effects. Third, when the same moderators were exam- ined, past synthesists sometimes drew opposite conclusions about their effects. Fourth, it was found that none of the past efforts were very comprehensive—no single one included more than 60% of the total re- search base uncovered by all the literature searches. Therefore, the new synthesis could be used to resolve conflicts between previous ones, to examine all at once the proposed moderators of homework's effects, and to include a more comprehensive research base. It was not claimed, however, that the past syntheses were of no use—they helped in the development of a conceptual framework for describing the homework process, laid out issues that needed to be addressed when the effects of homework were assessed, and suggested a comprehensive catalog of con- textual factors that might influence the utility of home study.

# THE RESEARCH SYNTHESIS
## CODING SHEET

Once the synthesist has formulated a problem and has an idea about what theorists, primary researchers, and previous synthesists have stated on the topic, the next step is to construct a coding sheet. The coding sheet is used to collect information from the primary research reports.

If the number of studies involved in the synthesis is small, it may not be necessary before the literature search begins to have a precise and complete idea about what information to extract from reports. The relevant reports, if only a dozen or so exist, can be retrieved, read, and reread until the synthesist has a good notion of what aspects of the studies would be interesting to code. Small sets of studies allow synthesists to follow up ideas that emerge only after several studies have already been read. They can return briefly to previously scrutinized studies to look for the new information.

If the synthesist expects to uncover a large amount of research, such a rereading of reports may be prohibitively time-consuming. In this instance, it is necessary for the synthesist to consider carefully what data will be retrieved from each research report before the formal search begins. It is important to pilot test these expectations against a few research reports and to modify the coding sheet so that a fairly standard and thorough examination of each research report can be conducted in a single reading. The rules for constructing a coding sheet are similar to those used in creating a coding frame and data matrix for a primary research effort (Bourque & Clark, 1992; Fowler, 1993).

The first rule in constructing a synthesis coding sheet is that any information that might have the remotest possibility of being considered relevant should be retrieved from the studies. Once the literature search has begun, it is exceedingly difficult to retrieve new information from studies that have already been coded. It is much less of a problem to include information that will not be used.

*Information to Include on the Coding Sheet.* There are certain pieces of information about primary research that every synthesist will want to include on a research synthesis coding sheet. Stock (1994) classified these items into seven categories: report identification, the setting of the study, subjects, methodology, treatment characteristics, statistical outcomes or effect sizes, and the coding process. The categories are explained as follows:

1. Report identification: First, the synthesist will want to retrieve information concerning the background characteristics of the research report itself: the authors of the report, the source of the report, when the report was published, and what information channel led to the report's discovery.

2. Setting of the study: This information most often includes the geographic location of the study (e.g., state or part of the country; urban, suburban, or rural). It can also include institutional surroundings (e.g., colleges vs. prisons for studies of rape attitudes) and even subtypes of institutions (e.g., public vs. private schools).

3. Subjects: Another area of information needed in syntheses involves the characteristics of the participants included in the primary research. It is clearly important to retrieve the number of participants in each condition of the study. The synthesist will also want to retrieve information concern-

ing the age of participants as well as any restrictions placed by the primary researchers on who could participate in the study.

4. Methodology: The synthesist will also want to retrieve information concerning the research design of the primary studies. The particular design characteristics of interest will vary from topic to topic. A comprehensive discussion of research designs and their interpretation can be found in Cook and Campbell (1979). Most research designs, however, are covered by five categories: one-group, pretest-posttest designs; correlational studies; nonequivalent control group or static-group comparisons (i.e., treatments are given to groups that existed before the research began); nonequivalent control group comparisons with matching or statistical control (i.e., a procedure was used to enhance the equivalence of intact groups); and random assignment designs.

   In some instances, this categorization will suffice. In other instances, different designs (e.g., time series) or finer distinctions in the designs described previously (e.g., distinctions between different matching or statistical control procedures) will need to be added.

   Other features of research design may also be relevant. Whether or not repeated measures or counterbalancing of treatments or both were used and the presence or absence of controls against experimenter bias might also be included.

5. Treatment characteristics: The synthesist will need to carefully describe the details of what went into manipulating or measuring the independent variables. What was the nature of the treatment? Did it vary in intensity and duration from study to study? Were manipulation checks taken and, if so, what did they reveal?

   Equally important are characteristics of how control or comparison groups were treated. Was there an alternate treatment? If so, what was it? If not, what did control groups do or how were they obtained? Differences among studies on any of these variables would be prime candidates for causes of differences in study outcomes.

   For studies involving personality or other multi-item scales, the synthesist will want to retrieve information concerning the names of the tests, whether or not they were standardized, the number of items they included, and the test's reliability, if this information is available. Similar information on the dependent variables used in experimental studies also needs to be cataloged carefully.

   Although experimental dependent variables are often answers to single questions or discrete behaviors, they too can vary in important ways from study to study. For example, experimental dependent variables can differ in their reactivity, sensitivity, or the length of delay before they are measured.

6. Statistical outcomes or effect sizes: Research synthesis coding sheets must also contain information on the outcomes of the study. First and most important, the coding sheet needs to identify the direction of outcomes of

comparisons. Was the hypothesis supported or refuted? What was the level of significance associated with the hypothesis test?

If a quantitative synthesis, or meta-analysis, of results is envisioned, the synthesist will also need to record more precise information on the statistical outcomes of studies. Because reporting of results varies from article to article and can take several different forms, it is possible to list the statistical outcomes of studies in terms of how desirable they are for use in quantitative synthesis. Listed from most to least desirable, these would be (a) the means, standard deviations, and sample sizes for each group in a comparison or hypothesis test; (b) an estimate of the treatment's impact or the association between variables (e.g., correlation coefficient); (c) the exact value of an inference test statistic (e.g., $t$ tests or $F$ tests) and its associated degrees of freedom; and (d) an inexact $p$ level and sample size.

Means and standard deviations allow the synthesist to precisely calculate any effect sizes for whatever comparisons they choose. Effect sizes calculated by the primary researchers, although an excellent source of information, may contain unknown errors, may not refer to the specific comparison of interest, or may not be in the metric chosen by the synthesist. Values of inference test statistics and degrees of freedom allow the synthesist to estimate effect sizes. Inexact $p$ levels, along with sample sizes, allow the estimation of inference test values. Also, the inference test values and $p$ levels sometimes refer to analyses containing multiple factors (e.g., analysis of variance with more than one independent variable), and unless these factors are the same across studies, this will add to the imprecision in estimates. Many issues involved in the extraction of statistical information from research reports will be discussed further in the chapters that follow.

7. Coding process: This information refers to the coding of the studies. The synthesist might be interested in who coded the study, how confident they were of their codes, and how long it took to complete the coding assignment. Later, the synthesist will examine the degree of reliability in coding decisions. Coding process information may help identify which coders had difficulty with their assignment, for which variables, and why.

Finally, each study report will also contain some miscellaneous but important information the synthesist will want to note on the coding sheet. In many instances, the coding sheet will be standardized to accommodate information about the main comparison of interest, but the research report will contain evidence concerning interactions between the main effect and other variables. Therefore, the coding sheet should contain space for noting the number of variables employed in a design or analysis and the outcomes of any interaction tests that involved the relation of interest. It is important to leave room for descriptive notes that allow the coders to report unique aspects of each study.

*Low- and High-Inference Codings.* The categories listed previously might be thought of as low-inference codings. That is, they require the coder only to locate the needed information in the research report and transfer it to the coding sheet. In some circumstances, coders might be asked to make some inferential judgments about the studies. These high-inference codings involve coders attempting to infer how a treatment or experimental manipulation might have been interpreted by the individuals subjected to it.

A synthesis by Carlson and Miller (1987) provides a good example. They summarized the literature on why negative mood states seem to enhance the likelihood that people will lend a helping hand. To test different interpretations of this research, they needed to estimate how sad, guilty, angry, or frustrated different experimental procedures might have made subjects. To do this, coders were asked to read excerpts from the methods sections of relevant articles. The coders then used a 1-to-9 scale to rate, for example, the "extent to which subjects feel specifically downcast, sad, or depressed as a result of the negative-mood induction" (p. 96).

These high-inference codings create a special set of problems for research synthesists. First, careful attention must be paid to the reliability of high-inference judgments. Also, coders are being asked to play the role of a research subject, and the validity of role-playing methodologies has been the source of much controversy (Greenberg & Folger, 1988). Miller, Lee, and Carlson (1991), however, have empirically demonstrated that high-inference codings can lead to valid judgments and can add a new dimension to synthesists' ability to interpret literatures and resolve controversies. If synthesists feel they can validly extract high-inference information from articles and persuasively explain their rationale for doing so, then this technique deserves a try.

*Revising and Pilot Testing the Coding Sheet.* When an area of research is large and complex, the construction of a coding sheet can be a difficult task. In the process of devising categories, synthesists make crucial decisions about what the important issues are in a field. Often, synthesists find that ideas they have about a topic and its research are only vague impressions. Constructing a coding sheet forces them to be more precise in their thinking.

The first draft of a coding sheet should never be the last. Synthesists need to show a first draft to knowledgeable colleagues for their input. Then, a few randomly selected studies need to be coded using the coding sheet. Categories will be added and category descriptors more precisely defined.

Finally, different coders should pilot test the coding sheet to uncover further ambiguities.

This process should not be viewed as a nuisance. It is an intrinsic part of clarifying the problem formulation. The development of a coding sheet should be viewed as no less important to the success of a research synthesis than the construction of a questionnaire is to survey research or an observation scheme to a study of naturalistic behavior.

Finally, a general coding sheet will never capture the unique aspects of all studies. Completed coding sheets are often filled with blank spaces and notes in margins. Perfection is never achieved. The synthesist can view these occurrences as failures (which they are not) or as targets of opportunity, highlighting the diversity of research in their topic area.

### Synthesis Examples

A possible coding sheet for the synthesis of research comparing students who do homework with students who do not do homework is presented in Table 2.1. I call this "a possible coding sheet" because even for the same synthesis there are multiple ways to arrange the variables and codes. In fact, although Table 2.1 illustrates most of the issues faced in arranging codes, it may not be the optimal coding sheet. As the variation in studies grows, so does the complexity of the codes. More complex issues and examples of how to address them can be found in Stock (1994).

The left-hand column in Table 2.1 is where all information that will be entered into the computer is recorded. Some information (such as the journal volume number and pages) may be recorded on the coding sheet but not transferred to the computer. The numbers under the blank lines signify the number and placement of computer columns that have been set aside for that variable in each row of the data matrix (with the second digit dropped for column numbers greater than nine to save space). In parentheses beneath each variable description is the name of the variable as it will appear in the computer file. For example, Table 2.1 indicates that the first three columns in the first row of the data matrix have been designated for a unique three-digit number identifying the research report (called RID in the computer). By setting aside three columns, I have the ability to distinguish 1,000 different research reports (with RIDs from 000 to 999). Column 4 is set aside to identify each separate study (study ID number) that might be reported in the same research report. In most instances, this entry will be "1," but if two studies are reported in one report the first study will have an entry of "1" and the second an entry of "2" in column 4. Column 5 is

## TABLE 2.1

Coding Sheet for Homework Versus No-Treatment Studies

| *Column No.* | | |
|---|---|---|

**Report identification**

|  |  |  |
|---|---|---|
| | Report ID#: | |
| 123 | (RID) | _____ Three-digit code |
| | Study ID#: | |
| 4 | (SID) | _____ One-digit code |
| | Sample ID#: | |
| 5 | (SAID) | _____ One-digit code |
| | Comparison ID#: | |
| 67 | (CID) | _____ Two-digit code |
| | First author _____ | |
| 890123 | (FA) | _____ First six letters |
| | Title _____ | |
| | Journal _____ | |
| 4567 | (JO) | _____ Four-letter code |
| | Year | |
| 89 | (YR) | _____ Last two digits |
| | Volume _____ | |
| | Pages _____ | |
| | Source of reference: | |
| 0 | (SO) | 1. Computer search |
| | | 2. Previous synthesis |
| | | 3. Reference list |
| | | 4. Personal communication |
| | | 5. Other |

**Research design:**

|  |  |  |
|---|---|---|
| | Design type: | |
| 1 | (DT) | 1. One group pretest-posttest |
| | | 2. Nonequivalent control |
| | | 3. Random assignment |
| | If nonequivalent control | |
| 2 | was used: | |
| | (NEC) | 1. No matching |
| | | 2. Matched on proxy pretest(s) |
| | | 3. Matched on pretest |
| | If random assignment | |
| 3 | was used: | 1. Students randomly assigned |
| | (RA) | 2. Classes randomly assigned |

**Other design features:**

|  |  |  |
|---|---|---|
| | Repeated measures: | |
| 4 | (RM) | 1. Yes |
| | | 2. No |

## TABLE 2.1
### *Continued*

| Column No. | | |
|---|---|---|
| | Counterbalancing: | |
| 5 | (CB) | 1. Yes |
| | | 2. No |
| | Teacher as experimenter: | |
| 6 | (TE) | 1. Yes |
| | | 2. No |
| | **Sample sizes:** | |
| | # of schools: | ____ |
| 789 | (NSCH) | |
| | # of classrooms: | ____ |
| 012 | (NCL) | |
| | # of students: | ____ |
| 3456 | (NSTU) | |
| | **School variables:** | |
| | Location (use state | ____ |
| 78 | abbreviations) | |
| | (LOC) | |
| | Source of funding: | |
| 9 | (FDS) | 1. Public |
| | | 2. Private |
| | **Student variables:** | |
| | Lowest included | |
| 01 | grade level: | ____ |
| | (LGR) | |
| | Highest included | |
| 23 | grade level: | ____ |
| | (HGR) | |
| | Socioeconomic status: | |
| 4 | (SES) | 1. Lower |
| | | 2. Middle |
| | | 3. Mixed |
| | Ethnic group: | |
| 5 | (ETH) | 1. White |
| | | 2. Black |
| | | 3. Other ____ |
| | | 4. Random sample or mixed |
| | Ability level: | |
| 6 | (ABL) | 1. Low |
| | | 2. Average |
| | | 3. High |
| | | 4. Mixed |

*(continued)*

## TABLE 2.1
*Continued*

| Column No. | | |
|---|---|---|
| | **Setting:** | |
| _____ | Subject matter: | |
| 7 | (SM) | 1. Math (general) |
| | | 2. Math computation |
| | | 3. Math problem solving |
| | | 4. Math concepts |
| | | 5. Reading (general) |
| | | 6. Reading comprehension |
| | | 7. Reading recognition |
| | | 8. Writing/spelling |
| | | 9. Language/vocabulary |
| | **Homework treatment:** | |
| _____ | Weeks of treatment: | _____ |
| 89 | (WKS) | |
| _____ | Frequency of assignments | |
| 0 | per week: | _____ |
| | (ASFR) | |
| _____ | Average length of assignments: | _____ minutes |
| 123 | (ASLG) | |
| | **Outcome measure:** | |
| _____ | Type of measure: | |
| 4 | (MEAS) | 1. Standardized achievement test |
| | specific _____ | 2. Class grade |
| | | 3. Teacher test |
| | | 4. Textbook test |
| | **Statistical outcomes:** | |
| _____ | Homework mean: | _____ |
| 56.78 | (HX) | |
| _____ | Homework standard deviation: | _____ |
| 90.12 | (HSD) | |
| _____ | Homework sample size: | _____ |
| 34567 | (HN) | |
| _____ | No homework mean: | _____ |
| 89.01 | (NHX) | |
| _____ | No homework standard deviation: | _____ |
| 23.45 | (NHSD) | |
| _____ | No homework sample size: | _____ |
| 67890 | (NHN) | |

## TABLE 2.1
### *Continued*

| Column No. | | |
|---|---|---|
| _____ 1 | Type of inference test:<br>(INF) | 1. *F*<br>2. *t*<br>3. Other _____<br>_____ |
| _____ 23.45 | Test value:<br>(INFVAL) | |
| _____ 67.89 | Test *df*:<br>(INFDF) | _____ |
| _____ .0123 | Test *p* level:<br>(INFP) | _____ |
| _____ 4 | Effect size direction:<br>(ESD) | 1. + (favors homework)<br>2. − (favors no homework) |
| _____ 56.78 | Effect size value:<br>(ESV) | _____ |

**Other statistical information:**
Other variables in analyses (list)

_____

_____

_____

Significant interactions involving homework:
Variable _____ Test value _____ *df* _____
Variable _____ Test value _____ *df* _____
Variable _____ Test value _____ *df* _____

**Coding information:**

| _____ 9 | Coder ID:<br>(CID) | _____ |
|---|---|---|

Notes and comments:

---

used to identify the independent sample (sample ID number) within the study. If information about comparisons between homework and no-homework conditions is given separately for separate groups of students within a single study (e.g., for first- and second-graders separately), this code will have a different value for each sample. Columns 6 and 7 give a unique identification for each comparison between homework and no-homework groups within a sample (comparison ID number). Therefore, this code permits one to distinguish between multiple outcome measures (e.g., standardized achievement tests and class grades) taken on the same group of students. The reasons for using four separate identification levels within each report will be explained more fully in Chapter 4.

The rationale behind most of the remaining variables and codes is self-evident, but some explanation concerning decisions about what information was retrieved and why may prove instructive. The section on research design contains no category for correlational studies, even though such a category was previously recommended. This is because studies that used correlational designs invariably examined the amount of time students reported spending on homework as a continuous variable. An entirely different coding sheet was devised for these studies. Studies correlating time on homework and achievement present a set of issues different from homework versus no-homework comparisons, including how samples of students were drawn from larger populations and whether teachers, students, or parents reported how much time the student spent on homework. Also, several of the categories in Table 2.1 were irrelevant to time-on-homework studies, such as the section on the reporting of means and standard deviations for two discrete groups.

This coding sheet needs slightly more detail regarding nonequivalent control group and random assignment designs than was suggested previously. When a nonequivalent control group was used with a matching procedure, coders were asked to distinguish between matchings based on (a) a pretest employing the same measure used as the dependent variable or (b) other pretest variables (perhaps gender, ethnic group, or socioeconomic status [SES] matches) related but not identical to the dependent variable. The two procedures might differ in their ability to produce equivalent groups and therefore might explain differences in the outcomes of studies. For a similar reason, a distinction was also made on the coding sheet among studies randomly assigning individual students or whole classrooms to homework and no-homework conditions.

There is no section in Table 2.1 for delineating how the control group was treated. This is because all control groups used in these comparisons were treated identically—they received no homework at all. A separate coding sheet was used for studies that included an in-school supervised-study control group. These sheets were very similar to Table 2.1 but included more codes distinguishing how the control group was treated. It would be possible to code both no-treatment and supervised-study control on the same coding sheet. Indeed, this would be necessary if one intended to make direct comparisons of the results of studies using the two types of control groups.

It must be pointed out that much of the information asked for on the coding sheet ultimately was never examined in the completed synthesis. This was true of all the information about students other than grade level (e.g. socioeconomic status, ethnic group, and ability level). Sometimes, too few studies reported information about the variable of interest (e.g., the SES of the students). In other cases, it was found that studies did not vary enough across values of a characteristic (e.g., most studies were done in public schools and very few in private schools) to allow valid inferences.

As noted previously, each one of the coding sheets was designed to contain information concerning a single comparison. In some studies, however, comparisons were reported, for example, for more than one grade level or more than one measure of achievement. When such a study was uncovered, the coder would fill out separate sheets for each two-group comparison. For example, a study with both standardized and class grade measures of achievement reported separately for students in fifth and six grades would have four coding sheets associated with it.

## VALIDITY ISSUES
## IN PROBLEM FORMULATION

Several decisions during problem formulation that affect the validity of a research synthesis have been mentioned. The two most central involve the breadth of concepts used in variable definitions and the operational detail used in the search for moderators of the primary relation under study.

First, synthesists who use only a few operations to define their concepts typically do so to ensure consensus about how their concepts are related to observable events. Such agreement is an attractive scientific goal. Most methodologists agree, however, that multiple realizations of concepts are desirable. As stated previously, numerous rival interpretations for the findings may be ruled out if multiple operations produce similar results. Also, narrow concepts provide little information about the generality or robustness of the results. Therefore, the greater the conceptual breadth of the definitions used in a synthesis, the greater its *potential* to produce conclusions that are more general than syntheses using narrow definitions.

The word potential is emphasized because of the second threat to validity associated with problem definition: If synthesists only cursorily detail study operations, their conclusions may mask important distinctions in results. An erroneous conclusion—that research results indicate negligible differences in outcomes—can occur if different results across studies are canceled in the use of very broad categories.

Of course, the most extreme attention to operational detail occurs when each study is treated as if it tested a completely different hypothesis. It is rare, however, for a synthesist to conclude that, due to the variation in methods across studies, no integration of the literature is possible. Therefore, most syntheses contain some threat to validity because they ignore differences between studies. The risk occurs in varying degrees in different syntheses, however.

A lack of overlap in the operational definitions considered relevant by different synthesists studying the same variables also creates variation in conclusions. When this happens, however, it ought not be called a "threat to validity" because it is impossible on objective grounds to say which of two synthesists used a more valid definition. They simply disagree about the operationalization of the same construct. Syntheses that do not overlap in operations are comparable only on the definitional level. It seems clear, however, that a synthesis is more desirable if it includes all the operations contained in another synthesis plus additional operations—if operational details receive appropriate treatment, of course. In practice, comparative evaluations will not be as clear-cut as these examples. Two syntheses involving the same concept may share some operations while each also includes operations the other does not.

### Protecting Validity

Synthesists can use the following guidelines to protect their conclusions from the threats to validity entering during problem formulation:

1. Synthesists should undertake their literature searches with the broadest possible conceptual definition in mind. They should begin with a few central operations but remain open to the possibility that other relevant operations will be discovered in the literature. When operations of questionable relevance are encountered, the synthesist should err toward making overly inclusive decisions, at least in the early stages of his or her project.

2. To complement conceptual broadness, synthesists should be thorough in their attention to the distinctions in study characteristics. Any suggestion that a difference in study results is associated with a distinction in study characteristics should receive some testing by the synthesist, if only in a preliminary analysis.

## EXERCISES

1. Identify two integrative research syntheses that claim to relate to the same or similar hypotheses. Which synthesis employs the broader conceptual definition? On what other dimensions concerning problem definition do the two syntheses differ? What aspect of problem definition in each synthesis do you find most helpful?

2. Identify a conceptual variable and list the operational definitions associated with it that are known to you now. Find several reports that describe research relevant to your topic. How many new operational definitions did you find? Evaluate these with regard to their correspondence to the conceptual variable.

3. For studies on a topic of interest to you, draw up a preliminary coding sheet. Find several reports that describe research that is relevant to the topic. How must you change the coding sheet to accommodate these studies? What did you leave out?

# 3

## *The Literature*
## *Search Stage*

**This chapter examines methods for locating studies relevant to a synthesis topic. The objectives of a literature search are outlined. Numerous informal, formal, and secondary channels for obtaining research reports are described, with special attention to how research enters the channel, how searchers access the channel, and what biases may be present in the kinds of information contained in the channel.**

In primary research, data are collected by asking people questions or observing their behavior. In research synthesis, data are collected by conducting a search for reports describing past studies relevant to the topic of interest. Regardless of whether social scientists are collecting new data or synthesizing previous data, the major decision they make during the data collection stage involves choosing the target population that will be the referent of the research (Fowler, 1993). The target population includes those individuals or groups that the researcher hopes to represent in the study. A precise definition of a target population might require the researcher to list all its members. Researchers rarely generate such lists. Because the truth or falsity of so many social science hypotheses depends on the population of interest (i.e., to whom the conclusion refers), however, it is important that researchers present clear, if general, population descriptions.

The sample frame of an investigation, whether it is a primary study or a research synthesis, includes those individuals or groups the researcher pragmatically is able to obtain or, in other words, that have a chance to be selected for inclusion in the study. In most instances, researchers will not be able to access all of a target population's elements. To do so would be too costly because some people are hard to find or refuse to cooperate.

## POPULATION DISTINCTIONS
## IN SOCIAL SCIENCE RESEARCH

*Similarities Between Primary Research and Research Synthesis.* Both primary research and research synthesis involve specifying target populations and sampling frames. In addition, both types of investigation require the researcher to consider how the target population and sampling frame may differ from one another. The trustworthiness of any claims about the population will be compromised if the elements in the sampling frame are not representative of the target population. Because it is easier to alter the target of an investigation than it is to sample hard-to-find people, both primary researchers and research synthesists may find they need to restrict or respecify their target population once an inquiry is complete.

*Differences Between Primary Research and Research Synthesis.* The most general target population for social science research could be characterized roughly as "all human beings." Most subdisciplines, of course, delineate the elements to be less ambitious, such as "all criminals" or "all students." Research topics might delineate the target population even more specifically—for example, "all rapists" or "all high school students."

Accessible sample frames in social science research are typically much more restricted than targets. Most social scientists are aware of the gap between the diversity of people to which they hope the results of their research refer and those people actually available to them.

As noted in Chapter 1, research syntheses involve two targets. First, synthesists hope their work will cover "all previous research" on the problem. Synthesists can exert some control over this goal through how they conduct their literature search—that is, through their choices of information sources. Just as different sampling methods in primary research can lead to differences in who is sampled (e.g., phone surveys sample different people from mail surveys), however, different literature searching techniques lead to different samples of studies. Likewise, just as it is more difficult to find and sample some people than others, it is also more difficult to find some studies than others. The following several sections describe some of the ways synthesists search the literature.

In addition to wanting to cover all previous research, synthesists want the results of their work to pertain to the target population of people that interests the topic area. A synthesist of homework research hopes that students at all grade levels, not just high school students, will be represented in past studies. The synthesist's influence is constrained at this point by the types of people sampled by primary researchers. Thus, research synthesis involves a peculiar process of sampling samples. The primary research covers samples of individuals or groups and the synthesist retrieves research. This process is akin to cluster sampling, with the clusters distinguishing people according to the research projects in which they participated.

In reality, synthesists typically are not trying to draw representative samples of studies from the literature. Instead, they attempt to retrieve an entire population of studies. This formidable goal is rarely achieved, but it is certainly more feasible in a synthesis than in primary research.

## METHODS FOR LOCATING STUDIES

How does a research synthesist go about finding studies relevant to a topic? There are numerous channels for sharing scientific information. These channels have undergone enormous changes in the past 20 years. In fact, it is safe to say that the way scientists transmit their work to one another has changed more in the past two decades than it did in the preceding three centuries, dating back to the late seventeenth century when scholarly journals first appeared. The change is primarily due to the use of computers to facilitate human communication.

This section presents some background on the major channels that a synthesist can use to find research. Many of the channels now require the searcher to have some familiarity with computers and the Internet. Readers unfamiliar with using the Internet will benefit from consulting one of the many excellent Internet guides (e.g., Hahn, 1996).

I will attempt to evaluate the kind of information contained in each channel by comparing its contents to that of "all relevant research," or to the entire population of studies the synthesist would find pertinent to the topic. Regrettably, there is little empirical data on differences in scientific information contained different channels, so most of the comparisons will involve some speculation on my part. The problem is further complicated by the fact that the effect of a channel's characteristics on its contents probably varies from topic to topic.

Also, the proliferation of ways to share information makes it increasingly difficult to find just a few descriptors that help us think about how the communication channels differ and relate to one another. Mechanisms for communication have arisen in a haphazard fashion, so no descriptive dimension perfectly captures all the important features.

There are several features that are useful in describing the different search channels. One important feature that distinguishes scientific communication channels relates to how research gets into the channel. Channels can have relatively open or restricted rules for entry. Open entry permits the primary researcher (the person who wants to put something in the channel) to enter the channel directly and place his or her work into its collection of information. Restricted entry requires primary researchers to meet the requirements of a third party—a person or entity between themselves and the user of their research—before their work can enter the information channel. The most important of these requirements is the use of peer review of research to ensure that it meets certain standards of quality. In fact, all channels have some restrictions on entries, but the type and stringency differ from channel to channel. It is these restrictions that most directly affect how the research in the channel differs from all relevant research.

A second important feature of communication channels concerns how searchers get into the channel. Channels have more or less open or restricted requirements regarding how to access their content. A channel is more restricted if it requires the literature searchers (the people seeking information from the channel) to identify very specifically what or whose documents they want. A channel is more open if the literature searchers can be more broad or general in their request for information. Some of these access requirements also can influence the type of research a searcher will find in a channel.

Finally, channels can differ in the kinds of information they contain about the research. Channels with detailed accounts of research will include complete journal articles or research reports. Channels with summarized accounts often include just research abstracts, research summaries, bibliographic information, or all three that can be used to obtain the full reports.

The importance of these distinctions will become clear as I describe how they relate to specific search channels. For purposes of exposition, I have grouped the channels under the following headings: informal channels, formal channels, and secondary channels. I will use my synthesis of research on homework as a practical example.

## INFORMAL CHANNELS

Informal channels of communication are distinguished by a lack of explicit rules governing the contact between the primary researcher and the

**TABLE 3.1**

Informal Channels for Locating Studies

| Channel | Restrictions on How Research Gets In | Restrictions on How Searcher Gets In | Types of Information Included |
|---|---|---|---|
| Personal contact | Researcher must be known to searcher | Must contact colleagues | Studies with similar methods and results |
| Personal solicitation | Researcher must hold status known to searcher | Must have address for contact | Studies consistent with organizational bias |
| Traditional invisible college | Research is accepted by prominent researchers | Must contact central researcher | Studies with similar methods and results |
| Electronic invisible college | Researcher must subscribe to computer list | Must subscribe to same computer list | Anything in topic area |
| The World Wide Web | Researcher must be computer user | Must use appropriate search terms | Anything at all |

literature searcher. There are no restrictions on the kinds of information that can be exchanged through informal channels. In all but one case, there is no third party that mediates the exchange of information. The five principle forms of informal communication are personal contacts, solicitation letters, traditional invisible colleges, electronic invisible colleges, and the World Wide Web. The distinctions between the forms of informal communication are summarized in Table 3.1.

**Personal Contact**

The most immediate information available to synthesists is their own research. Before anyone else sees research results, the primary investigators see it themselves. Thus, I would begin my synthesis on homework by including any of my own studies that were relevant to the issue (actually, no such studies had been conducted when I began the synthesis). Although this may seem like an obvious point, it is a critical one. Primary research that synthesists personally have conducted often has a strong, and perhaps overemphasized, impact on how they interpret the research literature as a whole (Cooper, 1986).

A researcher's own studies can differ markedly from all investigations relevant to a topic. Each researcher is likely to repeat the same operations across studies, using the same instruments or instructions or both to participants. Many operational and sample variations relevant to a topic area may go unexamined in any particular laboratory, even though these variations are well represented in all relevant research. For example, studies of homework that I conduct might exclusively use teacher grades as the measure of achievement. Other researchers might use textbook and standardized tests but not grades. Also, researchers often will tap the same subpopulation when recruiting participants—for example, the same school district in the case of homework research.

Other personal contacts happen outside a researcher's own laboratory but perhaps not far outside. Students and their professors share ideas and pass on to one another papers and articles they find that are of mutual interest. A colleague down the hall might run across an article on homework in a journal and, knowing of my interest in the topic, might pass it on to me or one of my students. Occasionally, readers of a researcher's past work will point out literature they think is relevant to the topic but was not cited in the report. This sometimes happens when the research report appears in print, but it also may occur as part of the manuscript review process. Thus, it would not be uncommon for a reviewer of a homework manuscript submitted for journal publication to suggest some additional relevant articles that are not referenced in the work. These would be added to my list of relevant research as I began my homework synthesis.

Personal contact is generally a very restricted communication channel. Primary researchers must know the searcher in some way to initiate the exchange of information. A searcher must also individually specify the researchers they know so as to obtain relevant information. Thus, much like a researcher's own work, information found through personal contacts or friends and colleagues generally will reflect the methodological and theoretical biases of the searcher's informal social system. It most likely will be more homogeneous in findings than all relevant research. Therefore, personal contacts with friends and colleagues must never be the sole source of studies in a research synthesis. Research synthesists who rely solely on these channels to collect relevant work are acting like surveyors who decide to sample only their friends.

### Personal Solicitation

Personal solicitations can produce less biased samples of information. These contacts involve, first, searchers identifying formal groups of individuals who might have access to relevant research reports. Then, searchers obtain lists of group members and contact the members individually—by mail, e-mail, or phone—even if the searchers do not know them personally. For the homework search, this technique was used in three ways. First, letters were sent to 25 deans of schools of education asking them to bring the project to the attention of their faculties and to request that relevant studies be sent to me. Seven fruitful leads were obtained in this way. Second, solicitation letters were sent to 53 state agencies throughout the United States that dealt primarily with education. Thirty-six agencies responded and 6 sent statewide homework assessments. Finally, a mailing list from a national association of directors of research and evaluation for school districts was obtained. Approximately half the districts responded to the solicitation letter and 11 provided homework research reports, although not all were relevant to the topic. For example, some reports evaluated the effectiveness of homework hotlines.

## Traditional Invisible Colleges

Another channel of informal communication, a bit less restrictive than personal contacts, is the invisible college. According to Crane (1969), traditional invisible colleges are formed because "scientists working on similar problems are usually aware of each other and in some cases attempt to systematize their contacts by exchanging reprints with one another" (p. 335). Through a sociometric analysis, Crane found that most members of invisible colleges were not directly linked to one another but were linked to a small group of highly influential members. In terms of group communication, traditional invisible colleges are structured like wheels—influential researchers are at the hub and less established researchers are on the rim, with lines of communication running mostly to the hub and less often among peripheral members.

The structural characteristics of the traditional invisible college are dependent on the fact that in the past the informal transmission of information between scientists occurred one-on-one, primarily through the mail and by telephone. These two mediums require that only two people at a time can exchange information (though multiple two-way communications might occur in parallel through, for example, mass mailings). Also, the two communicators had to know and choose to talk to one another. Thus, influential researchers could act as hubs, both restricting the input (entry) and directing the output of (access to) information to a known group of researchers.

When the synthesis of homework research began, I was unaware of who might be the central figures in a homework invisible college. As I gathered information from other sources, however, the same set of researchers began to appear over and over again. Sometimes, I would run across multiple studies by the same author. Often, reference lists contained citations of these same researchers' work. From this process, a list of 13 people who I thought might be hubs of homework research wheels was generated. I wrote to them and received back three research reports I found by no other means.

The influence of prominent researchers over the information communicated through traditional invisible colleges holds the key to assessing the biases in the information transmitted through this channel. A synthesist gathering research solely by contacting hubs of a traditional invisible college will probably find studies that are more uniformly supportive of the beliefs held by these central researchers than are studies gathered from all sources. This is because fledgling researchers who produce a result in conflict with that of the hub of an invisible college are less likely to try to enter their work into this channel. If they do, they are less likely to see their work widely disseminated throughout the network. Disconfirming findings may lead a researcher already active in an invisible college to leave the network. Also, because the participants in a traditional invisible college use one another as a reference group, it is likely that the kinds of operations and measurements employed in the members' research will be more homogeneous than that employed by all researchers who might be interested in a given topic.

### Electronic Invisible Colleges

Traditional invisible colleges still exist today. There also exists, however, a new type of invisible college. With the advent of the Internet, the need has diminished for communication hubs that hold together groups of scientists interested in the same topic. The Internet allows a primary researcher to send the same information simultaneously to a group of colleagues worldwide without knowing exactly who is receiving it. Likewise, literature searchers can seek the same information from a group whose members are unknown to them. Electronic invisible colleges operate primarily through the use of computerized list management programs— called listservs, listprocs, or Majordomos—or through newsgroups. These programs maintain mailing lists by automatically responding to e-mail requests and distributing new messages. The difference between mailing lists and newsgroups is that mailing lists send material to searchers automatically, whereas newsgroups wait for requests. Newsgroups also require the subscribers to learn more about the program before they can use it.

The electronic mailing list and newsgroup can be less restrictive than a traditional invisible college because, although an individual acts as the list coordinator, in unmoderated mailing lists the computer often serves as the hub of the communication wheel. It disseminates the communications that come to it without imposing any restrictions on content. In moderated mailing lists, the list of members can be held privately and admittance or content or both will be screened, so these function more like traditional invisible colleges.

Anyone can join mailing lists or newsgroups, once they know that the lists exist, by sending a simple command to their host computer. Thus, a literature searcher who uses mailing lists or newsgroups to gather research should obtain a more heterogeneous set of studies than would be the case using a traditional invisible college. The mailing list or newsgroup search, however, still will not produce studies as diverse in method and outcome as all relevant research. Subscribers may still share certain biases. For example, I might try to gather research investigating homework by contacting the listserv of the American Psychological Association (APA) Division of Educational Psychology. Subscribers to this list might overrepresent researchers who do large-scale surveys or experiments and underrepresent researchers who do ethnographic studies. I might also contact subscribers to the American Educational Research Association (AERA) Division on Learning and Instruction. Here, ethnographic studies might be better represented, but it might systematically miss studies conducted on special education students. Also, there is a tendency for electronic invisible colleges, not unlike traditional ones, to be dominated by a small group of active individuals.

How does the literature searcher know what mailing lists or newsgroups are out there? Lists can be found in printed directories (e.g., the Internet Yellow Pages), in Internet directories, (e.g., the Liszt Directory found at *http://www.liszt.com*), or by sending e-mail instructions to lists of lists (e.g., *listserv@listserv.net*). Directories devoted specifically to academic mailing lists and newsgroups can be found in the *Directory of Electronic Journals, Newsletters and Academic Discussion Groups* (Association of Research Libraries, 1997) or in the *Directory of Scholarly and Professional E-Conferences* at *http://n2h2.com/kovacs*. Mailing lists and newsgroups can also be found by visiting Internet websites of research organizations.

My search for homework research mailing lists and newsgroups was not very fruitful. I found the lists dedicated to homework related to issues of practices, not research. They focused on providing help with homework or suggesting good assignments for different subject areas. Thus, my best strategy for using the electronic invisible college would be to subscribe to the research association (APA and AERA) divisional mailing lists. I could then put out a request to other subscribers for homework research. The vast majority of subscribers who received my message probably could not help, but some might have information of interest to me. Another strategy would be to start a homework research listserv. This strategy would take longer to pay off but might reap great rewards when it did so.

Invisible colleges, whether traditional or electronic, are temporary, informal entities that deal with special problems. They can vanish when the problem is solved or the focus of the discipline shifts. Although specific invisible colleges come and go, there is no doubt that researchers spend a significant amount of their time in information exchanges mediated by invisible colleges.

## The World Wide Web

The World Wide Web is a system of links between computers that makes it simple to connect sites on the Internet. Computer programs that provide a resource, called servers, are linked to computer programs that wish to access that resource, called clients. The actual information exchanged between servers and clients is typically in the form of websites or webpages. Websites can be constructed by anyone who has (or knows someone who has) the required expertise. Thus, there is little restriction on whose information can enter the system. A literature searcher with access to an Internet browser (a client program used to access the Web) would type in the computer address of a particular website (known as a uniform resource locator). The client program then contacts the server program, which sends the webpage to the searcher's computer.

The major problem for a research synthesist using the Web is finding relevant website addresses. Search engines or navigators are programs that index websites. The searcher provides a search term or set of terms that the search engine compares to its index of terms. The search engine then gives the searcher a list of websites that fit the key word description, most often because the site contains the key word or words somewhere on the webpage.

Through my university, I have access to a program that connects me to the Internet. When I initiate this program, it provides me with access to several search engines. These include general search engines, such as Alta Vista, Excite, Infoseek, Lycos, Webcrawler, and Yahoo. General search engines have considerable overlap in how they run. Most important, they all in some way permit the searcher to employ Boolean syntax operators to expand or restrict the search.

Boolean operators allow the searcher to use set theory to help define the items that will be retrieved by a search. I can begin a search for homework research by asking a search engine to list for me all websites that are cataloged under the term "homework." I can expand my search by including the term "home study"—that is, by requesting "homework" or "home study." I can restrict my search to sites specifically related to "homework" and "research" by requiring that the terms "homework" and "research" both appear in the record. I can be even more particular by requiring that they appear adjacent to one another ("homework" next to "research") or by excluding sites that contain other search terms (e.g., "homework" and not "college").

How websites are cataloged in the directory and the precise commands used to do the Boolean syntax search will differ somewhat for each search engine. Some search engines use words to describe the Boolean operators, others use symbols (e.g., + and –). General search engines typically provide on-line assistance to help learn how to use them.

Another important aspect of the World Wide Web is its use of hypertext to link websites directly. Many websites (especially the listing produced by a search engine) contain references to related websites. If these references are highlighted in some way, typically by appearing underlined or in a unique color, the searcher can click on the reference and be sent directly to the new website. Often, websites that provide these links are called homepages.

Using the World Wide Web to find scientific research on a specific topic can be frustrating and time-consuming. The Web contains much more than research information. Also, placing a report or abstract directly on the Web is not yet a common practice among researchers. On the day I wrote this chapter, a general web search for information on homework uncovered tens of thousands of websites. A search for "homework" next to "research" cut this number to approximately 100 sites. "Homework" next to "research" also including "achievement" reduced the number of sites to 1. This site contained a research-based set of guidelines for homework practice meant to improve achievement.

To overcome this problem, a searcher can use one of the more specialized search engines that deal specifically with sites relevant to the social sciences. One site that lists these more specialized search engines is titled "Research Engines for the Social Sciences." It can be found at *www.carleton. ca/~cmckie/research.html.* A general search using the terms "research engines" and "social science" will lead to other sites that list search engines. The search engines listed in these sites primarily provide computer access to the research registers and reference databases that I will describe later.

The strategies for searching the World Wide Web I have described are only some examples of numerous approaches. With practice, searchers become more familiar with the resources available to them and how to construct searches that produce relevant material.

All the channels discussed so far share another important characteristic: They contain research that may not have undergone peer review to assess their methodological quality. There are no restrictions on what two colleagues send or say to one another or on what is contained in an e-mail message or website. Therefore, samples of studies found through personal contact, solicitations, invisible colleges, and webpages are more likely to contain studies with flawed methodology than will the corpus of all relevant research. Because of methodological flaws, these studies probably will never appear in more restricted communication channels, whereas more rigorous studies may appear in research journals but never circulate through invisible colleges or on the Web.

## FORMAL CHANNELS

Formal channels of communication have explicit rules that primary researchers must follow to enter information into the channels. These rules go beyond simple formatting requirements or knowledge of computers. They place restrictions on the kind or quality of information that is admitted to the system. The four major formal channels are professional conference paper presentation, personal journal libraries, electronic journals, and research report reference lists. Their characteristics are summarized in Table 3.2.

### Professional Conference Paper Presentations

There are a multitude of social science professional societies, structured by both career concerns and topic areas, and many of them hold yearly conventions. By attending these meetings or examining the titles of the papers given at them, research synthesists can discover what others in their field are doing and what research has recently been completed.

**TABLE 3.2**

Formal Channels for Locating Studies

| Channel | Restrictions on How Research Gets In | Restrictions on How Searcher Gets In | Types of Research Included |
|---------|-----------|-----------|-----------|
| Professional conference paper presentations | Research must pass weak peer review | Must be aware of meeting | Anything in discipline or topic area |
| Personal journal libraries | Research must pass strict peer review | Must subscribe or read same journal | Anything in subdiscipline or topic area |
| Electronic journals | List subscriber or pass peer review | Must subscribe or read same journal | Anything in subdiscipline or topic area |
| Research report reference lists | Research must be known to article's authors | Must subscribe or read same journal | Mostly studies in journal network |

In comparison to personal contacts and traditional invisible colleges, the research found through convention programs is less likely to reveal a restricted sample of results or operations. It is more likely to resemble the diversity to be found using the Internet. In comparison to solicitation letters and Internet searches, papers presented at meetings and conferences are more likely to have undergone peer review, so they should be of higher methodological quality.

The selection criteria for meeting presentations, however, is usually not as strict as that required for journal publication. A larger percentage of papers submitted to conferences are accepted than are manuscripts submitted to journals that use peer review. Also, the proposals that researchers submit for evaluation by a conference committee are often not very detailed. Finally, some researchers are invited to give papers by the people who develop the meeting. These invited addresses are not reviewed for quality. On the positive side, papers given at meetings are more likely to be current than journal articles because the researcher may present a paper before a publishable manuscript has been written. Journals also often have long lags between when a manuscript is submitted and when it is published.

For the homework synthesis, several years of convention programs of the American Educational Research Association were examined. No study was uniquely found through convention programs, though this does not mean that this channel would not prove valuable for other searches;

approximately 10% of research is presented at professional meetings and nowhere else (Cooper, DeNeve, & Charlton, 1997). I might have also examined regional education association meetings.

## Personal Journal Libraries

Synthesists can learn of research done in a topic area by examining the journals they subscribe to personally or the journals they regularly follow that are carried by their institutional library. Journals published on paper form the core of the formal scientific communication system. They are the traditional link between the primary researcher and research synthesist.

The *Report of the National Enquiry Into Scholarly Communication* (1979) found that the average scholar in several social science disciplines scanned approximately seven journals and followed four or five others on a regular basis. Most scholars said they spent between 10 and 12 hours per week reading scholarly books and journals. This reading material came largely from their personal subscriptions. King, McDonald, and Roderer (1981) surveyed active science researchers and found that 69% of the articles they read were from personal copies of journals.

There would be some serious biases in a search based on personal libraries as the sole or major source of research. The number of journals in which relevant research might appear is generally far in excess of those that a single scientist examines routinely. As early as 1971, Garvey and Griffith noted that scholars had lost the ability to keep abreast of all information relevant to their specialties through personal readings and journal subscriptions.

Information overload would not be such a serious problem if the journals read by each scientist were a random sample of all available journals. Scientists, however, tend to read journals that operate within networks of journals (Xhignesse & Osgood, 1967). Journal networks are composed of a small number of journals that tend most often to cite research published in other network journals.

Given that personal libraries are likely to include journals in the same network, it would not be surprising to find some biases associated with network membership. As with personal contacts and the invisible college, one would expect greater homogeneity in both research findings and operations within a given journal network than in all the research available on a topic area.

The appeal of using a personal journal library as a source of information lies in its accessibility. Its contents should also be credible to the reference group the synthesist hopes will read the work. Personal libraries of journals should be used to find research for a synthesis, but they should not be the sole source of information.

## Peer Review and Publication Bias

Most paper journals use peer review to decide whether or not to publish a particular research report. Upon submission, the journal editor sends the report to reviewers, who judge its suitability for publication. The primary criterion reviewers use is the methodological quality of the research. They look for flaws in methods that might compromise the inferences drawn by the researcher. Also, they look for the presence of safeguards against inferential errors.

The scientific rigor of the research is not the sole criterion for whether or not a study is published. Most notably, published research is biased toward statistically significant findings—findings that reject the null hypothesis—with a probability, $p < .05$. This bias is present in the decisions made by both reviewers and primary researchers.

Atkinson, Furlong, and Wampold (1982) conducted a study in which they asked consulting editors for two APA journals in counseling psychology to review manuscripts. The manuscripts were identical in all respects except whether the hypothesized relation was statistically significant. They found that significant results were more than twice as likely to be recommended for publication as nonsignificant ones. Furthermore, they reported that the manuscripts with statistically significant results were rated to have a better research design than the ones with nonsignificant results, even though the methods were the same.

Primary researchers are also susceptible to bias against the null hypothesis. Greenwald (1975) found that researchers said they were inclined to submit significant results for publication approximately 60% of the time. Researchers, however, said they would submit the study for publication only 6% of the time if the results failed to reject the null hypothesis. Examining actual decisions by researchers, Cooper et al. (1997) found approximately 74% of researchers submitted significant results for publication but only 5% submitted nonsignificant results. Researchers' decisions not to submit nonsignificant results are probably based on their beliefs that nonsignificant findings are less interesting than statistically significant ones. Also, they probably believe that journal editors are more likely to reject null results.

Prejudice against the null hypothesis is not the only source of bias that influences the results of published research. It has been known for many years that researchers whose findings conflict with the prevailing beliefs of the day are less likely to submit their results for publication than researchers whose work confirms currently held beliefs (Nunnally, 1960). Likewise, journal reviewers appear to look less favorably on studies that conflict with conventional wisdom than studies that support it. Bradley (1981) reported that 76% of university professors answering a mail questionnaire said they had encountered some pressure to conform to the subjective preferences of the reviewers of their work. These phenomena have been labelled collectively confirmatory bias.

The significance criteria for publication ensures that the size of correlations or differences between the mean scores of groups reported in published works will be larger than the differences that would be found in all relevant research. Begg and Berlin (1988) gave a detailed account of the statistical characteristics of prejudice against the null hypothesis. Lipsey and Wilson (1993) empirically demonstrated publication bias. They examined 92 meta-analyses that presented separate estimates of a treatment's effect found in published and unpublished research reports. The published estimates were approximately one-third greater than the unpublished ones.

The existence of bias against the null hypothesis and confirmatory bias mean that peer-reviewed journal articles should not be used as the sole source of information for a research synthesis, unless the synthesist can convincingly argue that these biases do not exist in the specific topic area. For the homework research synthesis, my personal journal library included five journals that were examined for relevant studies: *American Educational Research Journal, Educational Psychologist, Elementary School Journal, Journal of Educational Psychology,* and *Journal of Experimental Education.*

## Electronic Journals

Electronic journals, or e-journals, disseminate and archive full-text reports of scholarly work using computer storage media—for example, Internet computer servers or compact disc—read-only memory (CD-ROM) technology (see Schauder, 1994, for a complete description of the history of electronic journals). Some journals appear in both paper and electronic form. Other journals are strictly paper or strictly electronic.

There are two characteristics of electronic journals that distinguish them from paper journals. First, many electronic journals do not use peer-review procedures. It is critical for a synthesist to know which electronic journals do and do not evaluate submitted articles so they can assess both the potential methodological rigor of the studies in the e-journal and the likelihood of publication bias. Second, relative to paper journals, electronic journals have much shorter publication lags. Due to the storage capacity and favorable economics of computer technology, an article accepted for publication in an electronic journal can become available to readers much faster than articles accepted for paper journals.

A World Wide Web virtual library of electronic journals can be found at website *http://www.edoc.com/ejournal.* Among the categories of e-journals in this virtual library is "Academic and Reviewed Journals." Within this category can be found lists of scientific, technical, and medical e-journals distinguished by whether they are peer reviewed, student reviewed, or nonreviewed. The searcher can enter the virtual library by keying in a descriptor on the appropriate command line. My search for education e-journals listed the titles of all electronic journals related to education known to the service (new ones are being added all the time). By clicking on any specific e-journal title, the searcher is sent to the e-journal's homepage.

My search for education e-journals led me to the *Education Policy Analysis Archives.* It is a peer-reviewed journal published electronically since 1993 by the College of Education of Arizona State University. The e-journal's homepage is reproduced in Figure 3.1. Any of the eight boxes on the right side of the homepage can be used to link to resources for continuing the search. Another e-journal, titled *Education Research and Perspectives,* had been available on paper for more 40 years and is now available electronically as well. Both e-journals permit entry into their archives, but they differ in the sophistication they allow in search strategies. Neither journal contained research relevant to the effects of homework.

**Research Report Reference Lists**

Another search strategy is sometimes called the ancestry approach. It involves searchers examining the research reports they have already acquired to see if they contain references to studies still unknown. The searcher judges the entries in reference lists for their relevance to the problem. If they may be relevant, the searcher retrieves the abstract or full report. The reference lists of these reports can then be scrutinized for further leads. Through reiteration, searchers work their way back through a literature until either the important concepts disappear or the studies become so old they are judged to be obsolete.

Report references are rarely exhaustive lists of the relevant research. Rather, they are meant to provide context for interpreting the new primary research. Furthermore, journal article reference lists are likely to overrepre-

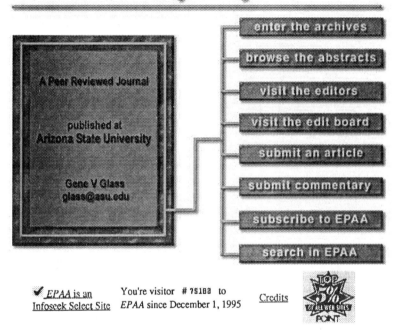

**Figure 3.1.** Homepage of Education Policy Analysis Archives
SOURCE: *http://olam.ed.asu.edu/epaa/*

sent work that appears in the journal's network. In general, if one examines
the references in a journal article, approximately one third of the citations
will be to other work that appeared in the same journal and approximately
one third of citations will be to other journals in the same network
(Xhignesse & Osgood, 1967). In any kind of research report, the primary
researchers will tend to cite other work available through the same outlet
or the small group of outlets that form their personal libraries and reference
groups. Therefore, searchers should expect more homogeneity among
research found through report reference lists than would be present in all
relevant studies. Likewise, searching reference lists will overrepresent
published research because it is generally easier to find than unpublished
work. Although reference lists in reports should not be used as a sole means

TABLE 3.3

Secondary Channels for Locating Studies

| Channel | Restrictions on How Research Gets In | Restrictions on How Searcher Gets In | Types of Research Included |
|---|---|---|---|
| Research bibliographies | Compiler must be aware of research | Must be aware of bibliography | Mostly published; recent research missing |
| Prospective research registers | Compiler must be aware of research | Must be aware of register | Mostly large-scale, funded research |
| Reference databases | Research must be in covered source | Must use appropriate search terms | Mostly published; recent research missing |
| Citation indexes | Research must be cited in publication | Must know article that cites research | Mostly published research; recent research missing |

for finding studies, they are generally a productive source of relevant research. Although I did not keep track of the precise numbers, I found many homework research articles by examining report reference lists.

SECONDARY CHANNELS

Secondary channels provide information about primary research documents, and some even contain the documents. They are constructed by third parties for the explicit purpose of providing literature searchers with relatively comprehensive lists of studies relating to a topic. It is this purpose that distinguishes secondary channels from Internet searches and report references. The major secondary channels, summarized in Table 3.3, are bibliographies, research registers, and reference databases, including citation indexes.

**Research Bibliographies**

Research bibliographies are nonevaluative listings of books and articles that are relevant to a particular topic area. Bibliographies are often maintained by single scientists or groups of individuals within a particular area rather than by a formal organization. It is possible to find bibliographies of bibliographies. The National Research Council Research Information Service publishes a bibliography of bibliographies in psychology that lists more than 2,000 bibliographies.

Another form of bibliography is the reference lists provided by previous research synthesists. Obviously, these can be especially fruitful sources of relevant studies. Searchers should not assume previous synthesis efforts are based on all relevant research, however. For my homework synthesis, the reference lists of nine previous syntheses were examined and the amount of overlap in the research referenced in each pair of syntheses was calculated. It was found that in a majority of cases, less than half the references were shared by any two papers.

The use of bibliographies prepared by others can be a tremendous time-saver to a research synthesist. The problem, however, is that most bibliographies are likely to be of much greater breadth than the synthesist's interest, and they may still contain some biases. Also, it is likely that most bibliographies will need updating for recent research. Even with these precautions, comprehensive bibliographies generated by other searchers can be a great help to the research synthesist. The compiler has spent many hours obtaining information, and the biases involved in generating the bibliographies may counteract biases that exist in the personal search of the synthesist.

## Government Documents

Related to bibliographies, the government system for publishing its own documents is a self-contained information retrieval system and might be missed entirely by a researcher who does not decide to enter this system.

Government documents fall into several categories—the most relevant to our present purpose is called research documents for specialists. Most government documents are handled by the Government Printing Office (GPO) or the National Technical Information Service (NTIS) or both. The *GPO Monthly Catalog* is available through computer searches as well as on paper. It indexes the most recently published GPO works. The NTIS database is available on-line. A complicating factor is that many government agencies are beginning to publish their own documents directly onto the World Wide Web without cataloging them in either the GPO or NTIS indexes.

The novice entering the maze of government documents for the first time will probably find the *Guide to U.S. Government Publications* to be the best starting point. This work does not describe the documents themselves but does describe the agencies that publish government documents.

In addition to federal government documents, state and local governments have published works that should be available in major research libraries.

## Prospective Research Registers

A research register is any database of studies focusing on a common feature, such as subject matter, funding source, or design (see Dickerson, 1994, for a thorough introduction to research registers). Prospective research registers are unique in that they attempt to include not only completed research but also research that is in the planning stage or is still under way. For example, a prospective research register might include information on studies that have recently received government funding or recently obtained approval for the use of human subjects.

From the searcher's point of view, identifying a research register with relevant studies can provide access to ongoing and unpublished research that is not filtered through personal contact. In this way, it provides information not unlike that obtained through solicitation letters and Internet sources. Research registers, however, are much more focused in content and are easier to use than the other channels. They also have the potential to be much more exhaustive.

Clearly, the comprehensiveness of the register is of greatest importance to the literature searcher. Therefore, it is critical that searchers determine (a) how long a register has been in existence and (b) how the research included in the register got to be there.

Currently, research registers are more prevalent in the medical than in the social sciences. Some government sources mentioned in regard to bibliographies, however, also serve as research registers. For example, a relatively simple search on the Web will reveal lists of recent research grants awarded by the U.S. Department of Education. I could use this list to look for homework studies. I could then contact any grantees to ask if they had any available results.

## Reference Databases

Finally, the sources of information likely to prove most fruitful to research synthesists are called reference databases. These are indexing and abstracting services maintained by both private and public organizations associated with the social sciences. An index or abstracting service will focus on a specific kind of document (e.g., journal articles and dissertations) or topic area and define its scope to be an explicit number of document outlets. Most documents that appear in the primary outlet will then be referenced in the system. Full-text databases are becoming more prevalent and will be the norm in the future. Even though reference databases are superb sources of studies, they still have limitations. First, there can be a long time lag between when a study is completed and when it will appear in the system. The study must be written up, submitted and accepted into its primary outlet, and then identified and cataloged into the reference database. Second, each database contains some restrictions on what is allowed to enter the system, based on topical or disciplinary restrictions. For instance, PsycINFO will include only psychology-related journals (although certainly an exhaustive accounting of these), whereas Educational Resources Information Center (ERIC) will have exhaustive coverage of education journals. Thus, a synthesist interested in an interdisciplinary topic needs to access more than one reference database. Third, some reference databases contain only published research and others only unpublished research (e.g., *Dissertation Abstracts*).

A fourth limitation on the exhaustiveness of searches based solely on reference databases derives not from what they contain but from how they are accessed by searchers. Even if a database were to have exhaustive coverage of the journals that are relevant to a topic, searchers will not necessarily be able to describe their topic in a manner that ensures they are able to uncover every relevant article in it. The search will lack the ability to "recall" all the wanted information. Like searching the Internet, searchers must enter the database by specifying search terms associated with particular pieces of research. Searchers who are unaware or omit terms that apply to operations relevant to their interests are likely to miss articles.

The search for homework studies used numerous secondary channels. PsycINFO and ERIC were searched and, although I was aware of no bibliographies or research registers devoted specifically to homework, I did examine the *U.S. Government Monthly Printing Catalog* and the National Technical Information Service. The two reference databases revealed hundreds of documents describing research on homework as well as related documents that provided excellent background information. The government databases provided approximately four dozen documents that were not available from the reference databases.

### Citation Indexes

Citation indexes are a unique kind of reference database that identifies and groups together all newly published articles that have referenced (cited) the same earlier publication. In this way, the earlier publication becomes the indexing term for the recent articles. In contrast to using research report reference lists to look for the ancestors of a report, the citation index employs a descendency approach, looking for the descendants of an article. The three citation indexes are the *Social Science Citation Index (SSCI), the Science Citation Index,* and the *Arts & Humanities Citation Index* published by the Institute for Scientific Information.

An example will make the citation search strategy clear. At the beginning of the search for homework research, I might have been aware of an important and well-known study that had a high likelihood of being cited in most subsequent investigations on the topic of homework. With this knowledge, I could enter a citation index by looking up the reference. The index would give a listing of all articles that had cited the earlier article during the period covered by the index. Each article that had cited the work would be listed by its author, source, and date of publication. I could then examine the recent articles to see if they contained results that could be used in my synthesis. I could have employed the same strategy again using several different important articles.

This strategy was not used for homework research because no truly central publications could be identified. The search for studies concerning individual differences in rape attitudes, however, did use the SSCI to great effect. Here, five measures of attitudes toward rape were identified, and the articles in which they appeared were used to access the citation index. The synthesists found 545 citations of the five scales and examined their abstracts to determine if the studies were relevant to the study of individual differences.

Citation indexes limit entry to references in published research, both journals and books. Their coverage, however, is quite exhaustive within these categories. Also, citation indexes will miss recent publications because of the time it takes to catalog documents.

## CONDUCTING SEARCHES
## OF REFERENCE DATABASES

This section provides more detail on how to conduct a reference database search. Several full-length treatments exist describing how social scientists can use the library. Notable among these is *Library Use: A Handbook for Psychology,* prepared under the auspices of the American Psychological Association (Reed & Baxter, 1992), and *The Educator's Information High-*

*way* (Wehmeyer, 1995). These texts cover in greater depth the issues in literature retrieval introduced later in this chapter. Also, individual vendors and reference database publishers provide readily available, detailed instructions on use.

All major research libraries have reference databases available. Reference librarians can help first-time users identify the databases most appropriate for their search and can provide the introductory instructions needed to access them. Your library will likely have reference databases available in several different mediums. Many databases are available in more than one medium.

The oldest medium is the print. Research libraries contain rows and rows of paper and microfiche databases. The searcher must go to the library to access paper and microfiche databases. Also, rather than accessing the printed databases directly, the searcher begins by employing printed indexes that indicate the whereabouts of information that might interest the searcher in the paper volumes or film files. For many reference databases, printed indexes are becoming a thing of the past, as are printed volumes.

Reference databases also come in CD-ROM format. Here, computer discs are used to store and retrieve indexes, references, abstracts, and even full-text documents. CD-ROM technology is increasingly being used to store smaller, specialized reference databases. Universities and other institutions purchase "licenses" to CD-ROM databases. The reference database vendor then updates the discs at regular intervals, typically monthly, quarterly, or semiannually. The compact discs are most often mounted on a single computer workstation, though they can also be made available on a local computer network. Typically, a portion of the library's reference section will contain a bank of computers, with many dedicated to a different CD-ROM reference database.

Finally, reference databases can be accessed on-line by dialing up commercial services or accessing them through the Internet. Almost all these services are available to any computer user with a modem and a willingness to pay local phone, access, and time charges. Some on-line services are leased to network sites, such as universities, for a flat fee. The institution then makes the service available to employees (and students), usually for free, by providing the software needed to access the database from home, office, or classroom computer workstations. Thus, with on-line services, searchers need not go to the library to access the reference database. They will have to visit the library, however, to obtain documents they think are relevant, unless the database contains full texts. On-line reference databases are also periodically updated, sometimes more frequently than their CD-ROM equivalents.

It is not necessary for the searcher to know much about how to operate a computer to access CD-ROM or on-line reference databases. Most commercial services contain step-by-step, menu-driven instructions that make them very easy to use. Also, research libraries employ trained specialists who can conduct the search or help the searcher through the process. Typically, the searcher tells the librarian the topic of interest and, most important, what terms, synonyms, and related terms are involved in the search. The librarian and the searcher can browse through thesauri (either in print or on-line) to identify terms that the searcher might not have considered. Searchers are also often asked by the librarian to provide examples of documents they hope to retrieve. This gives them some concrete idea about the material desired.

To begin my on-line search of reference databases for research on homework, I simply used my mouse arrow to click on the appropriate icon on my computer screen. This icon was associated with the on-line search service software package provided by my university. The computer automatically connected me to the on-line service. I was first informed of the latest updates to the reference databases. Another click on an icon led to a list of all the databases made available through this service. Highlighting any database provided a brief description of its contents, both the covered disciplines and dates of inclusion. With just a third click, the service retrieved the database, and I was ready to begin my search.

### Examples of Reference Databases

What follows is a brief description of a few reference database services. The ones I chose to highlight are among the most frequently employed in the social and behavioral sciences.

#### PsycINFO

The most familiar and frequently used indexing and abstracting service in the behavioral sciences is PsycINFO. The PsycINFO database contains more than 1 million records covering all types of documents related to psychology and allied fields. PsycINFO is actually a family of products, including printed, CD-ROM, and on-line mediums. The characteristics of these products are summarized in Table 3.4. Detailed information about PsycINFO can be found on its Internet homepage at *http://www.apa.org.*

PsycINFO is available on-line for the years 1967 to the present. In some instances, the searcher may be interested in older documents, and these

TABLE 3.4

Comparison of PsycINFO Institutional Products

| | PsycINFO | PsycLIT | Psychological Abstracts |
|---|---|---|---|
| Format | On-line or institutional lease | CD-ROM (compact disc) | Print |
| Coverage | Journals<br>Technical reports<br>Dissertations<br>Book chapters[a]<br>Books[a] | Journals<br>Book chapters<br>Books | Journals<br>Technical reports<br>Book chapters<br>Books |
| Coverage dates | 1967-present | Journals:<br>1974-present<br>Books:<br>1987-present | 1927-present |
| Updates | Monthly | Quarterly | Monthly |
| Languages | All languages | Journals:<br>All languages<br>Book chapters and Books:<br>English | English Only<br>(1988-present) |
| Availability | Commercial on-line services:<br>DIALOG  OCLC-EPIC<br>DataStar  Ovid Online<br>DIMDI  NlightN<br>HealthGate<br>Institutional lease | Subscription:<br>Aries Systems Corporation<br>EBSCO Publishing<br>National Information Services Corporation (NISC)<br>Ovid Technologies<br>SilverPlatter Information | Subscription from APA |

NOTE: For more information, contact PsycINFO User Services at 1-800-374-2722 or 202-336-5650.
a. Book chapter and book records are available on some on-line systems.

would have to be retrieved manually from the printed *Psychological Abstracts*. For recent material, however, computerized databases are more up-to-date than their print counterparts because the process of indexing articles is now done directly into computer storage, which then generates the printed volumes.

Returning to my homework search example, once I accessed the Psyc-INFO database using the on-line service, the screen displayed a box in which I entered my search term. A columned ledger was also displayed in which would appear the statistical results of my search. When I typed in the word *homework* in the entry box, another box was superimposed on the screen that told me homework was a valid subject heading. Next, the

computer asked me if I wanted to see all records filed under the term
*homework* or only those records for which homework was considered the
focus or major point of the article. To determine how this choice would
affect my search, I entered "homework", first specifying all records. I found
that the term *homework* occurred in 148 records (displayed on a line 1 in my
ledger). Then I entered homework again and requested a search restricted to
records with homework as the main focus. My ledger revealed that homework
was the major focus of 125 records (displayed on line 2). I decided to
continue my search using only the records that focused on homework.

Next, I typed the word "college" in the entry box. Another superimposed
box was immediately displayed that told me "college" was a subject
heading. The box also gave other information about the term, including the
date it was entered into the thesaurus as a subject heading and suggested
related terms I might want to use in my search, such as "university" and
"higher education". I was also asked to determine if I wanted to search for
college as a subject heading, assigned by the database vendor, or as a text
word, a word that appeared anywhere in the record. I chose to search for
college as a text word. Soon after, line 3 of my ledger indicated that 107,355
records contained the word "college".

In the entry box, I next typed the command, "2 not 3", thereby requesting
a count of records with the main focus of homework that did not contain
the word "college". Line 4 indicated that 118 such records existed. Across
the bottom of my screen, I had another array of options, one of which was
labeled "View Set". I clicked on this option. A list of the documents
captured by my search described on line 4 appeared immediately. First,
only bibliographic and institutional information on each record was listed,
but I could alter this presentation to include document abstracts, if so
desired. I scrolled through the list with the option of highlighting those
records I might want to save and later print.

When I chose the print option, I was first asked to select what information (called "fields" in a database) about each highlighted record I wanted
to print and what formatting options I wanted for my printed copy. After
choosing among these options, the results of my search were printed
through my office printer. The entire procedure took less than 30 minutes.

### ERIC

A multitude of information for both practitioners and researchers in the
field of education or any aspect of the human learning process can be found
in ERIC. The ERIC system collects, screens, organizes, and disseminates
literature through 16 clearinghouses, each focusing on a different facet of

education (e.g., adult education, reading, and science education). ERIC is produced and maintained by the United States Department of Education. It contains material dating back to 1966. ERIC publishes two printed guides to its contents. The first guide is called the *Current Index to Journals in Education* (CIJE). It presents a listing of the periodical literature covering major educational and education-related publications. The second is called *Resources in Education* (RIE). It presents the abstracts to recently completed research reports and other documents of educational significance. Both listings are indexed by subject, author, institutional source, and type of publication (e.g., book and convention paper), as well as other document characteristics.

Most documents stored in RIE can be retrieved in their entirety through the ERIC system. Typically, the full documents are contained in microfiche collections that can be found in major research libraries. The microfiche transparencies can be placed in reading machines to bring the document to full size. It is then possible to photocopy the magnified microfiche to obtain a paper copy of the document. ERIC documents from January 1996 to the present are available electronically, or the searcher can contact the ERIC Document Reproduction Service to obtain a copy.

The CIJE is entered in the same manner as the RIE, but the two printed guides need to be searched separately. In CIJE, after identifying relevant research, the searcher must find the journal containing the complete document. The ERIC indexes are also available through CD-ROM and on-line mediums. These are considerably easier and faster to use than the printed catalogs, integrate both the RIE and CIJE databases, and lead to the same journals and microfiche searches. General information on all ERIC information services is on the World Wide Web at *http://www.aspensys.com/eric2/welcome.html.*

After I printed out the results of my PsycINFO search, I conducted a similar search using the ERIC database. This time, I added a step by using a "Limit Set" option also displayed on the bottom of my screen. For example, my search for records with homework as their major focus in the ERIC database found 460 entries. I then clicked on the "Limit Set" box and my screen displayed a list of limiting options. I could limit my search to only RIE or CIJE records, to a specific language, to the last update of records, to specific education levels, to specific publication years, to publication types, or to records entered by specific ERIC clearinghouses. I chose to limit my search to only education levels below college. This command limited my search to 322 records.

Table 3.5 exhibits the record of one of the ERIC documents captured by my search exactly as it was printed on my office computer. Most of the

**TABLE 3.5**

Example of a Document Record in the ERIC System

---

\<1\>

**Accession Number**
    EJ491145

**Authors**
    Cooper, Harris. Nye, Barbara.

**Title**
    Homework for Students With Learning Disabilities: The Implications of Research
    for Policy and Practice.

**Source**
    Journal of Learning Disabilities. v27 n8 p470-79 Oct 1994.

**Local Messages**
    Owned by MU HSL.

**ERIC Subject Headings**
    Assignments                              *Parent Participation
    Elementary Secondary Education   Parent School Relationship
    *Homework                              Parent Student Relationship
    *Learning Disabilities                  *Teacher Role
    Models                                     Teaching Methods

**Abstract**
    A review of the literature on effects of homework for students with and without
    disabilities offers a homework process model, and suggests that homework policies
    and practices for students with learning disabilities should emphasize: simple, short
    assignments; careful monitoring by and prominent rewards from teachers; and
    parental involvement to provide structure, conducive environments, and immediate
    rewards. (Author/DB)

**Publication Type**
    JOURNAL ARTICLES. INFORMATION ANALYSES (State-of-the-Art Papers,
    Research Summaries, Reviews of the Literature on a Topic). VIEWPOINTS
    (Opinion Papers, Position Papers, Essays, etc.).

**Document Delivery**
    Available from: UMI.

**ISSN**
    0022-2194

**Language**
    English

**Clearinghouse Code**
    Handicapped and Gifted Children.

**Entry Month**
    9502

record fields are self-explanatory. The accession number tells me where to look for this document in the ERIC collection. The local message tells me that I can find the *Journal of Learning Disabilities* in the University of Missouri Health Sciences Library.

## Dissertation Abstracts International

Although many reference databases contain abstracts of dissertations, *Dissertation Abstracts International* (DAI) focuses exclusively on this type of document. Both the printed and the computerized versions, called *Dissertation Abstracts Online* (DAO), have records dating back to the year 1861. The computerized version also includes master's theses abstracts back to 1962. DAI and DAO are very broad databases in that all dissertations, regardless of academic discipline, are abstracted in them.

The materials in DAI and DAO are indexed according to author and important search terms in the title and abstract. No indexer reads each dissertation to assign descriptive terms. Instead, a dissertation will appear in DAI's printed subject indexes only under those important words that appear in the dissertation title. Also, most libraries maintain paper and microfilm copies of only those dissertations completed at their university. Therefore, when an abstract appears relevant, the searcher usually must contact, through interlibrary loan, the university at which the dissertation was conducted to obtain a full-length copy. Alternatively, the searcher can purchase a copy from University Microfilms International (UMI) in Ann Arbor, Michigan. (Universities that maintain agreements with UMI may not loan dissertations through interlibrary loan.)

Although the contents of DAI and DAO are exceptionally broad, it is possible to somewhat circumscribe a search. For instance, when I searched DAO for document records containing the key word homework, the database located 837 records. DAO, however, permits the searcher to limit a search to a certain document type (only dissertations or only master's theses), to only those records containing an abstract (as opposed to just a title), to the latest update of the database, to a specific language or languages, or to specific years. Therefore, when I limited my search to records in English, seven records were removed. When I added the commands "not postsecondary" and "not college," the number of relevant records was reduced to 689. Finally, I limited the search to dissertations and theses produced in 1966 or later. A total of 675 records remained. Then, I examined the record titles and abstracts, marked the documents of interest to me, and printed my third bibliography, just as I had done with my PsycINFO and ERIC searches.

## SSCI

Given the nature of citation indexing, perhaps the most remarkable thing about the SSCI is the breadth of its social science coverage. The SSCI indexes every article from more than 1,500 journals that cover 50 different social science disciplines. The SSCI selectively covers nearly 6,000 other journals that might or might not have social science information in them. Through this process, the SSCI compiles more than 130,000 new journal articles every year. In print, the SSCI dates back to 1972, and on CD-ROM it dates back to 1981.

The SSCI also contains a subject index that uses the significant words in article titles to index documents. Subject searches of the SSCI can be accomplished only through the use of free text terms from article titles. Subject searches can be specified to include only a certain type of document, such as journal articles or book reviews.

To use the citation index component of SSCI, the searcher must provide the reference whose citation history is of interest. A problem with the use of the citation indexes is that numerous errors are contained in the bibliographic information included in journal articles (Boyce & Banning, 1979). Therefore, to be sure that most citations have been located, it might be necessary for searchers to retrieve information on the cited first author, not the specific article of interest, and then sift through these to identify citations that are not listed accurately.

For a recent homework search, I decided to go to the library and use the printed SSCI to identify authors of journal articles who had cited my research synthesis on homework. I could then retrieve these articles to see if they described research on homework that had been published since the appearance of the synthesis. The synthesis had appeared in 1989 both as a book and as a much briefer article published in *Educational Leadership*. To discover who had cited these publications, I looked up "Cooper H" in each SSCI annual volume beginning in 1990.

The two columns from the 1995 volume containing the records for citations to H. Cooper are reproduced in Table 3.6. In the printed SSCI, the document being cited is displayed in bold. Therefore, under "Cooper H", I worked my way down the listing until I got to "89 Educ Leadership 47 85". This tells me that H. Cooper was the author of an article that appeared in 1989, in *Educational Leadership*, volume 47, and the article began on page 85. Listed under this article are entries describing the five articles whose records were entered during 1995 that cited the *Educational Leadership* piece. The work listed next is the homework book. It was cited three times. One author cited both the book and the journal article. Note also that for some cited documents the searcher is alerted to the fact that additional citations to the work can be found in the *Science Citation Index.* The codes in the far right margin of each column indicate the type of source item—"B" is for book review, "R" is for review, "N" is for technical note, and so on.

There are two other interesting things to note about the SSCI entries. First, in the second column displayed in Table 3.6, there is a list of entries associated with the name "Cooper HM". My middle initial is "M" and I used it for many of my earlier publications. Although the author credit for both the homework book and the article did not use my middle initial, Table 3.6 indicates that one author included my middle initial in citing the book. Also, there is one reference each to "Cooper HA" and "Cooper HC". These are both incorrect citations to works by "Cooper HM" (in fact, they are references to the book you are currently reading). Second, because I am intimately familiar with the work of one H. M. Cooper, it is clear to me that at least one other H. M. Cooper publishes in social science journals.

Space limitations make it impossible to examine each of the thousands of abstracting services available in the social sciences. Most of these are available through on-line computer searches. The content of these services varies from broad coverage of disciplines, such as in ERIC, to highly specialized topic areas, such as aging (Ageline), substance abuse (DRUGINFO), and marriage and the family (Family Resources Database). Information on abstracting services can be obtained from your librarian, from the *Introduction to Reference Work: Volume 1* (Katz, 1997), or from the *Directory of Online Databases,* among other sources.

### Limitations of Computer Searches

It is impossible to overemphasize the value of the computer search to the research synthesist. With phenomenal speed, the synthesist can obtain extensive lists of potentially relevant documents. Because of the amount of time saved and the convenience of having a hard copy of the search outcome, which can then be evaluated at the synthesist's convenience, a computer search can be much broader than if the same database searches were undertaken manually.

Computer searching is not without problems. In particular, if computerized searches are used exclusively, the possibility of making accidental discoveries is greatly diminished (Menzel, 1966; Stoan, 1982). Performing

## TABLE 3.6
### Example of *Social Science Citation Index* Entries During 1995

| | | VOL | PG | YR |
|---|---|---|---|---|
| **COOPER H** ——— | | | | |
| **46 THOSE PRESENT OFFICI** | | | | |
| WHITE GM | PUBL CULTUR | 7 | 529 | 95 |
| **59 S AFR MED J** | | 33 | 349 | |
| **67 S AFR MED J** | | 41 | 902 | |
| LOUW J | S AFR J PSY | 25 | 99 | 95 R |
| **79 REV EDUC RES** | | 49 | 389 | |
| STASSEN MLA | REV HIGH ED | 18 | 361 | 95 |
| **83 PYGMALION GROWS** | | | | |
| BABAD E | J EDUC PSYC | 87 | 361 | 95 |
| **83 PYGMALION GROWS STUD** | | | | |
| PAPAIOAN.A | J SPORT EXE | 17 | 18 | 95 |
| **83 TEACHER STUDENT PERC** | | | | |
| GOTTFRED.DC | J EDUC RES | 88 | 155 | 95 |
| **84 RES MOTIVATION ED** | | | p209 | |
| URDAN TC | REV EDUC RE | 65 | 213 | 95 R |
| **84 RES MOTIVATION ED** | | 1 | 209 | |
| FONTAINE AM | EUR J PSY E | 9 | 225 | 94 |
| **85 J RES DEV EDUC** | | 18 | 25 | |
| TATAR M | BR J SOC ED | 16 | 93 | 95 |
| **88 J PERS SOC PSYCHOL** | | 55 | 937 | |
| HART AJ | J PERS SOC | 68 | 109 | 95 |
| **89 EDUC LEADERSHIP** | | 47 | 85 | |
| BAUCH PA | EDUC EVAL P | 17 | 1 | 95 |
| GAJRIA M | J LEARN DI | 28 | 291 | 95 |
| GEARY DC | AM PSYCHOL | 50 | 24 | 95 R |
| HOOVERDE.KV | ELEM SCH J | 95 | 435 | 95 |
| SALEND SJ | REM SPEC ED | 16 | 271 | 95 |
| **89 HOMEWORK** | | | | |
| HOOVERDE.KV | ELEM SCH J | 95 | 435 | 95 |
| JAYANTHI M | REM SPEC ED | 16 | 102 | 95 |
| PRESSLEY M | EDUC PSYCH | 30 | 207 | 95 |
| **89 INTEGRATING RES GUID** | | | | |
| BISHOPCL.C | COMP HUM BE | 11 | 241 | 95 |
| **90 RES METHODS PERSONAL** | | | | |
| TANG SH | APPL COGN P | 9 | 365 | 95 |
| **91 COCHLEAR IMPLANTS PR** | | | | |
| (ANON) | J BR ASSN T | 19 | 135 | 95 |
| **91 J PERS** | | 59 | 109 | |
| ROMAN RJ | J PERSONAL | 63 | 113 | 95 |
| **93 WALL STREET J** | | 0316 | 8 | 1 |
| SCHALOCK RL | J MENT HEAL | 22 | 358 | 95 |
| **94 HDB RES SYNTHESIS** | | | | |
| WIELAND D | EVAL HEALTH | 18 | 252 | 95 |
| **94 HD RES SYNTHESIS** | | | | |
| SEE SCI FOR 6 ADDITIONAL CITATIONS | | | | |
| BALAS EA | J AM MED IN | 2 | 307 | 95 |
| " | MED CARE | 33 | 687 | 95 |
| COOPER H | AM PSYCHOL | 50 | 111 | 95 N |
| EAGLY AH | " | | 50 | 145 | 95 R |
| ELKIS H | ARCH G PSYC | 52 | 735 | 95 R |
| GLASS GV | CONT PSYCHO | 40 | 736 | 95 B |
| LEPPER MR | APPL COGN P | 9 | 411 | 95 |

| | | VOL | PG | YR |
|---|---|---|---|---|
| PREISS RW | EVAL HEALTH | 18 | 315 | 95 |
| SCHULTZ PW | J ENVIR PSY | 15 | 105 | 95 |
| SHADISH WR | J MAR FAM T | 21 | 345 | 95 |
| SLAVIN RE | J CLIN EPID | 48 | 9 | 95 |
| VEVEA JL | PSYCHOMETRI | 60 | 419 | 95 |
| WEISZ JR | PSYCHOL B | 117 | 450 | 95 R |
| **94 HDB RSE SYNTHESIS** | | | | |
| YEATON WH | EVAL HEALTH | 18 | 283 | 95 |
| **94 HOUSE CAT** | | | | |
| SHORT K | READ TEACH | 48 | 422 | 95 B |
| **94 HDB RES SYNTHESIS** | | | p87 | |
| HASSELBLV | MED CARE | 33 | 202 | 95 |
| **94 J LEARN DISABIL** | | 27 | 470 | |
| GAJRIA M | J LEARN DI | 28 | 291 | 95 |
| JAYANTHI M | REM SPEC ED | 16 | 102 | 96 |
| SALENG SJ | REM SPEC ED | 16 | 271 | 95 |
| SODERLUN.J | J E BEN DIS | 3 | 190 | 96 |
| **94 WALL STREET J 8014** | | | p1 | |
| RABE GA | DEVIANT BEH | 16 | 223 | 95 |
| **94 WALL ST J 1282A** | | 1 | | |
| GRANT JM | INDIANA LAW | 70 | 1353 | 95 |
| **94 WALL ST J 0002A** | | 2 | | |
| CHARNOVI.S | CORNELL I L | 27 | 489 | 94 |
| **95 AM PSYCHOL** | | 50 | 111 | |
| LIPSEY MW | AM PSYCHOL | 50 | 113 | 95 N |
| **COOPER HA** ——— | | | | |
| **89 INTEGRATING RES** | | | | |
| WHITLEY BE | PSYCHOL B | 117 | 146 | 95 R |
| **COOPER HC** ——— | | | | |
| **89 INTEGRATING RES GUID** | | | | |
| PETROSIN.AJ | EVAL REV | 19 | 274 | 95 |
| **COOPER HF** ——— | | | | |
| **92 MATS BRIEF MAY** | | | p27 | |
| RABERT B | AUSSEN-POLI | 46 | 71 | 95 |
| **COOPER HM** ——— | | | | |
| **75 J EDUC PSYCHOL** | | 67 | 312 | |
| COOPER H | J EXP EDUC | 63 | 231 | 95 |
| HARRISON L | QUEST | 47 | 7 | 95 |
| **79 J PERS SOC PSYCHOL** | | 37 | 131 | |
| BURT DB | PSYCHOL B | 117 | 285 | 95 R |
| COLLIN CA | SOC BEH PER | 22 | 355 | 94 |
| EAGLY AH | AM PSYCHOL | 50 | 145 | 95 R |
| GLADSTON.TR | J ABN C PSY | 23 | 597 | 95 |
| ZHANG J | ADOLESCENCE | 29 | 885 | 94 |
| **79 J EDUC PSYCHOL** | | 71 | 375 | |
| LINEHAN SL | J SPEC EDUC | 29 | 295 | 95 |
| **80 NOCTURNAL MALAGASY** | | | p191 | |
| RUMBAUGH D | SOCIAL RES | 62 | 711 | 95 |
| **80 PSYCHOL BULL** | | 87 | 442 | |
| SEE SCI FOR 1 ADDITIONAL CITATION | | | | |
| BUSHMAN BJ | PSYCHOL B | 117 | 530 | 95 |
| COOPER H | AM PSYCHOL | 50 | 111 | 95 N |
| FAITH MS | J COUN PSYC | 42 | 390 | 95 R |
| PREISS RW | EVAL HEALTH | 18 | 315 | 95 |

**TABLE 3.6**

*Continued*

| | VOL PG YR | | | VOL PG YR |
|---|---|---|---|---|
| **82 REV EDUC RES** | 52 291 | | JOHNSON BT | J APPL PSYC | 80 94 95 |
| BAKER D  INT J SCI E | 17 695 95 | | KRYWANIO ML | NURS RES | 43 133 94 |
| DIFABIO RP  PHYS THER | 75 865 95 | | LEFRANCO.R | CAN J AGING | 14 52 95 |
| PREISS RW  EVAL HEALTH | 18 315 95 | | LEPPER MR | APPL COGN P | 9 411 95 |
| **83 PYGMALION GROWS STUD** | | | ROSENTHA.R | PSYCHOL B | 118 183 95 |
| HART RD  COMMUN EDUC | 44 140 95 | | "  | PSYCHOL SCI | 5 329 94 |
| PIANTA RC  DEV PSYCHOP | 7 295 95 | | SMITH MC | CANCER NURS | 18 167 95 |
| **84 ELEM SCHOOL J** | 85 77 | | **89 INTEGRATIVE RES REV** | | |
| WEINSTEI.RS  AM EDUC RES | 32 121 95 | | GANONG LH | FAM RELAT | 44 501 95 |
| **84 INTEGRATIVE RES REV** | | | **89 INTEGRATING RES GUID** | v2 | |
| BURT DB  PSYCHOL B | 117 285 95 R | | SWANSON JM | ADV CL CH P | 17 265 95 R |
| HEESACKE.M  COUNS PSYCH | 23 611 95 | | **91 PERS SOC PSYCHOL B** | 17 245 | |
| OROURKE TW  J SCH HEALT | 65 33 95 N | | WHITE MJ | AM J MENT R | 100 293 95 |
| SLAVIN RE  J CLIN EPID | 48 9 95 | | **93 J COMP NEUROL** | 328 313 | |
| WEISSING.E  LEISURE SCI | 17 141 95 | | SEE SCI FOR 8 ADDITIONAL CITATIONS | | |
| **84 INTEGRATIVE RES REV** | v2 | | BENSHLOM.R | BEHAV GENET | 25 239 95 |
| FRANCES A  PSYCHIAT AN | 25 15 95 | | **93 NATURE** | 361 156 | |
| **89 EDUC PSYCHOL** | 24 79 | | SEE SCI FOR 12 ADDITIONAL CITATIONS | | |
| BLATCHFO.P  OX REV EDUC | 20 411 94 | | BARTON RA | PHI T ROY B | 348 381 95 |
| WILD KP  Z ENTWICK P | 27 78 95 | | BENSHLOM.R | BEHAV GENET | 25 239 95 |
| **89 HOMEWORK** | | | **94 HDS RES SYNTHESIS** | | |
| SODERLUN.J  J E BEH DIS | 3 150 95 | | SEE SCI FOR 2 ADDITIONAL CITATIONS | | |
| **89 INTEGRATING RES GUID** | | | HASSELBL.V | PSYCHOL B | 117 167 95 |
| SEE SCI FOR 1 ADDITIONAL CITATION | | | **COOPER HSF** ——————— | | |
| BUSHMAN BJ  PSYCHOL B | 117 530 95 | | **87 LIFT OFF** | | |
| BUSSE RT  J SCH PSYCH | 33 269 95 | | NICHOLAS JM | AVIAT SP EN | 66 63 95 R |
| CROUCH GI  ANN TOURISM | 22 103 95 | | | | |
| GOREY KM  PERS INDIV | 19 345 95 R | | | | |
| HUGHES C  AM J MENT R | 99 623 95 R | | | | |

SOURCE: Reprinted with permission of the Institute for Scientific Information.

a computer search, however, does not prevent the searcher from browsing through journals and library shelves, and browsing is recommended before the computer search begins. Not only can browsing expand the searcher's search terms for the computer but also the searcher can identify relevant articles that should appear on the computer printout. If they do not appear, something has gone awry.

## DETERMINING THE ADEQUACY
## OF LITERATURE SEARCHES

The question of which and how many sources of information to use in a search has no general answer. The appropriate sources will partly be a function of the topic under consideration and partly of the resources of the synthesist. As a rule, however, searchers must always employ multiple channels with different entry and access restrictions so that they minimize any systematic differences between included and unincluded studies. If a synthesist has uncovered different studies through channels that do not share similar restrictions, then the overall conclusions of the synthesis should be replicable by another synthesist using different, but also complementary, sources for primary research. This rule embodies the scientific criterion of replicability.

Secondary channels, especially reference databases and research registers if they are available, should form the backbone of any comprehensive literature search. These sources probably contain the information most closely approximating all research. Typically, they cast the widest net, within their stated, restricted but known goals.

Previously, I mentioned that concentrating on only formal sources would produce a set of studies that overrepresented published, statistically significant results. Due to peer review, however, it can be counterargued that published research has undergone the most rigorous methodological appraisal by established researchers and probably is of the highest quality. As shall be shown in Chapter 4, however, publication does not ensure that only studies of high quality will be included in the synthesis. Faulty studies often make their way into print. Well-conducted studies may never be submitted for publication.

A focus on only published research might be legitimate in two circumstances. First, published research often contains several dozen or, in some cases, hundreds of relevant works. In such an instance, it is likely that although the published research may overestimate the magnitude of a relation, it probably will not incorrectly identify the direction of a relationship. The suggested magnitude of the relation can be adjusted for publication bias or interpreted cautiously. Also, enough instances of a hypothesis test will be covered to allow a legitimate examination of which study characteristics covary with study outcomes.

Second, there are many hypotheses that have multiple testings in the literature that were not the primary focus of the research. For instance, many psychological and educational studies include gender as a variable in the research design and report hypothesis tests of gender differences, although these are only an ancillary interest of the primary researchers. The bias toward significant results in publications probably does not extend much beyond the primary hypothesis. Therefore, a hypothesis that appears in many articles as a secondary interest of the researchers will be affected by the publication bias to a lesser degree than the researcher's primary focus.

Generally speaking, however, focusing on only published studies is not advisable. In addition, synthesists should not restrict their searches to published outlets, even if they ultimately decide to include only published work in their syntheses. To make a well-informed choice about what to put in and leave out of a synthesis, and even to help decide what the important issues are in a field, the synthesist needs to have the most thorough grasp of the literature.

Finally, the information contained in informal channels is not likely to reflect information gleaned from all potential sources. Research found informally, however, might complement that gained through formal and secondary channels because it is likely to be more recent. Therefore, searchers should also conduct informal searches but should carefully examine the percentage of the total relevant literature that is made up of information retrieved in this manner. If this percentage is large, it is a warning sign indicating that the searcher should go to other formal and secondary sources before terminating the search.

## VALIDITY ISSUES IN STUDY RETRIEVAL

At the beginning of this chapter, I mentioned that literature searches have two different targets—previous research and individuals or groups relevant to the topic area. Therefore, it is necessary for research synthesists to address the adequacy of their accessed studies with respect to each of the targets. The synthesist must ask (a) how the retrieved studies might differ from all studies and (b) how the individuals or groups contained in retrieved studies might differ from all individuals or groups of interest.

Much of this chapter has dealt with how to answer the first of these questions. Every study does not have an equal chance of being retrieved by the synthesist. It is likely that studies easily obtained through the synthesist's retrieval channels are different from studies that never become available. Therefore, the synthesist must pay careful attention to what the inaccessible studies might have said and how this might differ from what is contained in studies that have been retrieved.

The synthesist's second population of interest, referring to individuals or other basic units of analysis, injects a note of optimism into the discussion. There is good reason to believe research syntheses will pertain more directly to a target population than will the separate primary research efforts in the topic area. The overall literature can contain studies conducted at different times, on adults and children, and in different countries with varied racial and ethnic backgrounds. A literature can also contain research conducted under different testing conditions with different methods. For certain problem areas containing numerous replications, the population of referent individuals accessible to a synthesist may closely approximate the target population of the primary researcher. Although we might be resigned to population restrictions in primary research, we need not be so acquiescent about the referent population of research syntheses.

Of course, we must bear in mind that the biases against the null hypothesis and contradictory findings may affect the available samples of people as well as the sampled studies of the synthesis. To the extent that more retrievable studies are associated with particular subpopulations of elements, the retrieval bias will restrict the accessible populations of individuals.

The first threat to validity associated with the literature search is that the studies in the synthesis probably will not include all studies pertinent to the topic of interest. Again, synthesists should access as many information channels as needed to ensure that no obvious, avoidable bias exists, within the limits set by cost-effectiveness.

The second threat to validity occurring during the retrieval of research is that the individuals or groups in the retrieved studies may not represent all individuals or elements in the target population. Of course, the primary researcher's choice of units is beyond the control of the research synthesist, but the synthesist is obligated to describe carefully the missing populations and to qualify any conclusions based on missing or overrepresented samples.

### Protecting Validity

1. The most powerful protection against threats to validity caused by unrepresentative samples of studies in syntheses comes from a broad and exhaustive search of the literature. Although the law of diminishing returns applies here, a complete literature search has to include at least a search of reference databases, a perusal of relevant journals, the examination of references in past primary research and research syntheses, and informal contacts with active and interested researchers. The more exhaustive a search, the more confident a synthesist can be that another synthesist using similar, but perhaps not identical, sources of information will reach the same conclusions.

2. In their manuscripts, synthesists should be explicit about how studies were gathered, including information on the reference databases searched, for what years, and with what search terms. Without this information, readers of the synthesis have no way of comparing the validity of the conclusion

of a particular synthesis with the conclusions that may be contained in other syntheses.

3. Synthesists should present indices of potential retrieval bias if they are available. For instance, many research syntheses examine whether any difference exists in the results of studies that are published versus those that are unpublished.

4. The research synthesist should summarize the sample characteristics of individuals used in the separate studies. Given the general gloom that accompanies most discussion of sample representativeness in the social sciences, many synthesists will find this summary reveals an unexpected strength of their research syntheses.

## EXERCISES

1. Define a topic area by specifying the search terms and the necessary Boolean syntax operators that would guide a literature search. Pick a few years and do a manual search and a computer search of a reference database. Perform a parallel search of the World Wide Web. How are the outcomes different? Which was more useful and cost-effective?

2. For a topic of your choice, choose the channels you would use to search the literature and the order in which you would access them. For each step in the search, describe its strengths, limits, and cost-effectiveness.

# 4

# *The Data Evaluation Stage*

This chapter describes and evaluates different approaches to judging the methodological adequacy of primary research. It also points out problems encountered in retrieving information from research reports. It examines how to identify independent hypothesis tests when multiple tests of the same hypothesis occur in the same sample or study. The chapter concludes with a discussion of validity issues that arise during the data evaluation stage.

The data evaluation stage of a scientific endeavor involves making judgments about whether or not individual data points are trustworthy enough to be included in the research. This activity must be carried out regardless of whether the data points are the scores of individual participants on measured variables, as in primary research, or the outcomes of studies, as in research synthesis. Data evaluation requires the investigator to establish criteria for judging the adequacy of the procedures used to gather the data. The researcher must examine all the potential errors or irrelevancies that might have influenced each data point. Then, the researcher must determine whether these influences are substantial enough to dictate that the data point be dropped from the inquiry.

## EVALUATING DATA IN
## SOCIAL SCIENCE RESEARCH

*Similarities Between Primary Research and Research Synthesis.* Both primary researchers and research synthesists examine their data looking for extreme values, errors in recording, or other indicators that suggest unreliable measurements. Individual data points are examined to see if they are statistical outliers (Barnett & Lewis, 1984). The researcher wants to discover if the most extreme data points are of questionable trustworthiness, either because they are full of error or because they are not really members of a target population. To do this, the researcher can use statistical procedures and conventions to compare the most extreme data points to the overall sample distribution.

The search for statistical outliers in research synthesis involves similar procedures. Instead of examining individual data points, however, synthesists examine the size of relationships or treatment effects revealed in each study. They try to determine if the most extreme study outcomes are too different from the overall distribution of outcomes to be considered trustworthy.

As an example, statistical outliers sometimes occur because errors are made when data are transferred from data sheets to computer files. A primary researcher may observe that a given individual's score on an aggression measure takes a value not on the scale, for instance, when the scale ranges from 0 to 20 and the individual has a score of 90 in the computer file. The researcher might then go back to the original data sheets and discover that a score of 09 was mistakenly recorded as 90. Similarly, a research synthesist may find that the average of 20 correlations that relate dogmatism to acceptance of myths about rape is $r = .15$. The synthesist might also note that one correlation is recorded as $r = .90$, and this seems much too large. A check of the coding sheets might reveal that the actual value was $r = .09$, and the numbers were transposed in the computer files. The average correlation would then have to be recalculated.

*Differences Between Primary Research and Research Synthesis.* Other means for identifying unreliable data are different for the two types of research. In primary research, a participant's responses are sometimes discarded because the researcher has evidence that the individual did not attend to the appropriate stimuli or that the response instructions were misunderstood. If deception or some other form of misdirection was used in the research, individual data may be discarded because the participant did not believe the cover story or deduced the hidden hypothesis.

In research synthesis, there is only one potential criterion, beyond error in recording, for discarding data: the validity of the study's methods. Synthesists decide whether each study was conducted in a careful enough manner so that the result can be trusted to shed light on the hypothesis of interest. Synthesists can make either discrete decisions—whether or not to include the study—or continuous ones—whether to weight studies differently depending on their relative degree of trustworthiness. A large part of this chapter will be devoted to criteria for judging the methodological quality of a study.

Most social scientists agree that methodological quality should be the primary criterion for decisions about how much trust to place in a study's results. In practice, however, the predispositions of synthesists about what the outcome of the synthesis should be often have a strong impact on how studies are evaluated. It is important to examine the sources and effects of synthesists' prior beliefs about a research area.

## PREDISPOSITIONS OF
## THE SYNTHESIST

Almost every primary researcher and research synthesist begins an inquiry with some expectation about its outcome. In primary research, methodologists have constructed elaborate systems of controls to eliminate artifactual results created by these experimenter expectancy effects.

In research syntheses, protections against expectancy bias are fewer and less foolproof. Synthesists are fully aware of their biases and often are also aware of the outcomes of studies as the research is being collected and evaluated. This leads to the possibility that the evaluation of a research project's methodology will be colored by the evaluator's predisposition toward its outcomes. The impact of predispositions on syntheses were so great in the past that Glass (1976) made the following remark about the process:

> A common method for integrating several studies with inconsistent find-
> ings is to carp on the design or analysis deficiencies of all but a few
> studies—those remaining frequently being one's own work or that of
> one's students or friends—and then advance the one or two "acceptable"
> studies as the truth of the matter. (p. 4)

Mahoney (1977) performed an experiment that directly tested the impact of predispositions on the evaluation of research. He sampled guest editors for the *Journal of Applied Behavior Analysis* and asked them to rate several aspects of a controlled manuscript. Mahoney found that the methods, discussion, and contribution of the manuscript were evaluated more favorably if the study confirmed the synthesist's predisposition about the results. In a related study, Lord, Ross, and Lepper (1979) found that readers rated studies that supported their attitudes as more methodologically sound than studies with counterattitudinal results. More striking, the undergraduates who participated in the Lord and colleagues study showed polarization in attitudes despite the fact that they all read the same research abstracts. That is, even though all participants read one study that supported their prior belief and one that refuted it, after reading the two studies participants saw more support for their initial positions.

One way to minimize the impact of predispositions on the evaluation of research would be to have information gathered from studies by coders who are unaware of the studies' outcomes. This can be done by having separate coders unfamiliar with the research area code different parts of the research article. For example, one coder codes the methods section and another codes the results section. Schramm (1989) evaluated this "differential photocopying" procedure. She found it created new problems and did not lead to much higher interrater reliability.

Thus, it appears that predispositions favoring a result can influence the synthesists' judgments about the methodological quality of a piece of research. If a study disconfirms the synthesist's predisposition, the synthesist is more likely to attempt to find some aspect of the study that renders it irrelevant or methodologically unsound. Studies that confirm predispositions, however, may be included even though their relevance is questionable or their methods are flawed.

## JUDGING RESEARCH QUALITY

Problems with quality judgments may be even more extensive than those associated with synthesist predispositions. It may be the case that even "disinterested" judges of research could not agree on what is and is not a quality study.

*Studies of Evaluator Agreement About Research Quality.* Numerous studies have examined the reliability of evaluations made about manuscripts submitted to journals in the fields of psychology (Fiske & Fogg, 1990; Scarr & Weber, 1978), education (Marsh & Ball, 1989), and medicine (Justice, Berlin, Fletcher, & Fletcher, 1994). These studies typically calculate some measure of agreement between the recommendations made by manuscript readers concerning whether or not a manuscript should be accepted for publication.

In an interesting demonstration, Peters and Ceci (1982) resubmitted 12 published articles to the journals in which they initially appeared. The manuscripts were identical to the originals except that the names of the submitters were changed and their affiliations were changed from "high-status" to "low-status" institutions. Only 3 of the 12 articles were detected as being resubmissions. Of the 9 articles that completed the rereview process, 8 were not accepted for publication.

In many respects, the judgments of manuscript evaluators are more complex than those of research synthesists. The manuscript evaluator must consider several dimensions that do not interest the research synthesist, including the clarity of writing and the interests of the journal's readership. Also, a journal editor will sometimes deliberately choose evaluators who represent different perspectives. The editor, however, still hopes that the evaluators will agree on the disposition of the manuscript. Also, of course, if perfectly objective criteria were available (and were employed), the evaluators would come to concurring decisions.

Some of the differences between judgments by manuscript evaluators and research synthesists were controlled in a study conducted by Gottfredson (1978). He removed much of the variability in judges' ratings that might be due to differing initial biases by asking authors to nominate experts competent to evaluate their work. Gottfredson was able to obtain at least two expert evaluations for each of 121 articles. The experts evaluated the quality of the articles on a three-question scale that left the meaning of the term *quality* ambiguous. An interjudge agreement coefficient of $r = .41$ was obtained. On a 36-item evaluation scale that tapped many explicit facets of research quality, an interjudge agreement coefficient of $r = .46$ was obtained.

Why do overall judgments of quality differ? In addition to differences in predispositions, it is possible to locate two sources of variance in evaluators' quality judgments: (a) the relative importance they assign to different research design characteristics and (b) their judgments about how well a particular study met a design criterion. To demonstrate the first source of variance, I conducted a study in which six experts in school desegregation research were asked to rank order the importance of six design characteristics for establishing the "utility or information value" of a school desegregation study (Cooper, 1986). The six characteristics were (a) the experimental manipulation (or in this case, the definition of deseg-regation); (b) the adequacy of the control group; (c) the validity of the outcome measure; (d) the representativeness of the sample; (e) the repre-sentativeness of the environmental conditions surrounding the study; and (f) the appropriateness of the statistical analyses. The intercorrelations of the rankings among the experts varied from $r = .77$ to $r = -.29$, with the average correlation being $r = .47$.

In summary, the studies of judgments of methodological quality indicate evaluator agreement is less than one would like. Sometimes, however, judges are picked to represent varying perspectives. Also, the statistical measures of agreement have been criticized as being too conservative (Whitehurst, 1984). Finally, the reliability of judgments can be enhanced by adding more judges. That is, a decision to accept or reject an article for publication based on samples of 10 evaluators' ratings will, on average, correspond more with the consensus of 10 other evaluators than will samples based on 2 evaluators' decisions. It is rare, however, that such large pools of evaluators are used to make quality judgments about research, either by journal editors or by research synthesists.

*A Priori Exclusion of Research Versus A Posteriori Examination of Research Differences.* The studies of agreement about research quality and the role of predispositions in the evaluation process demonstrate instances in which subjectivity intrudes on attempts to be scientifically objective. The point is important because research synthesists often debate whether or not a priori judgments of research quality should be used to exclude studies from their work.

This debate was best captured in an exchange of views between Hans Eysenck (1978) and Gene Glass and Mary Smith (1978a) concerning Smith and Glass's (1977) early meta-analysis of research on psychotherapy. Smith and Glass (1977) synthesized more than 300 studies of psychotherapy with no a priori exclusion of studies due to poor methodology. Eysenck felt this strategy represented an abandonment of scholarship and critical judgment:

> A mass of reports—good, bad, and indifferent—are fed into the computer in the hope that people will cease caring about the quality of the material on which the conclusions are based. . . . "Garbage in—garbage out" is a well-known axiom of computer specialists; it applies here with equal force. (p. 517)

Eysenck concluded that "only better designed experiments than those in the literature can bring us a better understanding of the points raised" (p. 517).

In rebuttal, Glass and Smith (1978a) made several points already mentioned in this chapter and in previous ones. First, as noted in Chapter 2, the poor design characteristics of different studies can "cancel" one another out if the results of different studies are consistent. Second, the a priori quality judgments required to exclude studies are likely to vary from judge to judge and be influenced by personal biases. Finally, Glass and Smith claimed they did not advocate the abandonment of quality standards. Instead, they regarded the impact of design quality on study results as "an empirical a posteriori question, not an a priori matter of opinion" (Glass, McGaw, & Smith, 1981, p. 222). They suggested that synthesists thoroughly code the design aspects, good and bad, of each study and then demonstrate if, in fact, the outcomes of studies are related to how the studies were conducted.

The position of Glass and colleagues seems more consistent with a rigorous approach to research synthesis. The decision to include or exclude studies on an a priori basis requires the synthesist to make an overall judgment of quality that is often too subjective to be trustworthy. Instead, a careful enumeration of study characteristics can be devised by a synthesist, and study characteristics can be compared to study results to determine if they covary with one another. If it is empirically demonstrated that "good" studies produce results different from "bad" studies, the results of the good studies can be believed. When no difference is found, it is sensible to retain the bad studies because they contain other variations in methods (such as different samples and locations) that, by their inclusion, will help answer many other questions surrounding the problem area.

The only circumstance in which a priori exclusion of studies may be appropriate is when the criteria for excluding studies are defined before the literature is searched so that the rules do not shift to suit the synthesist, and the number of acceptable studies is large enough to still permit the synthesist to adequately substantiate any general conclusions. In most cases, however, letting the data speak—that is, including all studies and examining empirically the differences in results associated with methods—substitutes a discovery process for the predispositions of the synthesist.

## APPROACHES TO CATEGORIZING RESEARCH METHODS

The decision to test empirically the impact of methodology on research results does not relieve the synthesist of all evaluation responsibilities. The synthesist must still decide what methodological characteristics of studies need to be coded. As I pointed out previously, these decisions will depend on the nature of the question under scrutiny and the types of associated research. If a problem has been addressed mainly through experimental manipulations in laboratory settings, a different set of methodological characteristics may be important than if a correlational, field study, or some mix of the two types of research has been used. In the past, research synthesists have employed two approaches to coding to help them capture differences between good and bad studies. The first approach requires the synthesist to make judgments about the threats to validity that exist in a study. The second approach requires the detailing of the objective design characteristics of a study, as described by the primary researchers.

## The Threats-to-Validity Approach

When Campbell and Stanley (1963) introduced the notion of "threats to validity," they literally transformed the social sciences. They suggested that an identifiable set of extraneous influences associated with each research design could be found that "might produce effects confounded with the experimental stimulus" (p. 5). Different research designs had different validity threats associated with them, and designs could be compared according to their inferential capabilities. More important, less-than-optimal designs could be "triangulated" so that strong inferences could result from multiple studies when the single, "perfect" study could not be performed.

Campbell and Stanley's (1963) notion held the promise of increased sensitivity and objectivity in discussions of research quality. It was not long, however, before some problems in the application of their scheme became apparent. The problems related to creating an exhaustive list of threats to validity and identifying what the implication of each threat might be.

Initially, Campbell and Stanley (1963) proposed two broad classes of validity threats. Threats to *internal* validity related to the direct correspondence between the experimental treatment and the experimental effect. To the extent that this correspondence was compromised by deficiencies in research design, the ability to interpret a study's results would be called into question. Campbell and Stanley listed eight threats to internal validity. Threats to *external* validity related to the generalizability of research results. Evaluating external validity required assessing the representativeness of a study's participants, settings, treatments, and measurement variables. Although the external validity of a study could never be assessed definitively, Campbell and Stanley suggested four classes of threats to representativeness.

Next, Bracht and Glass (1968) offered an expanded list of threats to external validity. They felt that "external validity was not treated as comprehensively as internal validity in the Campbell-Stanley chapter" (p. 437). To rectify this omission, Bracht and Glass identified two broad classes of external validity: *population* validity, referring to generalization to persons not included in a study, and *ecological* validity, referring to nonsampled settings. Two specific threats to population validity were described along with 10 threats to ecological validity.

Later, Campbell (1969) added a ninth threat to internal validity, called *instability,* defined as "unreliability of measures, fluctuations in sampling persons or components, autonomous instability of repeated or equivalent measures" (p. 411).

Next, Cook and Campbell (1979) offered a list of 33 specific threats to validity grouped into four broad classifications. The notions of construct validity and statistical conclusion validity were added to internal and external validity. *Construct* validity referred to "the possibility that the operations which are meant to represent a particular cause or effect construct can be construed in terms of more than one construct" (p. 59). *Statistical conclusion* validity referred to the power and appropriateness of the data analysis technique.

From this brief history, the problems in using the threats-to-validity approach to assess the quality of empirical studies should be clear. First, different researchers may use different lists of threats. For instance, should the threat of instability offered by Campbell (1969) constitute 1 threat, as originally proposed, or 3 threats, as redefined by Cook and Campbell (1979)? Should ecological validity constitute 1 threat or up to 10 different threats? A second problem is the relative weighting of threats: Is the threat involving historical confounds weighted equally with the threat involving restricted generalizability across constructs? Expert methodologists may even disagree on how a particular threat should be classified. For instance, Bracht and Glass (1968) listed experimenter expectancy effects as a threat to external validity, whereas Cook and Campbell (1979) listed it as a threat to the construct validity of causes.

All these problems aside, the threats-to-validity approach to the evaluation of research still represents an improvement in rigor and is certainly preferable to the a priori single judgment of quality it replaces. Each successive list of threats represents an increase in precision and accumulation of knowledge. Also, the list of validity threats gives the synthesist an explicit set of criteria to apply or modify. In that sense, synthesists who use the threats-to-validity approach make their rules of judgment open to criticism and debate. This is a crucial step in making the research evaluation process more objective. Wortman (1994) gives a good summary description of how this approach can be applied.

### The Methods-Description Approach

In the second approach to study evaluation, the synthesist codes exhaustively the objective characteristics of each study's methods as they are described by the primary researchers. This methods-description approach was discussed earlier in connection with the study coding sheet (see Chapter 2). Now, a more detailed examination is in order.

In Campbell and Stanley's (1963) original work, 3 preexperimental designs, 3 true experimental designs, and 10 quasi-experimental designs were described. The list of designs was expanded by Cook and Campbell (1979). In most areas of research, considerably fewer than all the available designs will be needed to describe exhaustively how independent and dependent variables have been paired in the relevant research.

As Campbell and Stanley (1963) noted, experimental designs relate mainly to eliminating threats to internal validity. They hold little information about the three other classes of threats to trustworthiness. Some of these were alluded to in Chapter 2, but more detail should be added here. Examining the credibility of, for example, experimental manipulations and measurements requires a description of the procedures that the primary researchers used to create independent variables and measure dependent variables. With regard to manipulated independent variables, synthesists can code the number and type of empirical realizations used: In how many ways was the independent variable manipulated? Was the manipulation accomplished through written instruction, film, or the creation of a live-action situation? Similarly, synthesists can record the presence or absence of controls to keep the experimenter unaware of the treatment conditions and whether deception or misdirection was used to lead the participant away from guessing the hypothesis. Obviously, these considerations are relevant only when treatment manipulations were employed in the studies of interest.

Distinctions in measurement techniques can be codified by recording the number of measures used; whether they were verbal, written, behavioral, or interpersonal judgments; whether they were standardized, informal, or constructed for the particular study; and their reliabilities, if such assessments are available. Other measurement characteristics might be of interest to particular research areas.

With regard to the population and ecological generalizability of results, it has been suggested that the synthesist can record any restrictions on the types of individuals sampled in the primary studies, when and where the studies were conducted, and when the dependent variable measurements were taken in relation to the manipulation or measurement of the independent variables.

Finally, to assess a study's statistical power, synthesists should record the number of participants, whether a between- or within-subjects design was employed, the number of other factors (sources of variance) extracted by the analyses, and the statistical test used.

One problem with the methods-description approach to evaluating studies is shared with the threats-to-validity approach: Different synthesists may choose to list different methodological characteristics. The methods-description approach, however, has several advantages. First, when studies are being coded the methods-description approach does not require as much integration of material or inferential judgment. Making a judgment about the threat to validity called "low statistical power" provides a good example. The coder can judge whether a study has a good chance to reject a false null hypothesis only through a combination of several explicit study characteristics: size of the sample, between- or within-subjects design, inherent power of the statistical test (e.g., parametric vs. nonparametric), number of other sources of variance extracted in the analysis, or all these. Two coders of the same study might disagree on whether or not a study is low in power but perfectly agree on a coding of the separate components that make up the decision.

The objective design characteristics of studies can be coded with less ambiguity of meaning and, therefore, greater reliability. The question then becomes: Is the integration of methodological information when studies are first coded necessary to assess the presence or absence of a validity threat? For a majority of threats, the answer is no. If an analysis of study results shows that, for example, only studies using within-subjects designs found significant results, then the synthesist can examine this design feature for all of its implications for validity. That is, between-subjects designs may have been too low in power to reveal an effect, or the premeasure in the within-subjects designs may have sensitized the participants to the independent variable manipulation. Thus, although it may be difficult to retrieve the particular aspect of a research design that created a threat to validity, the synthesist often can still examine validity threats when coding methodological distinctions.

### Mixed-Criteria Approach

The optimal strategy for categorizing studies appears to be a mix of the two a posteriori approaches. First, the synthesist should code all potentially relevant, objective aspects of research design. There are threats to validity, however, that may not be captured by this information alone. For instance, the threats to internal validity involving how a control group is treated—that is, diffusion of treatments, compensatory rivalry, or resentful demoralization in the less desirable treatment—are probably best coded directly as threats to validity, although deciding whether they are present or absent still relies heavily on the description of the study presented by the primary researcher. Although this mixed-criteria approach does not remove all problems from study evaluation, it is another step toward explicit, objective decision making in an area previously rife with subjective and arbitrary judgments.

## Synthesis Examples

Two of the four syntheses provide good examples of how research evaluations can be conducted.

First, the synthesis of the effects of homework included three codings related to the internal validity of studies. These were: the type of experimental design (e.g., random assignment or nonequivalent control groups); whether treatments were counterbalanced; and whether the experimenter was also the teacher of the classes receiving the treatments. Other codings of the homework studies related to the construct, external, and statistical conclusion validity of studies (see Table 2.1).

Note that the coders of homework studies made no inferences whatsoever about methods or their validity; they simply gathered information exactly as reported by the primary researchers. Studies that used random assignment, counterbalanced treatments, and experimenters who were not also the class teacher were clearly preferable. Studies that fell short of this ideal, however, were also included in the synthesis, and I examined the impact of the design factors on the actual outcomes of studies. Only if important relations were found between design and outcome were the differences in study results weighted in regard to their relative trustworthiness.

The reliability of personality measurements was a critical methodological issue for the synthesis of research on personality moderators of interpersonal expectancy effects. It is known that, all else being equal, less reliable measures produce smaller correlations with other variables than do more reliable measures. Therefore, if a measure of one personality dimension was less reliable than a measure of a second personality dimension, and if the second measure produced a larger correlation with expectancy bias, it could not be known if the lower correlation was caused by a "true" difference in the impact of the personality dimensions or by more error in how the first dimension was measured.

To assess the effect of measurement reliability on synthesis results, each personality measure was coded for: (a) whether reliability data on the instrument was available (often, this had to be tracked down in sources other than the research report that was being coded); (b) the type of reliability (i.e., internal consistency or test-retest); and (c) the reliability estimate. Internal consistency estimates associated with 48 comparisons and test-retest estimates associated with 22 comparisons were found. Reliability estimates could not be found for 36 of the personality measures. No significant relationship was found when the synthesists tested whether the size of correlations between personality dimensions and interpersonal expectancies was associated with the reliability of the personality measure. Thus, the synthesists could rule out variations in measurement reliability as a threat to the validity of the conclusion that different relations exist between different personality dimensions and expectancy bias.

## PROBLEMS IN DATA RETRIEVAL

Thus far, I have discussed procedures that allow synthesists to find and then evaluate research. Some deficiencies in both retrieval and evaluation procedures have been noted that will frustrate synthesists regardless of how thorough and careful they try to be. Some potentially relevant studies do not become public and defy the grasp of even the most conscientious search procedures. With regard to evaluating studies, it is impossible to remove all subjectivity from the process, and some judgments are inherently ambiguous. A third set of problems span both the retrieval and the evaluation phases of research synthesis. These problems, almost completely beyond the control of the synthesist, involve (a) the inability of libraries to ensure that all documents of potential relevance to the synthesist are on hand, (b) the incomplete or careless reporting of data by primary researchers, and (c) the less-than-perfect information processing skills of the people who retrieve information from studies. Each of the three problems will be dealt with separately.

### Problems in Library Retrieval

Every research synthesist will find that some documents of potential relevance (based on their title or abstract) cannot be obtained from their personal or institutional library. To what lengths should the synthesist go to retrieve these documents? The use of interlibrary loans is a viable route. As noted earlier, interlibrary loan can even be used to obtain dissertations and masters theses, or dissertations can be purchased from University Microfilms International.

Contacting the primary researchers directly is another possibility, although personal contact often results in only a low rate of response. Whether or not a primary researcher can be located and induced to send a document is influenced in part by the age of the requested material and the status of the requester. In general, when deciding how much effort should be expended trying to retrieve documents that are difficult to obtain, the searcher should consider (a) the likelihood that the needed document actually contains relevant information and if so how much, (b) the percentage of the total known documents that are difficult to find, (c) the cost involved in undertaking extraordinary retrieval procedures (e.g., interlibrary loan is cheap, buying dissertations is expensive), and (d) any time constraints operating on the synthesist.

### Incomplete and Erroneous Research Reports

Perhaps the most frustrating occurrence in data retrieval occurs when synthesists obtain primary research reports but the reports do not contain the needed information. Incomplete reporting will be of primary concern to research synthesists who intend to perform meta-analyses. Reports can be missing information on statistical outcomes, preventing the meta-analyst from estimating the magnitude of the difference between two groups or the relationship between two variables. Also, reports can be missing information on study characteristics, preventing the meta-analyst from determining if study outcomes were related to how the study was conducted. What should the meta-analyst do about missing data? Several conventions can be suggested to handle the most common problems.

#### Incomplete Reporting of Statistical Outcomes

Research reports sometimes contain insufficient information about the results of statistical procedures carried out by the primary researchers. Statistical data are most often omitted when the results are nonsignificant. The synthesist has limited options when a relationship or comparison is reported as "nonsignificant" and the primary researchers do not give the associated means and standard deviations, inference test value, $p$ level, or effect size.

One option is to contact the primary researchers and request the information. As I noted previously, the success of this tactic will depend partly on whether the researcher can be located and the status of the requester. The likelihood of compliance with the request will also depend on how easy it is for the researcher to retrieve the information. There is less chance a request will be met if the study is old, if the desired analyses are different from those originally conducted, or if much data is asked for.

Another option is to treat the comparison as having uncovered an exact null result. That is, for any statistical analysis involving this comparison, a probability of .5 (in the one-tailed instance) and a relationship strength of zero is assumed. It is reasonable to expect that this convention has a conservative impact on the results of the meta-analysis. In general, when this convention is used, the average relationship strength will be closer to zero than if the exact results of nonsignificant relationships were known.

A third option is to leave the comparison out of the meta-analysis. This strategy will likely lead to a higher average relationship than if the missing value was known. All else being equal, nonsignificant findings will be associated with the smaller relationship estimates in a distribution of sampled estimates.

Most meta-analysts choose the third option, especially if the number of missing values is small relative to the number of known values. If meta-analysts can classify missing-value comparisons according to the direction of their findings, however—that is, if they know which group had the higher mean or whether the relationship was positive or negative—these comparisons can be included in vote-count procedures (discussed in Chapter 5). Using vote counts, it is possible to estimate the strength of a relationship (see Bushman & Wang, 1995).

If many comparisons with missing results are found, meta-analysts can calculate average relationships both with the missing values left out and with them counted as exact null findings. In this way, meta-analysts can determine whether their overall conclusion is the same using different assumptions about the data. When statisticians analyze the same data using different assumptions, it is called sensitivity analysis.

In addition to incompleteness, some reports are inexact in their statistical data. Many reports will describe statistical tests as reaching the $p < .05$ level of significance rather than describing the exact probability associated with the outcome of the inference test. In this case, meta-analysts who must rely on $p$ levels to calculate their desired statistics can recalculate the $p$ levels to reflect their exact value.

Sometimes, reports will contain the statistical outcomes of a comparison, but the meta-analyst still might not have the information he or she needs because of the testing procedure used by the primary research. Synthesists who want to perform quantitative combinations often find two primary analyses are incommensurable because they are based on different analytic designs. This would be the case if one study reported a simple $t$-test comparison of an alcohol and control group on a measure of aggression, whereas another study reported an analysis of variance employing the sex and age of participants as additional factors in the design. All else being equal—and assuming some sex and age effect—the second experiment will produce a lower probability level and a larger alcohol effect because the alcohol-versus-control difference is compared to a smaller error term in the second analysis.

Glass et al. (1981) outlined procedures for equating statistical results from studies using different numbers of factors in their analytic design. In practice, however, primary researchers rarely report their results in enough detail to carry out the needed transformations. The meta-analyst should determine empirically whether the statistical results of a study are related to the number of factors in the analysis. If a relation is found, the synthesist should report separately the results obtained from analyses of studies that used only the single factor of interest.

Another problem arises when some primary researchers use parametric statistics (those that assume normal distributions) and others use nonparametric statistics (ones that make no assumptions about distributions) to test and express the same relationship. For instance, this would be the case if one researcher measures aggression in an alcohol study by calculating the average shock intensity administered by each participant (dictating the use of parametric tests) and another simply records whether each participant did or did not aggress (dictating use of nonparametric tests). Most often, statistical techniques based on one set of assumptions will predominate greatly over the other. Then, the statistics from the lesser-used approach can be converted to their dominant-approach equivalents and aggregated as though they shared the dominant assumptions. As long as the number of conversions is small, there will be no great distortion of results. If the split between parametric and nonparametric tests is relatively even, the two sets of studies should be examined separately.

Finally, there is the problem of errors in statistical analyses. Although no one knows exactly how common errors are in statistical analyses, meta-analysts should cross-check the statistics presented in research reports to ensure that none of the results imply wild values and all of the results reported about a comparison are consistent with one another.

*Incomplete Reporting of*
*Other Study Characteristics*

Research reports can also be missing information concerning the details of studies other than their outcomes. For example, reports often will be missing information on the composition of samples (e.g., their gender, age, or ethnic makeup) or treatment characteristics (e.g., treatment fidelity or intensity). Meta-analysts want this information so they can examine whether treatment effects or relationship magnitudes are related to the conditions under which the comparisons or estimates were made. When study information of this type is missing, the meta-analyst must leave that comparison out of the analysis, although it may be included in other analyses for which the needed information is available.

The amount of concern a meta-analyst should have over missing study characteristics will depend partly on why the data are missing. Some data will be missing at random. That is, there will be no systematic reason why some reports include information on the characteristic, whereas others do not. If this is the case, then the outcome of an analysis examining the relationship between study outcomes and study values on the characteristic will be unaffected by the missing data, except, of course, for a loss of statistical power.

If the reason data are missing relates systematically to study outcomes, or to the values of the missing data themselves, then the problem is more serious. In this case, the missing data might be affecting the results of the analysis. For example, suppose primary researchers are more likely to report that the participants in their study were all males if the result indicates a significant affect of alcohol on aggression. Nonsignificant effects are more often associated with mixed-sex samples, but this is unknown to the meta-analyst because researchers who find nonsignificant results are less inclined to report the sample's composition. In such a case, the meta-analyst would have a hard time discovering the relationship between gender and the magnitude of the alcohol effect.

Pigott (1994) suggested several strategies for dealing with missing study characteristics. First, as mentioned for study outcomes, the comparison can be left out of the analysis. Second, missing values can be filled in with the mean of all known values on the characteristic of interest. This strategy does not affect the outcome of the analysis, except to raise its power. It is most appropriate when the meta-analyst is examining several study characteristics together in one analysis. In such a case, a single missing value may delete the entire study and this may not be desirable. Third, the missing value can be predicted using regression analysis. In essence, this strategy uses known values of the missing variable found in other studies to predict the most likely value for the missing data point. Pigott also describes several more complicated ways to estimate missing data.

In most instances, I would advise meta-analysts to stick with the simpler techniques for handling missing data. As techniques become more complex, more assumptions are needed to justify them. Also, when more complicated techniques are used, it becomes more important to conduct sensitivity analysis. It is always good to compare results using filled-in

missing values with results obtained when missing values are simply
omitted from the analysis.

## Unreliability in Coding Study Results

### Sources of Coding Error

Just as researchers sometimes make errors in their data analysis, it is also
the case that errors are made in the recording of data. Transcription errors
are a problem for research synthesists when they extract information from
research reports. Rosenthal (1978) synthesized 21 studies that examined
the frequency and distribution of recording errors. These studies uncovered
error rates ranging from 0% to 4.2% of all the data recorded; 64% of the
errors in recording were in a direction that tended to confirm the study's
initial hypothesis.

Recording errors are not the only source of unreliability in study coding.
Sometimes, codes cannot be reliably applied because the descriptions
written by primary researchers are not clear. Other times, ambiguous
definitions provided by the research synthesist lead to disagreement about
the proper code for a study characteristic. Finally, as I noted earlier, the
predispositions of coders can lead them to favor one interpretation of an
ambiguous code over another.

Stock, Okun, Haring, Miller, and Kinney (1982) empirically examined
the number of unreliable codings made in a research synthesis. They had
three coders (one statistician and two post-PhD education researchers)
record data from 30 documents into 27 different coding categories. Stock
and colleagues found that some variables, such as the means and standard
deviations of the ages of participants, were coded with perfect or near-per-
fect agreement. Only one judgment, concerning the type of sampling
procedure employed by the researchers, did not reach an average coder
agreement of 80%.

### Minimizing and Estimating Coder Error

Although coders of primary research are fairly reliable in their retrieval
of information, it is good practice to take steps to ensure reliable codings.
This is especially true if the number of studies to be coded is large or if
persons with limited research training are called on to do the coding.
Regardless, the synthesist should treat the coding of studies as if it were a
standard exercise in data gathering. Synthesists should follow the rules
described in Chapter 2 for developing thorough and exhaustive coding

sheets. Coding sheets should be accompanied by code books explaining the meaning of each entry. Prior to actual coding, discussions and practice examples should be worked out with coders.

Also, it is often important to obtain numerical estimates of coder reliability. Before actual coding begins, assessments of reliability should be taken on controlled sets of studies. Coding should not begin until an acceptable level of intercoder reliability has been established. After coding begins, the synthesist might want to check coder reliability on randomly chosen studies.

There are many ways to quantify coder reliability, and none appears to be without problems (see Orwin, 1994, for a general review of evaluating coding decisions). Two methods appear most often in research syntheses. Most simply, research synthesists will report the agreement rate between pairs of coders. The agreement rate is the number of agreed-on codings divided by the total number of codings. Also useful is Cohen's kappa, a measure of reliability that adjusts for the chance rate of agreement. Kappa is defined as the improvement over chance reached by the coders.

Some synthesists will report both the agreement rate and kappa and will do so separately for each coded study characteristic. Other synthesists will have each study examined by two coders, will compare codings, and then will have discrepancies resolved in conference or by consulting a third coder. This procedure leads to very high reliability. Other synthesists have individual coders mark the codes they are least confident about and discuss these codes in group meetings. This procedure also leads to highly trustworthy codings.

### Synthesis Examples

In the synthesis of the effects of homework, less than a dozen potentially relevant manuscripts were identified in the literature search that could not be retrieved for examination. Most of these were very old, were published outside North America, or were unpublished documents. These documents represented less than 5% of all the documents actually judged potentially relevant.

The synthesis of personality moderators of interpersonal expectancy effects had the most difficulty with missing data. This occurred because correlation coefficients were often reported as nonsignificant, and the magnitude of the correlation was not given. One technique that helped fill in these missing data was to determine if a published journal article was a report of a dissertation. If it was, the full dissertation was obtained. These often contained more complete descriptions of data outcomes.

Finally, the homework synthesis included a formal test of the reliability with which studies were coded. Kappa coefficients and percentages of agreement were calculated between two coders on 13 categories. The reliability estimates indicated perfect agreement on 7 of the categories. The poorest reliability, $\kappa = .71$ and 79% agreement, occurred on the coders' retrieval of the number of assignments students did each week. Whenever disagreements occurred, the two coders examined the study together and resolved their difference.

## IDENTIFYING INDEPENDENT COMPARISONS

Another important decision that must be made during the data evaluation stage involves how to identify independent comparisons or estimates of a relationship strength. Sometimes, a single study may contain multiple tests of the same comparison or relation. This can happen for two reasons. First, more than one measure of the same construct might be employed and each measure analyzed separately. For example, an alcohol researcher might measure aggression through both self-reports and observation. Second, different samples of people might be used in the same study and their data analyzed separately. This would occur, for instance, if a rape-attitude researcher gave the same instruments to all participants but then separately examined results for males and females. In both instances, the separate estimates in the same study are not completely independent—they share historical and situational influences, and in the former case they even share influences contributed by having been collected on the same people.

The problem of nonindependence of comparisons can be taken further. Sometimes, a single research report can describe more than one study. Sometimes, multiple research reports describe studies conducted in the same laboratory. A synthesist might conclude that studies conducted at the same site, even if they appear in separate reports over a number of years, still contain certain constancies that imply the results are not completely independent. The same primary researcher with the same predispositions may have used the same laboratory rooms while drawing participants from the same population.

Synthesists must decide when statistical tests will be considered independent events, especially in instances when they intend to perform a meta-analysis. Several alternatives can be suggested regarding the proper unit of analysis in research syntheses.

## Laboratories as Units

The most conservative way to identify independent statistical tests employs the laboratory or researcher as the smallest unit of analysis. Advocates of this most conservative approach would suggest that the information value of repeated studies in the same laboratory is not as great as an equal number of studies reported from separate laboratories. (An intraclass $r$ can be computed to assess the empirical degree of independence of studies from the same laboratory.) This approach requires the synthesist to gather all studies done at the same research laboratory and to come to some overall conclusion concerning the results at that particular site. Therefore, one drawback is that it requires the synthesist to conduct syntheses within syntheses because decisions about how to synthesize results first must be made within laboratories and then between laboratories.

This approach is rarely used in practice. It is generally considered too conservative and too wasteful of information that can be obtained by examining the variations in results from study to study, even within the same site. Also, it is possible to ascertain whether laboratories or researchers are associated with systematic differences in study outcomes by using the researcher as a study characteristic in the search for outcome moderators.

## Studies as Units

Using the study as the unit of analysis requires the synthesist to make an overall decision about the results of all related comparisons reported in separate studies but not aggregate results over more than one study. If a single study contains information on more than one test of the same comparison, the synthesist can calculate the average result and have that represent the study. Alternatively, the median result can be used. If there is a preferred type of measurement, for example, a particular rape-attitude scale with good characteristics, this result can represent the study.

Using the study as the unit of analysis ensures that each study contributes equally to the overall synthesis result. For example, a study estimating the relationship between rape attitudes and need for power using two age groups and two different attitude scales would include four related correlations. Cumulating them in some fashion so that a single correlation comes from the report ensures equal consideration will be given to another report with one age group and one attitude measure.

There will be some subjectivity in the synthesist's judgment of what constitutes a study. For instance, one synthesist might consider all results in a single journal article or manuscript as one study. Another synthesist might consider a report that divides results into separate studies as containing more than one study. Regrettably, the delineation is not as clear as we might like.

## Samples as Units

Using independent samples as units permits a single study to contribute more than one statistical test, if the tests are carried out on separate samples of people. Thus, a rape-attitude synthesist would consider statistical tests on males and females within the same study as independent but not tests that used alternate measures of the same attitude construct given to the same people.

Using independent samples as units assumes that the largest portion of the variance shared by statistical tests in the same study comes from data collected on the same subjects. This shared variance is removed, but other sources of dependency that exist at the study level are ignored.

When a meta-analyst calculates an average comparison or relationship across units, it is good practice to weight each independent unit—be it a sample within a study or the entire study—by its sample size (this procedure is discussed further in Chapter 5). Then, weightings are functionally equivalent whether independent samples within studies or entire studies are used as units of analysis.

## Comparisons as Units

The least conservative approach to identifying independent units of analysis is to use the individual comparison or estimate of relationship strength. Each separate estimate calculated by primary researchers is regarded as an independent estimate by the research synthesist. This technique's strength is that it does not lose any of the within-study information regarding potential moderators of the study's outcomes. Its weakness is that the assumption that estimates are independent, needed for most statistical syntheses of results, will be violated. Also, the results of studies will not be weighted equally in any overall conclusion about results. Instead, studies will contribute to the overall finding in relation to the number of statistical tests contained in it. In the example concerning rape attitudes and need for power, the study with four related comparisons will have four times the influence on the overall results as the second, independent study with one comparison. This is not necessarily a good weighting criterion.

**Shifting Unit of Analysis**

A compromise approach to identifying comparisons is to employ a shifting unit of analysis. Specifically, each statistical test is initially coded as if it were an independent event. Thus, a single study that contained four statistical comparisons would have four separate coding sheets filled out for it. Each coding sheet would be slightly different, depending on the aspects of the samples, measurements, or design characteristics used to distinguish the statistical results. Then, when an overall cumulative result for the synthesis is generated, the statistical results are weighted so that each study or sample contributes equally (or is weighted only by sample size, not its number of statistical tests) to the general finding. The study containing four comparisons would have these averaged and then added as a single number into the analysis across all studies.

When examining potential moderators of the overall outcome, however, a study's or sample's results would be aggregated only within the separate categories of the moderator variable. For example, suppose a meta-analyst has chosen to use studies as the basic unit of analysis. If a rape-attitude and need-for-power study presented correlations for males and females separately, this study would contribute only one correlation to the overall analysis—the average of the male and female correlations—but two correlations to the analysis of the impact of attitude-holder sex on the size of the correlation—one for the female group and one for male group. To take the process one step further, assume this study reported different correlations for rape myth acceptance and victim blame within each sex—that is, four correlations in all. Then, the two correlations for different attitude scales would be averaged for each sex when the analysis for the influence of sex on outcomes was conducted. The two sex-related correlations would be averaged for each scale when the type of attitude was examined as a moderator.

In effect, the shifting-unit technique ensures that for analyses of influences on comparisons or relationship strengths, a single study can contribute one data point to each of the categories distinguished by the moderating variable. This strategy is a good compromise that allows studies to retain their maximum information value while keeping to a minimum any violation of the assumption of independence of statistical tests. The approach is not without problems, however. First, creating and re-creating average effect sizes for analysis of each different moderator can be confusing. Also, when the meta-analyst wishes to study multiple influences on study outcomes in a single analysis, rather than one influence at a time, the unit of analysis can quickly decompose into individual comparisons.

## Statistical Adjustment

Raudenbush, Becker, and Kalaian (1988) have proposed a statistical solution to the problem of nonindependent hypothesis tests (see also Gleser & Olkin, 1994). They have devised a procedure based on generalized least squares regression that statistically adjusts for interdependence among multiple outcomes within studies and for different numbers of outcomes across studies. The key to successfully using their technique lies in the synthesist having credible numerical estimates of the interdependence of statistical tests.

For instance, assume a study of correlates of rape attitudes includes both a measure of myth acceptance and victim blame. To use Raudenbush and colleagues' (1988) technique, the synthesist must estimate the correlation between the two scales for the sample in this study. Data of this sort often are not provided by primary researchers. When not given, it might be estimated from other studies, or the analysis could be run with low and high estimates to generate a range of values.

## Synthesis Examples

All four illustrative research syntheses employed the sample as the basic independent unit. The unit, however, was allowed to shift (become smaller) depending on the analysis. The synthesis of studies examining correlates of rape attitudes included 65 research reports containing 72 studies with data on 103 independent samples. Primary researchers calculated a total of 479 correlations. For the overall analysis, the 103 independent samples were used as the unit, and all correlations were averaged within samples. An analysis of differences in average correlations for different rape attitude scales, however, was based on 108 correlations because five primary researchers had given two scales to the same sample of participants.

The synthesis of personality moderators of interpersonal expectancy effects uncovered 17 research reports that described 24 studies testing expectancy effects in a photo-rating situation. One report, a book, included 6 studies. The 24 studies contained 106 correlations. The median number of correlations in a study was 2, but in four studies 10, 15, 16, and 18 different correlations were found. The most important analysis examined four categories of experimenter personality (need for social influence, expressiveness, likability, and other) and three categories of subject personality (influenceability, decoding skills, and other). Correlations were averaged within each category for each study. Thus, 48 independent (average) correlations were used in this analysis.

## VALIDITY ISSUES IN
## EVALUATING RESEARCH

In this chapter, I have discussed several sets of problems requiring decisions by synthesists that have an impact on the validity of their work. The threats relate to the evaluation of the quality of primary studies, missing data, the reliability of information retrieval, and the choice of a unit of analysis.

First, the use of any evaluation criteria other than methodological quality to exclude or weight studies in a synthesis introduces a potential threat to the validity of the synthesis outcome. As Mahoney (1977) stated, "To the extent that researchers display [confirmatory] bias our adequate understanding of the processes and parameters of human adaptation may be seriously jeopardized" (p. 162). It is safe to assume that evaluation bias has pernicious effects on our understanding.

Second, incomplete reporting by primary researchers compromises the validity of syntheses. We have seen that many research reports omit discussions of some statistical tests or give only incomplete information on the tests that are mentioned. The greater the percentage of such incomplete reports within a research synthesis, the wider are the confidence intervals that must be placed around its conclusions.

Relatedly, the validity of a synthesis is threatened by unreliability in the coding of research results. In most instances, coding can be done with fairly high reliability, but this is not assured and can vary across coders and coding tasks.

Finally, synthesis results become suspect if there is reason to believe that the synthesist has miscalculated the appropriate unit of independent data. Using a unit that falsely inflates the number of data points taken as independent leads to violations of statistical assumptions and overestimates the power of statistical tests.

### Protecting Validity

In the course of this chapter, I have mentioned numerous procedures designed to increase the trustworthiness of decisions made during data evaluation. These included the following:

1. Synthesists should make every effort to ensure that only a priori, conceptual, and methodological judgments influence the decision to include or exclude studies from a synthesis and not the results of the study. If studies

are to be weighted differently, the weighting scheme should be explicit and justifiable.

2. The approach used to categorize study methods should exhaust as many design characteristics as possible. The synthesist should detail each design distinction that was related to study results and describe the outcome of the analysis.

3. The synthesist should state explicitly what conventions were used when incomplete or erroneous research reports were encountered. To be safe, analyses should be conducted using multiple approaches to missing data.

4. Training and assessment procedures should be used to minimize unreliable retrieval of information from studies. When possible, more than one coder should examine each study. Intercoder agreement should be quantified and reported. Codes that lead to disagreement or low confidence should be discussed by multiple parties.

5. The unit of analysis decision should be based on both statistical considerations and the nature of the particular problem under study. The approach chosen by the synthesist should be carefully described and justified.

## EXERCISES

1. List a set of criteria that you think distinguish good and bad research. Rank order the criteria with regard to their impact on research quality. Compare your criteria and rankings with those of a classmate. What is similar and different about your lists?

2. With your classmate, agree on a set of criteria and evaluation scales. Also, identify a set of studies on the same topic. Independently apply the criteria to the studies. Compare your ratings. How did they differ and what led to the differences? How might the criteria be revised to minimize differences in future use?

3. Using the same set of studies, and again in conjunction with a classmate, record the following information from each report: (a) sample size, (b) any restrictions on who was sampled, (c) an overall rating of the study's quality, (d) the means of comparison groups (or other data) on the primary variable of interest, (e) whether or not the hypothesis was confirmed, and (f) the type and significance level of the inference test of primary interest. How many values did you agree and disagree on? Which values led to the most disagreement? Why?

# 5

# *The Data Analysis Stage*

**This chapter presents some statistical methods that can help synthesists summarize research results. Among the techniques discussed are counting study outcomes, combining probabilities from inference tests, averaging effect sizes, and examining the variability in effect sizes across studies. The chapter concludes with an outline of validity issues that arise during data analysis.**

Data analysis involves reducing the separate data points collected by the inquirer into a unified statement about the research problem. Analysis requires that the researcher order, categorize, and summarize the data. As noted in Chapter 1, data analysis requires that decision rules be used to distinguish systematic data patterns from "noise" or chance fluctuation. Although different decision rules can be used, the rules involve assumptions about what noise looks like in the target populations (e.g., normally distributed errors) and what criteria must be met before the existence of a pattern in the data is said to be reliable. The purpose of data analysis is to get the data into a form that permits valid interpretation.

## DATA ANALYSIS TECHNIQUES
## IN SOCIAL SCIENCE RESEARCH

Just as any scientific inquiry requires the leap from concrete operations to abstract concepts, both primary researchers and research synthesists must leap from patterns found in samples of data to more general conclusions about whether these patterns also exist in target populations. Until the mid-1970s, however, there had been almost no similarity in the analysis techniques used by primary researchers and research synthesists. Primary researchers were obligated to present sample statistics and to substantiate any inferences drawn from their data by providing the results of statistical tests. Frequently, primary researchers (a) compared sampled means and standard deviations or calculated measures of relationship, (b) made the assumptions needed for conducting inference tests relating the sample results to populations, and (c) reported the probabilities associated with whether systematic differences distinguished from error in the sample could be inferred about the population as well.

Traditional statistical aids to primary data interpretation have not gone uncriticized. Some have argued that significance tests are not very informative because they only tell what the likelihood is of obtaining the observed results when the null hypothesis is true (e.g., Cohen, 1994; Oakes, 1986). These critics argue that in a population of people the null hypothesis is almost never true, and therefore the significance of a given test is mainly influenced by how many participants have been sampled. Also, critics who are skeptical about the value of significance test statistics point to limitations in the population of events referred to by most statistical tests. No matter how statistically significant a relation may be, the results of a study are generalizable only to people like those who participated in that particular research effort.

Skepticism about the value of statistics helps those who use them to refine their procedures and keep their output in proper perspective. Nonetheless, most primary researchers use statistics, and most would feel extremely uncomfortable about summarizing primary data without some assistance (or credibility) supplied by statistical procedures.

In contrast to primary researchers, until recently research synthesists were not obligated to apply any standard statistical techniques in the analysis of their data. Traditionally, synthesists interpreted data using intuitive rules of inference unknown even to themselves. Analysis methods were idiosyncratic to the particular perspective of the individual synthesist. Therefore, a description of the common rules of inference used in research syntheses was not possible.

The subjectivity in analysis of research literatures led to skepticism about the conclusions of many syntheses. To address the problem, methodologists introduced quantitative methods into the synthesizing process. The methods build on the primary research statistics contained in the individual studies.

## META-ANALYSIS

I suggested in Chapter 1 that the two events that had the strongest impact on research synthesis were growth in the amount of research and the rapid advances in computerized research retrieval systems. A third strong impact was the introduction of quantitative procedures, called meta-analysis, into the research synthesis process.

The explosion in social science research focused considerable attention on the lack of standardization in how synthesists arrived at general conclusions from series of related studies. For many topic areas, a separate verbal description of each relevant study was no longer possible. One traditional strategy was to focus on one or two studies chosen from dozens or hundreds. This strategy failed to portray accurately the accumulated state of knowledge. Certainly, in areas where hundreds of studies exist, synthesists must describe "prototype" studies so that readers understand the methods used by primary researchers. Relying on the results of prototype studies as representative of all studies, however, may be seriously misleading. First, as has been shown, this type of selective attention is open to confirmatory bias: A particular synthesist may highlight only studies that support his or her initial position. Second, selective attention to only a portion of all studies places little or imprecise weight on the volume of available testings. Presenting one or two studies without a cumulative analysis of the entire set of results gives the reader no estimate of the confidence that should be placed in a conclusion. Finally, selectively attending to evidence cannot give a good estimate of the strength of a relationship. As evidence on a topic accumulates, researchers become more interested in "how much" rather than simply "yes or no."

Traditional synthesists also faced problems when they considered the variation between the results of different studies. Synthesists would find distributions of results for studies sharing a particular procedural characteristic but varying on many other characteristics. They found it difficult to conclude accurately whether a procedural variation affected study outcomes because the variability in results obtained by any single method meant that the distributions of results with different methods would overlap.

It seemed, then, that there were many situations in which synthesists had to turn to quantitative synthesizing techniques. The application of quantitative inference procedures to research synthesis was a necessary response to the expanding literature. If statistics are applied appropriately, they should enhance the validity of synthesis conclusions. Quantitative research synthesis is an extension of the same rules of inference required for rigorous data analysis in primary research. If primary researchers must specify quantitatively the relation of the data to their conclusions, the next users of the data should be required to do the same.

## A Brief History of Meta-Analysis

At the beginning of the twentieth century, Karl Pearson (1904) was asked to review the evidence on a vaccine against typhoid. He gathered data from 11 relevant studies, and for each study he calculated a recently developed statistic called the correlation coefficient. He averaged these measures of the treatment's effect across two groups of studies distinguished by their outcome variable. On the basis of average correlations, Pearson concluded that other vaccines were more effective. This is the earliest known quantitative research synthesis.

Gene Glass (1976) introduced the term *meta-analysis* to mean the statistical analysis of results from individual studies "for purposes of integrating the findings" (p. 3). Glass (1977) also wrote, "The accumulated findings of . . . studies should be regarded as complex data points, no more comprehensible without statistical analysis than hundreds of data points in a single study" (p. 352). Procedures for performing meta-analysis had appeared in statistics texts and articles long before 1976 (Fisher, 1932; Pearson, 1933; for a review, see Olkin, 1990), but instances of their application were rare. It took the expanding database and the growing need for research syntheses to provide impetus for the general use of meta-analysis.

Seventy-five years after Pearson's (1904) research synthesis, Rosenthal and Rubin (1978) undertook a synthesis of research studying the effects of interpersonal expectations on behavior in laboratories, classrooms, and the workplace. They found not 11 but 345 studies that pertained to their hypothesis. Almost simultaneously, Glass and Smith (1978b) conducted a review of the relation between class size and academic achievement. They found not 345 but 725 estimates of the relation based on data from approximately 900,000 students. Smith and Glass (1977) also gathered assessments of the effectiveness of psychotherapy. This literature revealed 833 tests of the treatment. Hunter, Schmidt, and Hunter (1979) uncovered 866 comparisons of the differential validity of employment tests for black and white workers.

Each of these research teams drew the inescapable conclusion that the days of the traditional research synthesis were over. Largely independently, the three teams rediscovered and reinvented Pearson's solution to their problem. They were quickly joined by others. Among these were Light and Pillemer (1984), who prepared a text that focused on the use of research synthesis in the social policy domain. Hedges and Olkin (1985) provided the rigorous statistical proofs that established meta-analysis as an independent specialty within the statistical sciences. I proposed that the research synthesis process be conceptualized in the same manner as original data collections and be held to the same standards of scientific rigor (Cooper, 1982).

Meta-analysis was not without its critics, and some criticisms persist. The value of quantitative synthesizing was questioned along lines similar to criticisms of primary data analysis (e.g., Barber, 1978; Mansfield & Bussey, 1977). Much of the criticism, however, stemmed less from issues in meta-analysis than from more general inappropriate synthesizing procedures, such as a lack of operational detail, which were erroneously thought to be by-products of the use of quantitative procedures (see Cooper & Arkin, 1981).

Evidence indicates that meta-analysis is now an accepted procedure, and its application within the social and medical sciences continues to grow (Mann, 1990). Greenberg and Folger (1988) stated that "if the current interest in meta-analysis is any indication, then meta-analysis is here to stay" (p. 191).

## When Not to Do a Meta-Analysis

Much of this chapter will describe some basic meta-analysis procedures and how they are applied. It is important to state explicitly, however, some circumstances in which the use of quantitative procedures in syntheses is not appropriate.

First, quantitative procedures are applicable only to research syntheses and not to syntheses with other focuses or goals (see Chapter 1). For instance, if a synthesist is interested in tracing the historical development of the concept "self-fulfilling prophesies," it would not be necessary to do a quantitative synthesis. If the synthesist also intended to make inferences about whether different definitions of interpersonal expectancy effects lead to different likelihoods that self-fulfilling prophesies will occur, however, then a quantitative summary of relevant research would be appropriate.

Second, the basic premise behind the use of statistics in research syntheses is that a series of studies address an identical conceptual hypothesis. If the premises of a synthesis do not include this assertion, then there is no need for cumulative statistics. Also, a synthesist should not quantitatively combine studies at a broader conceptual level than readers would find useful. At an extreme, most social science research could be categorized as examining a single conceptual hypothesis—social stimuli affect human behavior. Indeed, for some purposes, such a hypothesis test might be very enlightening. This should not be used, however, as an excuse to lump together concepts and hypotheses without attention to those distinctions that will be meaningful to the users of the synthesis (see Kazdin, Durac, & Agteros, 1979, for a humorous treatment of this issue). For instance, the synthesis of personality moderators of interpersonal expectancy effects provides an example of when a quantitative combination of studies was possible but not profitable. Thirty-three studies were found that tested the broad conceptual hypothesis. Twenty-four of these examined experimenter expectancy effects on photo-rating tasks, 6 used other laboratory settings, 1 used an instructional setting, and 2 used simulated therapeutic settings. Rather than lump them all together, only the studies on photo-rating tasks were meta-analyzed. To have accumulated results at any broader level of experimental context and to have claimed ecological generalizability based on this cumulation would have been misleading because more than two thirds of all comparisons were conducted in a specific kind of setting.

The alcohol and aggression synthesis illustrates another example of when quantitative syntheses may be ill-advised. In this synthesis, separate analyses were conducted on comparisons of alcohol versus no-treatment controls and alcohol versus placebo controls. Even though both comparisons assessed the effects of alcohol, it would not be informative to lump them together. When a hypothesis involves a comparison with controls, the synthesist might find that a distinction in the type of control is important enough not to be obscured in a quantitative analysis.

## The Impact of Integrating
## Techniques on Synthesis Outcomes

Although the relative validity of traditional and quantitative research synthesis strategies is difficult to assess, Cooper and Rosenthal (1980) did demonstrate some of their objective differences. In this study, graduate students and university faculty members were asked to evaluate a literature on a simple hypothesis: Are there sex differences in task persistence? All synthesists evaluated the same set of studies, but half the synthesists used quantitative procedures and half used whatever criteria appealed to them. No synthesist in the latter condition chose quantitative techniques. The authors found that statistical synthesists thought there was more support for the sex-difference hypothesis and a larger relationship between variables than did nonstatistical synthesists. Statistical synthesists also tended to view future replications as less necessary than nonstatistical synthesists, although this finding did not reach statistical significance.

It is also likely that the different statistical procedures employed by quantitative synthesists will create variance in synthesis conclusions. Several different paradigms have emerged for quantitatively synthesizing research with a parametric model (Hedges & Olkin, 1985; Hunter & Schmidt, 1990; Rosenthal, 1984), and other paradigms can be used with a Bayesian perspective (Louis & Zelterman, 1994; Raudenbush & Bryk, 1985). There are numerous techniques available for combining the separate study probabilities to generate an overall probability for the run of studies (see Becker, 1994). The different techniques generate probability levels that vary somewhat. Thus, the rules adopted to carry out quantitative analysis can differ from synthesist to synthesist, and this may create variance in how synthesis results are interpreted. We can assume as well that the rules used by nonquantitative synthesists also vary, but their inexplicit nature makes them difficult to compare formally.

## SYNTHESIZING MAIN EFFECTS AND INTERACTIONS

Before examining several of the quantitative techniques available to synthesists, it is important to take a closer look at some of the unique features of accumulated research results. In the chapter on problem formulation, I pointed out that most research syntheses first focus on tests of main effects. This is primarily because conceptually related replications of main effects occur more frequently than tests of three or more interacting variables. Of course, once synthesists have discerned whether or not a main effect relationship exists, they next turn to potential moderators of the relation or to interaction effects.

In research syntheses, the most obvious feature of both main effects and interactions is that the results of separate tests of the same comparison or relationship will vary from one testing to the next. This variability is sometimes dramatic and requires us to ask from where the variability comes.

### Variability in Main Effect Tests

Differences in the outcomes of tests of main effects can be caused by two classes of influences. The simplest cause is the one most often overlooked—sampling error. Even before the current interest in quantitative synthesis, Taveggia (1974) recognized this important influence:

A methodological principle overlooked by writers of . . . reviews is that research results are *probabilistic*. What this principle suggests is that, in and of themselves, the findings of any single research are meaningless—they may have occurred simply by chance. It also follows that if a large enough number of researches has been done on a particular topic, chance alone dictates that studies will exist that report inconsistent and contradictory findings! Thus, what appears to be contradictory may simply be the positive and negative details of a distribution of findings. (pp. 397-398)

Taveggia highlights one of the implications of using probability theory and sampling techniques to make inferences about populations.

For example, suppose it was possible to measure the academic achievement of every American student. Also, suppose that if such a task were undertaken, it would be found that achievement was exactly equal for students who do and do not do homework—that is, exactly equal group means existed for the two populations. Still, if 1,000 samples of 50 homeworkers and 50 no-homeworkers were taken, very few samples would reveal exactly equal group means. Furthermore, if the sample means were compared statistically using the $p < .05$ significance level (two-tailed), approximately 25 comparisons would show a significant difference favoring homeworkers, whereas approximately 25 would favor no-homeworkers.

This variation in results is an unavoidable consequence of the fact that the means estimated by the samples will vary somewhat from the true population values. Therefore, just by chance some comparisons will pair sample estimates that vary from their true population values by large amounts and in opposite directions.

In the example given, it is unlikely that the synthesist would be fooled into thinking anything but chance caused the result—after all, 950 comparisons would reveal null effects, and significant results would be distributed equally for both possible outcomes. In practice, however, the pattern of results is rarely this clear. First, as we discovered in the chapter on literature searching, the synthesist might not be aware of all null results because they are hard to find. Also, even if an overall relation does exist between two variables (i.e., the null hypothesis is false), some studies can still show significant results in a direction opposite to the overall conclusion. To continue the example, if the average achievement of homeworkers is greater than that of no-homeworkers, some samplings will still favor no-homeworkers, the number depending on the size of the relation and how many comparisons have been performed. In summary, one source of variance in the results of studies can be chance fluctuations due to the inexactness of sampled estimates.

A second source of variance in main effects is of more interest to synthesists. This variance in results is created by differences in how studies are conducted or who participates in them or both. In Chapter 2, the notion of synthesis-generated evidence was introduced to describe what we learn when we find associations between study characteristics and study outcomes. For instance, the homework synthesist might find that studies comparing achievement among students who do and do not do homework have been conducted with high school or elementary school students, with class grades or standardized tests as measures of achievement, and with math classes and English classes. Each of these differences in studies could create systematic variation in study results if they are related to how much homework influences achievement.

The existence of the two sources of variance in research results raises an interesting dilemma for the synthesist. When so-called contradictory findings occur (as they invariably will), should the synthesist seek an explanation for them by attempting to identify differences between the methods used in studies? Should the synthesist simply assume the contradictory findings are produced by chance variations due to sampling error? Some tests have been devised to help synthesists answer these questions. In effect, these tests use "sampling error" as the null hypothesis. If the variation in results across studies is too great to be explained by sampling error, then the synthesist knows to seek explanations elsewhere—that is, in methodological or substantive differences between studies. I will discuss these procedures later, but for now it should simply be noted that two distinct sources of variance in study results need to be considered by synthesists.

### Variability in Interaction Tests

Obviously, the factors that create variability in main effects can also affect variability in tests of interaction. Interaction effects are as susceptible to sampling error and procedural variation as main effects. Examining interactions in research syntheses, however, presents some unique problems. For ease of presentation, I will discuss these by referring to tests of two-way interactions, but the remarks generalize to higher-order interactions as well.

Figure 5.1 illustrates the results of two hypothetical studies demonstrating interactions. In Study I, the amount of material retained by two groups of children is examined: One group received homework assignments and one received in-school supervised study as an alternative treatment. The homework and in-school study groups were compared in the first week and

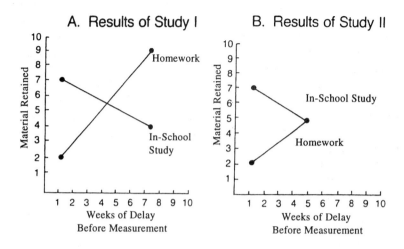

**Figure 5.1.** Results of Two Hypothetical Studies Comparing Homework and In-School Study

the seventh week after the lesson. In Week 1, children doing homework knew less of the material than in-school study children, but in Week 7 children doing homework recalled considerably more material than those doing in-school study. Thus, the effect of the treatments reversed itself over the course of the study.

Hypothetical Study II used the same treatments and a similar research design. In Week 1, children doing homework knew less material than children doing in-school study, but in Week 5 no difference was found between the groups. The effect of different treatments "disappeared" between the first and second measurement, but it did not reverse itself.

A synthesist uncovering two studies with these findings might be tempted to conclude that they produced inconsistent results. After all, Study I indicated that in-school study was initially effective but with the passage of time it actually became less effective than homework. Study II evidenced no counterproductive effect, just a vanishing of the differences between study techniques. A closer examination of the two figures, however, illustrates why it might not be appropriate to conclude that the studies are inconsistent. The results of Study II probably would have been closely approximated by the researchers in Study I if they had taken a measurement of retention in Week 5. Likewise, had Study II contained a Week 7 measurement, these researchers probably would have produced results quite similar to the Week 7 results contained in Study I.

In general, researchers who find that the experimental effect appears at only one level of an interacting variable can only speculate about whether sampling from more extended levels of that variable might lead to a reversal of the effect. Research synthesists, however, may have an opportunity to draw such conclusions more confidently. As the example demonstrates, synthesists must not assume that different forms or strengths of interaction uncovered by different studies necessarily imply inconsistent results. Instead, they need to examine the differing levels of variables employed in different studies and, if possible, to chart results taking the different levels into account. In this manner, one of the benefits of research synthesis is realized. Although one study might suggest that the difference between treatments dissipates over time and another study might suggest that the effects reverse themselves, the research synthesist can find that the two results are in fact perfectly commensurate.

Figure 5.1 can also be used to highlight the distinction between study-generated and synthesis-generated evidence. First, the figure depicts study-generated evidence pertaining to the existence of an interaction between the effect of the treatments and the time of measurement. Each study contains within it evidence on this relation. The figure, however, also reveals inconsistency in the study-generated evidence, with one study suggesting a disappearance of differences and one a reversal. Synthesis-generated evidence is then used to explain the inconsistency. We rely on information about a study characteristic, the length of interval between treatment and measurement, to help us out.

This benefit of research synthesis also underscores the importance of primary researchers presenting detailed information concerning the levels of variables used in their studies. Without specific information, research synthesists may not be able to conduct an across-study analysis similar to the one presented previously. If the primary researchers in Study I and Study II neglected to specify how long a delay was used between measurements, perhaps referring to the two measurement intervals as, for example, "short" and "long," the commensurability of the results would have been impossible to demonstrate.

Research synthesists must also carefully examine the statistical analyses that accompany reports of interactions. For instance, all else being equal, it is more likely that the researchers of Study I reported a significant interaction between time of measurement and treatment than did the researchers in Study II. In fact, assuming equal error terms, the $F$ value in Study I for the interaction should be several times greater than that in Study II. Therefore, it is extremely important that synthesists retrieve detailed data about interactions, regardless of statistical significance. The problem, of course, is that unless the interaction was the chief concern of the primary researchers or unless the interaction proved significant, there is small chance that information detailed enough to perform the kind of analysis portrayed in Figure 5.1 will be contained in the report.

### Interactions in Meta-Analysis

The statistical combination of interactions in meta-analysis is a very complex task. In fact, synthesists rarely combine the statistical results of studies examining the same interaction. This is partly due to the infrequency with which studies have tested the same interaction and partly to the incomplete reporting of many tests of interaction.

There are two different ways that interactions could be statistically combined across studies. First, the separate *p* levels and relationship strengths associated with each study's interaction test could be aggregated. An alternative strategy would be to aggregate separately the relation of two variables at each level of the third variable. For instance, a homework synthesis could generate an estimate of the difference in retention of homework versus in-school study by aggregating all measures taken with a 1-week delay and comparing this to an aggregation of all measures taken with a 7-week delay. This would probably be more useful and easily interpretable than a direct estimate of the magnitude of the interaction effect. To do this, however, the primary research reports must contain the information needed to isolate the different simple main effects.

### TECHNIQUES FOR COMBINING SIGNIFICANCE LEVELS OF INDEPENDENT FINDINGS

In this section and several that follow, I will briefly introduce some of the quantitative techniques that are available to synthesists. I have chosen the techniques because of their simplicity and broad applicability. The treatment of each technique will be conceptual and introductory. The reader who wants a more complete description of these techniques as well as many others should consult the primary sources cited in the text. For the discussion that follows, I have assumed the reader has a working knowledge of the basic inferential statistics employed in the social sciences.

Three assumptions are crucial to the validity of a conclusion based on a cumulation of individual statistical findings. First and most obvious, the individual findings that go into a cumulative analysis should all test the same comparison or estimate the same relationship. Regardless of how conceptually broad or narrow their ideas might be, synthesists should be comfortable with the assertion that all the included statistical tests address the same question.

Second, the separate tests that go into the cumulative analysis must be independent of one another. Identifying independent comparisons was discussed in Chapter 4. Meta-analysts must take care to identify comparisons so that each one contains unique information about the hypothesis.

Finally, the synthesist must believe that the primary researchers made valid assumptions when they computed the results of the test. Thus, if the synthesist wishes to combine the probabilities associated with a series of $t$-test comparisons, the synthesist must assume that the observations, residuals, or errors of the two groups are independent and normally distributed and that the variances are approximately equal.

One reason why statistical techniques are used in research syntheses is to combine the significance levels associated with separate tests of comparisons or relationships. This is done to generate an overall probability relating to the existence of a group difference or relationship. For instance, if three tests of a relationship find statistically significant results and seven find nonsignificant results, what is the synthesist to conclude? The techniques for combining significance levels allow the synthesist to cumulate the results of numerous tests so that overall conclusions can be drawn.

## Vote-Counting Methods

The simplest methods for combining independent statistical tests are the vote-counting methods. Vote counts can take into account the statistical significance of findings or focus only on the direction of the findings.

For the first method, the synthesist would take each finding and place it into one of three categories: statistically significant findings in the expected direction (referred to as positive findings), statistically significant findings in the unexpected (negative) direction, and nonsignificant findings (i.e., ones that did not permit rejection of the null hypothesis). The synthesist then would assert that the category with the largest number of findings tells what the direction of the relationship is in the target population.

This vote count of significant findings has much intuitive appeal and has been used quite often. The strategy, however, is unacceptably conservative. The problem is that chance alone should produce only approximately 5%

of all findings falsely indicating a significant effect. Therefore, depending on the number of findings, much less than one-third positive and statistically significant findings might indicate a real difference in the target population. This vote-counting strategy, however, requires that at least 34% of findings be positive and statistically significant before the expected result is declared a winner.

Hedges and Olkin (1980) demonstrated the conservative nature of this approach. Assume that a correlation of $r = .30$ exists between two variables in a population, and 20 samplings have been conducted with 40 people in each sample. The probability that the vote count associated with this series of studies will conclude a positive relation exists—if the criterion described previously is used—is less than 6 in 100. Thus, the vote count of significant findings could, and often does, lead synthesists to suggest abandonment of hypotheses (and effective treatment programs) when, in fact, no such conclusion is warranted.

Adjusting the expected frequencies of the three findings so that the disproportionately high number of expected nonsignificant findings is taken into account solves the statistical problem but it raises a practical one. We have seen that null results are less likely to be reported by researchers and are less likely to be retrieved by synthesists. Therefore, if the appropriate theoretical values are used in a vote-count analysis, it should often occur that both positive and negative significant findings appear more frequently than expected. Thus, it seems that using the frequency of nonsignificant findings in a vote-count procedure is of dubious value.

An alternative vote-counting method is to compare the frequency of statistically significant positive findings against the frequency of significant negative ones. This procedure assumes that if the null hypothesis prevails in the population, then the frequency of significant positive and negative findings (Type I errors) is expected to be equal. If the frequency of findings is found not to be equal, the null hypothesis is rejected in favor of the prevailing direction.

A problem with this vote-count approach is that the expected number of nonsignificant findings, even when the null hypothesis is not true, can still be much greater than the expected number of either positive or negative significant findings. Therefore, this approach will ignore many findings (all nonsignificant ones) and will be relatively low in statistical power.

A final way to perform vote counts in research synthesis involves tallying the number of positive and negative findings regardless of their statistical significance. In this analysis, the synthesist categorizes findings based solely on their direction. Again, if the null hypothesis is true—that is, if no relationship exists between the variables in the sampled population—we would expect the number of findings in each direction to be equal.

Once the number of results in each direction are counted, the meta-analyst performs a sign test to discover if the cumulative results suggest one direction occurs more frequently than chance would suggest. The formula for computing the sign test is as follows:

$$Z_{vc} = \frac{(N_p) - (\frac{1}{2} N)}{\frac{1}{2}\sqrt{N}} \qquad\qquad [5.1]$$

where

$Z_{vc}$ = the standard normal deviate, or $z$ score, for the overall series of findings;
$N_p$ = the number of positive findings; and
$N$ = the total number of findings (positive plus negative findings).

The $Z_{vc}$ can be referred to a table of standard normal deviates to discover the probability (one-tailed) associated with the cumulative set of directional findings. If a two-tailed $p$ level is desired, the tabled value should be doubled. The values of $Z$ associated with different $p$ levels are presented in Table 5.1. This sign test can be used in a vote count of either the simple direction of all findings or the direction of only significant findings.

Suppose 25 of 36 comparisons find that people who have recently consumed alcohol acted more aggressively than people in a placebo group. The probability that this many findings would be in one direction given that in the target population there is equal aggressiveness exhibited by people in the two conditions is $p < .02$ (two-tailed), associated with a $Z_{vc}$ of 2.33. This result would lead the meta-analyst to conclude a positive relation was supported by the series of comparisons.

The vote-count method that employs the direction of findings regardless of significance has the advantage of using information from all statistical findings. Like the other vote counts, however, it does not weight a finding's contribution by its sample size. Thus, a finding based on 100 participants is given weight equal to one with 1,000 participants. Furthermore, the revealed magnitude of the comparison or relationship (or impact of the treatment under evaluation) in each finding is not considered—a finding showing a large increase in aggressiveness due to alcohol is given equal weight to one showing a small decrease. Finally, a practical problem with

**TABLE 5.1**

Standard Normal Deviate Distribution

| $\gamma$ | $\alpha'' = 1 - \gamma$ | $\alpha' = \frac{1}{2}(1 - \gamma)$ | $z$ |
|---|---|---|---|
| .995 | .005 | .0025 | 2.807 |
| .99 | .01 | .005 | 2.576 |
| .985 | .015 | .0075 | 2.432 |
| .98 | .02 | .01 | 2.326 |
| .975 | .025 | .0125 | 2.241 |
| .97 | .03 | .015 | 2.170 |
| .965 | .035 | .0175 | 2.108 |
| .96 | .04 | .02 | 2.054 |
| .954 | .046 | .023 | 2.000 |
| .95 | .05 | .025 | 1.960 |
| .94 | .06 | .03 | 1.881 |
| .92 | .08 | .04 | 1.751 |
| .9 | .1 | .05 | 1.645 |
| .85 | .15 | .075 | 1.440 |
| .8 | .2 | .10 | 1.282 |
| .75 | .25 | .125 | 1.150 |
| .7 | .3 | .150 | 1.036 |
| .6 | .4 | .20 | 0.842 |
| .5 | .5 | .25 | 0.674 |
| .4 | .6 | .30 | 0.524 |
| .3 | .7 | .35 | 0.385 |
| .2 | .8 | .40 | 0.253 |
| .1 | .9 | .45 | 0.126 |

$\gamma$ = area between $-z$ and $z$
    = confidence coefficient
$\alpha' = \frac{1}{2}(1 - \gamma)$
    = area above $z$
    = area above $-z$
    = significance level for one-sided test
$\alpha'' = 1 - \gamma = 2\alpha'$
    = area beyond $-z$ and $z$
    = significance level for two-sided test

SOURCE: Noether (1971). Copyright 1971 by Houghton Mifflin Co. Reprinted with permission.

the directional vote count is that primary researchers frequently do not report the direction of results, especially if a comparison proved statistically nonsignificant.

Still, the vote count of directional findings can be an informative complement to other meta-analytic procedures and can even be used to generate an estimate of the strength of a relationship. Bushman and Wang (1995) provide formulae and tables that estimate the size of a population correlation given that the meta-analyst knows (a) the number of findings, (b) the directional outcome of each finding, and (c) the sample size of each finding. For example, assume that each one of the 36 comparisons between an alcohol and placebo group was based on a sample size of 50 participants. Using Bushman and Wang's table, I find that when 25 of the 36 comparisons (69%) reveal more aggression in the alcohol group, the most likely population value for a correlation between group membership and aggressiveness is $r = .07$.

In summary, meta-analysts can perform vote counts to aggregate results across individual findings by comparing the number of simple directional findings or the number of significant directional findings or both. Both of these procedures will be very imprecise and conservative—that is, they will miss relations that exist. The simple direction of results will not appear in many research reports in the first case, and nonsignificant findings cannot contribute to the analysis in the second case. Vote counts should be described in meta-analyses, but they should be used to draw inferences only when there is a large number of studies. Also, they should always be accompanied by more sensitive meta-analysis procedures.

### Combined Significance Levels

One way to address the shortcomings of vote counts is to consider combining the exact probabilities associated with the results of each comparison or estimate of a relation. Becker (1994; also see Rosenthal, 1984) cataloged 16 methods for combining the results of inference tests so that an overall test of the null hypothesis can be obtained. By using the exact probabilities, the results of the combined analysis take into account the different sample sizes and relationship strengths found in each comparison.

Of the 16 methods, the most frequently applied is called the method of Adding $Z$'s. The method was first introduced by Stouffer and colleagues (1949). The Adding $Z$'s method uses the following formula:

$$Z_{st} = \frac{\sum_{i=1}^{N} Z_i}{\sqrt{N}} \qquad [5.2]$$

where

$Z_{st}$ = the standard normal deviate, or $z$ score, for the overall series of findings;

$Z_i$ = the standard normal deviate for the $i$th finding; and

$N$ = the total number of findings in the series.

The steps to carry out the analysis are simple. The synthesist must

1. choose which direction for the findings will be considered positive and which negative;

2. record the probability associated with each finding;

3. halve the reported probability if it is two-tailed;

4. look up the $z$ score associated with each probability;

5. sum the $z$ scores, remembering to place a minus sign before negative results; and

6. divide this sum by the square root of the number of findings.

The resulting $Z_{st}$ can then be referred to a table of standard normal deviates (see Table 5.1) to identify the probability associated with the cumulative set of individual probabilities. If a two-tailed probability is desired, the tabled $p$ level should be doubled. The probability describes the combined likelihood that the series of results included in the analysis could have been generated by chance if the null hypothesis is true in the target population. Table 5.2 presents a hypothetical application of the Adding $Z$'s method. Note that I have set the hypothetical results of Studies 2 and 7 to exact null findings. I assume these two studies simply reported "nonsignificant" results with no associated significance levels. Studies 1 and 5 produced statistically significant results, and Study 4 produced a result opposite to that predicted.

The method of Adding $Z$'s can be modified to allow the meta-analyst to differentially weight the results of different statistical tests. For instance, if several findings come from a single study, the meta-analyst might want to weight these less than another finding that is the only contribution of another study. Also, the meta-analyst might want to give added weight to findings based on larger sample sizes (though the combined $z$ score is already affected by sample size because sample size influences significance levels).

The formula for the Adding Weighted $Z$'s method is

**TABLE 5.2**

A Hypothetical Example of the Combination of Eight Findings

| Finding | Number of Participants $(n_i)$ | $n_i^2$ | One-Tailed p Level | Associated z Score | $n_iZ$ |
|---|---|---|---|---|---|
| 1 | 48 | 2,304 | .025 | 1.96 | 94.08 |
| 2 | 28 | 784 | .50 | 0 | 0 |
| 3 | 32 | 1,024 | .33 | .44 | 14.08 |
| 4 | 24 | 576 | .90 | −1.28 | −30.72 |
| 5 | 64 | 4,096 | .01 | 2.33 | 149.12 |
| 6 | 40 | 1,600 | .39 | .28 | 11.20 |
| 7 | 20 | 400 | .50 | 0 | 0 |
| 8 | 30 | 900 | .15 | 1.04 | 31.20 |
| Σ | 286 | 11,684 | | 4.77 | 268.96 |

Adding $Z$'s: $Z_{st} = \dfrac{4.77}{\sqrt{8}} = 1.69$, $p < .0461$, one-tailed

Adding Weighted $Z$s: $Z_w = \dfrac{268.96}{\sqrt{11684}} = 2.49$, $p < .0064$, one-tailed

$N_{FS.05} = \left(\dfrac{4.77}{1.645}\right)^2 - 8 = .41$ (or 1)

NOTE: The one-tailed p level of .90 is from a study finding a direction opposite to that predicted (thus, the associated z score is negative).

$$Z_w = \frac{\sum\limits_{i=1}^{N} W_i Z_i}{\sqrt{\sum\limits_{i=1}^{N} W_i^2}} \qquad\qquad [5.3]$$

where

$Z_w$ = the z score for the weighted combination of findings;
$W_i$ = the weighting factor associated with each finding; and
all other terms are defined as before.

Table 5.2 presents a hypothetical example of the Adding Weighted $Z$'s method, with the weighting factor being the sample size of the study.

The combining significance levels procedure overcomes the improper weighting problems of the vote count. It has severe limitations of its own, however. First, whereas the vote-count procedure is overly conservative, the combining significance levels procedure is extremely powerful. In fact, it is so powerful that, for hypotheses or treatments that have generated a large number of tests, rejecting the null hypothesis is so likely that it becomes a rather uninformative exercise.

### Fail-Safe $N$

It has been mentioned several times that not all findings have an equal likelihood of being retrieved by the synthesist. Nonsignificant results are less likely to be retrieved than significant ones. This fact implies that the Adding $Z$'s method may produce a probability level that underestimates the chance of a Type 1 error. Rosenthal (1979a) wrote,

> The extreme view of this problem . . . is that the journals are filled with the 5% of studies that show Type 1 errors, while the file drawers back in the lab are filled with the 95% of studies that show insignificant (e.g., $p < .05$) results. (p. 638)

The problem is probably not this dramatic, but it does exist.

One of the advantages of the Adding $Z$'s method is that it allows the calculation of a Fail-safe $N$ (see Cooper, 1979; Rosenthal, 1979a). The Fail-safe $N$ answers the question, "How many findings totalling to a null hypothesis confirmation (e.g., $Z_{st} = 0$) would have to be added to the results of the retrieved findings in order to change the conclusion that a relation exists?" Rosenthal (1979a) called this the "tolerance for future null results." The formula for calculating this number, when the chosen significance level is $p < .05$, is

$$N_{FS.05} = \left( \frac{\left( \sum_{i=1}^{N} Z_i \right)^2}{1.645} \right) - N \qquad [5.4]$$

where

$N_{FS.05}$ = the number of additional null-summing findings needed to raise the combined probability to just above $p < .05$;

1.645 = the standard normal deviate associated with $p < .05$ (one-tailed); and all other quantities are defined as before.

Obviously, the Fail-safe $N$ cannot be computed when findings are weighted unequally, unless the synthesist wishes to estimate what the average weight of unretrieved findings might be—a dubious estimate at best. A hypothetical example of a Fail-safe $N$ is presented in Table 5.2.

The Fail-safe $N$ is a valuable descriptive statistic. It allows the users of a synthesis to evaluate the cumulative result of the synthesis against their assessment of how exhaustively the synthesist has searched the literature. The Fail-safe $N$, however, also contains an assumption that restricts its validity. That is, its user must find credible the proposition that the sum of the unretrieved studies is equal to an exact null result. It might be the case that unretrieved studies have a cumulative result opposite to that contained in the meta-analysis—perhaps because primary researchers did not want to publish studies that contradicted studies already in print. Also, unretrieved studies might cumulatively add support to the conclusion because the synthesist ignored information channels that paralleled those that were used. The plausibility of these alternatives should always be assessed when a Fail-safe $N$ is interpreted.

When is a Fail-safe $N$ large enough so that synthesists and readers can conclude a finding is resistant to unretrieved null results? Rosenthal (1979b) suggested that the resistance number equal 5 times the number of retrieved studies plus 10. No steadfast rule is intuitively obvious, so synthesists should argue anew for the resistance of their findings each time the formula is applied. The best argument for a resistant finding is a large Fail-safe $N$ coupled with a comprehensive search strategy.

## Synthesis Examples

The synthesis of personality moderators of interpersonal expectancy effects in laboratory experiments calculated five combined $z$ scores and probabilities, one for each of five personality dimensions. The study was used as the unit of analysis, and each study was weighted equally. It was found that experimenters with a greater need for social influence were more likely to generate interpersonal expectancy effects. The combined $z$ score, based on eight studies, was 2.94, with an associated $p$ level of .0032 (two-tailed). The Fail-safe $N$, the number of null-summing studies needed to raise the combined probability above $p = .05$, was 10.02, or 11 (because 10 studies would be just below $p = .05$).

Tests of the expressiveness and likability of the experimenter indicated nonsignificant relations to experimenter bias, though in both cases the relation was positive (for expressiveness: $N = 3$, $Z_{st} = 1.79$, $p < .0734$, two-tailed; for likability: $N = 4$, $Z_{st} = 1.71$, $p < .0872$, two-tailed). The influenceability and decoding skills of the subject were both positively related to the appearance of expectancy effects (for influenceability: $N = 11$, $Z_{st} = 2.21$, $p < .015$, two-tailed; for decoding skill: $N = 7$, $Z_{st} = 2.60$, $p < .0094$, two-tailed).

## Combined Significance Levels and Study-Generated Evidence

The results of vote-count and combined significance level techniques produce study-generated evidence. That is, each individual test being integrated has something to say about the hypothesis under consideration. Therefore, if the individual studies have used random assignment of participants to conditions to uncover causal mechanisms, the combined results of vote counts and Adding Z's relate to these causal mechanisms. On the basis of these results, the synthesist can make assertions about causality if in fact the primary research included experimental manipulations.

## MEASURING RELATIONSHIP STRENGTH

The primary function of the meta-analysis procedures described so far is to help the synthesist accept or reject the null hypothesis. Most researchers interested in social theory have been content to simply identify relations that have some explanatory value. The prevalence of this "yes or no" question is partly due to the relatively recent development of the social sciences. Social hypotheses are crudely stated first approximations to the truth. Social theorists rarely ask how potent theories are for explaining human behavior or how competing explanations compare with regard to their relative explanatory value. Today, as their theories are becoming more sophisticated, social scientists are more often making inquiries about the size of relations.

Giving further impetus to the "How much?" question is a growing disenchantment with the null hypothesis significance test itself. As I noted earlier, whether or not a null hypothesis can be rejected is tied closely to the particular research project under scrutiny. If an ample number of participants are available or if a sensitive research design is employed, a rejection of the null hypothesis often is not surprising. This state of affairs becomes even more apparent in a meta-analysis that includes a combined significance level, in which the power is great to detect even very small relations. A null hypothesis rejection, then, does not guarantee that an important social insight has been achieved.

Finally, when used in applied social research, the vote-count and combined significance level techniques give no information on whether the effect of a treatment or the relationship between variables is large or small or important or trivial. Answering the null hypothesis question, "Does homework improve achievement, yes or no?" is often not the question of greatest importance. Instead, the important question is "How much does homework improve achievement?" The answer might be zero or it might suggest a small or large impact. Furthermore, research synthesists should ask, "What factors influence the effect of homework?" The answer to this question could help them make recommendations about how best to construct homework assignments so they are most effective. Given these questions, synthesists would turn to the calculation of average effect sizes. Also, as shall be shown later, the null hypothesis question, "Is the relationship different from zero?" can be answered by placing a confidence interval around the "How much?" estimate, obviating the need for a separate combined significance level test.

### Definition of Effect Size

To meaningfully answer the "How much?" question, we must agree on definitions for the terms magnitude of difference and relationship strength, what generally is called the effect size. Also, we need methods for quantitatively expressing these ideas once we have defined them. Jacob Cohen (1988), in *Statistical Power Analysis for the Behavioral Sciences,* presented the most thorough definition of effect sizes (also see Lipsey, 1990). He defined an effect size as follows:

> Without intending any necessary implication of causality, it is convenient to use the phrase "effect size" to mean "the *degree* to which the phenomenon is present in the population," or "the degree to which the null hypothesis is false." By the above route it can now readily be clear that when the null hypothesis is false, it is false to some specific degree, i.e., *the effect size (ES) is some specific non-zero value in the population.* The

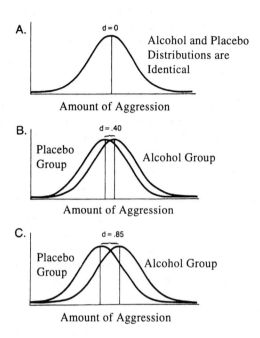

**Figure 5.2.** Three Hypothetical Relations Between Alcohol and Placebo Groups in Aggression Experiments

larger this value, the greater the *degree* to which the phenomenon under study is manifested. (pp. 9-10)

Figure 5.2 presents three hypothetical relationships that illustrate Cohen's (1988) definition. Suppose the results come from three experiments comparing the effects on aggression of alcohol versus a placebo. Figure 5.2A presents a null relationship. That is, the participants given the alcohol have a mean and distribution of aggression scores identical to the placebo-treated participants. In Figure 5.2B, the alcohol group has a mean slightly higher than that of the placebo group, and in Figure 5.2C the difference between treatments is even greater. A measure of effect size must express the three results so that greater departures from the null are associated with higher effect size values.

Cohen's (1988) book contains many different metrics for describing the strength of a relation. Each effect size index is associated with a particular research design in a manner similar to $t$ tests being associated with two-group comparisons, $F$ tests associated with multiple-group designs, and chi squares associated with frequency tables. I will describe the three primary metrics and one secondary metric for describing effect sizes. These metrics are generally useful—almost any research outcome can be expressed using one of them. For more detailed information on these effect size metrics, as well as many others, the reader should consult Cohen's book. Cohen, however, describes several metrics that permit effect size estimates for multiple degree of freedom tests and these should not be used for reasons discussed later. Thus, my description of metrics is restricted to those commensurate with single degree of freedom tests.

### The $d$ Index

The $d$ index measure of an effect size is appropriate when the means of two groups are being compared. The $d$ index is typically used in association with $t$ tests or $F$ tests based on a comparison of two conditions. The $d$ index expresses the distance between the two group means in terms of their common standard deviation. For example, if $d = .40$, it means that $4/10$ of a standard deviation separate the two means.

The hypothetical research results presented in Figure 5.2 illustrate the $d$ index. For the research result that supports the null hypothesis (Figure 5.2A), the $d$ index = 0. That is, there is no distance between the alcohol and placebo group means. The second research result (Figure 5.2B) reveals a $d$ index of .40—that is, the mean of the alcohol group lies $4/10$ of a standard deviation above the placebo group's mean. In the third example, a $d$ index of .85 is portrayed. Here, the group with the higher mean (alcohol) has a mean that rests $85/100$ of a standard deviation above the mean of the lower-meaned (placebo) group.

Calculating the $d$ index is simple. The formula is as follows:

$$d = \frac{X_1 - X_2}{\dfrac{SD_1 + SD_2}{2}}$$

[5.5]

where

$X_1$ and $X_2$ = the two group means; and
$SD_1$ and $SD_2$ = the average standard deviation of the two groups.

The formula for the $d$ index assumes that the two groups have equal (or approximately equal) sample sizes and standard deviations.

The $d$ index is not only simple to compute but also scale-free. That is, the standard deviation adjustment in the denominator of the formula means that studies using different measurement scales can be compared or combined.

In many instances, synthesists will find that primary researchers do not report the means and standard deviations of the separate groups. For such cases, Rosenthal (1984, 1994) has provided a computation formula for the $d$ index that does not require the meta-analyst to have specific means and standard deviations. This formula is as follows:

$$d = \frac{2t}{\sqrt{df_{error}}} \qquad [5.6]$$

where

$t$ = the value of the $t$ test for the associated comparison; and

$df_{error}$ = the error degrees of freedom associated with the $t$ test.

In instances in which $F$ tests with a single degree of freedom in the numerator are reported, the square root of the $F$ value ($t = \sqrt{F}$) can be substituted for the $t$ value in the above formula if the meta-analyst knows the direction of the mean difference.

The $d$ index may leave something to be desired in terms of its intuitive appeal. For this reason, Cohen (1988) also presented a measure associated with the $d$ index called $U_3$. $U_3$ tells the percentage of the sample with the lower mean that was exceeded by 50% of the scores in the higher-meaned group. More informally, $U_3$ answers the question "What percentage of the scores in the lower-meaned group was exceeded by the average score in the higher-meaned group?" Values for converting the $d$ index to $U_3$ are presented in Table 5.3. For example, the $d$ index of .40 presented in Figure 5.2B has an associated $U_3$ value of 65.5%. This means that 65.5% of the scores in the lower-meaned (placebo) group are exceeded by the average score in the higher-meaned (alcohol) group. For Figure 5.2C, the $d$ index of .85 is associated with a $U_3$ of 80.2. Thus, 80.2% of the scores in the lower-meaned (placebo) group are exceeded by the average score in the higher-meaned (alcohol) group.

**TABLE 5.3**

Equivalents Among Some Effect Size Metrics

| $d$ | $U_3$ (%) | $r$ | $r^2$ |
|-----|-----------|------|-------|
| 0 | 50.0 | .000 | .000 |
| .1 | 54.0 | .050 | .002 |
| .2 | 57.9 | .100 | .010 |
| .3 | 61.8 | .148 | .022 |
| .4 | 65.5 | .196 | .038 |
| .5 | 69.1 | .243 | .059 |
| .6 | 72.6 | .287 | .083 |
| .7 | 75.8 | .330 | .109 |
| .8 | 78.8 | .371 | .138 |
| .9 | 81.6 | .410 | .168 |
| 1.0 | 84.1 | .447 | .200 |
| 1.1 | 86.4 | .482 | .232 |
| 1.2 | 88.5 | .514 | .265 |
| 1.3 | 90.3 | .545 | .297 |
| 1.4 | 91.9 | .573 | .329 |
| 1.5 | 93.3 | .600 | .360 |
| 1.6 | 94.5 | .625 | .390 |
| 1.7 | 95.5 | .648 | .419 |
| 1.8 | 96.4 | .669 | .448 |
| 1.9 | 97.1 | .689 | .474 |
| 2.0 | 97.7 | .707 | .500 |
| 2.2 | 98.6 | .740 | .548 |
| 2.4 | 99.2 | .768 | .590 |
| 2.6 | 99.5 | .793 | .628 |
| 2.8 | 99.7 | .814 | .662 |
| 3.0 | 99.9 | .832 | .692 |
| 3.2 | 99.9 | .848 | .719 |
| 3.4 | a | .862 | .743 |
| 3.6 | a | .874 | .764 |
| 3.8 | a | .885 | .783 |
| 4.0 | a | .894 | .800 |

SOURCE: Cohen (1988). Copyright by Erlbaum and Associates. Reprinted with permission.
NOTE: a. Greater than 99.95.

### The $r$ Index

A second effect size, the $r$ index, is simply the Pearson product-moment correlation coefficient. The $r$ index is the most appropriate metric for expressing an effect size when the researcher is interested in describing the relationship between two continuous variables.

The $r$ index is familiar to most social scientists, but the formula for it requires variances and covariances, so it can rarely be computed from information typically presented in primary research reports. Luckily, primary researchers do report their $r$ indexes in most instances where they are applicable. If only the value of the $t$ test associated with the $r$ index is given, the $r$ index can be calculated using the following formula:

$$r = \sqrt{\frac{t^2}{t^2 + df_{error}}} \qquad [5.7]$$

where all terms are defined as before.

**The Odds Ratio**

A third effect size metric is applicable when both variables are dichotomous—for example, when people who have and have not consumed alcohol are simply compared on whether or not they have exhibited aggressive behavior. This measure of effect, called an odds ratio, is used most in the medical sciences, in which the researcher is often interested in the effect of a treatment on mortality or the appearance or disappearance of disease.

As its name implies, the odds ratio describes the relationship between two sets of odds. Suppose a meta-analyst comes across a study of the effects of alcohol on whether or not a person engages in aggressive behavior. Two hundred people consumed either alcohol or a placebo and then were observed for any evidence of aggression. The results of the study were as follows:

|                 | Alcohol | Placebo |
|-----------------|---------|---------|
| Aggressed       | 75      | 60      |
| Did not aggress | 25      | 40      |

To calculate an odds ratio, the meta-analyst first determined that the odds of a participant aggressing in the alcohol condition were 3 to 1 (75 to 25). The odds of exhibiting aggressive behavior in the placebo condition were 1.5 to 1 (60 to 40). The meta-analyst then simply forms the ratio of the alcohol odds over the placebo odds. In this case, the odds ratio is 2, meaning the odds of aggressing are twice as large in the alcohol as in the placebo condition. When the odds are the same in both conditions (i.e., when the null hypothesis is true), the odds ratio will be 1. The odds ratio can be calculated more directly by dividing the product of the main diagonal elements by the product of the off-diagonal elements—in this example (75 × 40) ÷ (60 × 25).

Because the odds ratio is rarely used in the social sciences and was not used in the synthesis examples, it will not be treated extensively here. Most of the techniques discussed later, however, are readily adapted to its use.

### Practical Issues in Estimating Effect Sizes

The formulas for calculating effect sizes are straightforward. In practice, meta-analysts face many technical issues when they attempt to calculate a magnitude of effect. The most important of these is missing data. Other issues arise because different studies use somewhat different designs, because of biases in sample estimates, and because of some unique characteristics of the effect size metrics themselves. I will describe a few of these.

*Choosing a Metric When Studies Have Different Designs.* One issue that arises for many meta-analysts is that different primary researchers choose different designs to study the same phenomena. For instance, in the synthesis of the relation between personality and interpersonal expectancy effects, some primary researchers dichotomized personality scores into "high" and "low" groups and used a $t$ test to determine if the groups were significantly different. Other researchers left the personality scales in their continuous form and correlated them with continuous measures of expectancy effects.

When different designs occur, the synthesist must convert one metric into the other so that a single metric can be used in the meta-analysis. Conveniently, the different effect size metrics are easily converted from one to the other. The $r$ index can be transformed into a $d$ index by the following formula:

$$d = \frac{2r}{\sqrt{1 - r^2}}$$

[5.8]

or the $d$ index can be transformed into the $r$ index by

$$r = \frac{d}{\sqrt{d^2 + 4}}$$ [5.9]

Table 5.3 gives some of the equivalents among these two measures of effect. When a chi-square statistic associated with a 2 × 2 contingency table is given, the $r$ index can be estimated as follows:

$$r = \sqrt{\frac{\chi^2}{n}}$$ [5.10]

where
$\chi^2$ = the chi-square value associated with the comparison; and
$n$ = the total number of observations in the comparison.

Cohen (1988) also gives an effect size (not an odds ratio), called the $w$ index, associated with chi-square. This metric is identical to an $r$ index when $df = 1$.

Even though metrics can easily be converted, meta-analysts must still pick a single metric in which to describe their results. The choice of how to express the effect size is determined by which metric best fits with the measurement and design characteristics of the variables under consideration. The metric of choice is based on the characteristics of the conceptual variables. Therefore, when we related personality to expectancy effects, the $r$ index was most appropriate because the two variables were conceptually continuous in nature. The first study described previously created two "artificial" groups, with the probable intention of maximizing the chance that a significant difference would be found. For this study, we would calculate a $d$ index from the high and low personality group means and standard deviations and then convert it to an $r$ index using Equation 5.9.

*Choosing an Estimate for the Standard Deviation of the d Index.* An important influence on effect sizes is the choice of the standard deviation used to estimate the variance around group means. As noted previously, most synthesists have no choice but to make the assumption that the two group standard deviations are equal to one another because the effect size must be estimated from an associated significance test, which also makes this assumption. In instances in which information about standard deviations is available and they appear to be unequal, however, the synthesist should choose one group's standard deviation to serve as the denominator in the $d$ index for purposes of standardizing the mean difference. If a treatment and control group are compared, the control group standard deviation should be used. For the $U_3$ index, this allows the synthesist to state the impact of the treatment in comparison to the untreated population—for example, "The average treated person scored higher than $X\%$ of the untreated population."

*Estimating Effect Sizes When Studies Compare More Than Two Groups.* Suppose we find a study of alcohol effects on aggression that compared three groups—for example, a brewed alcohol group versus a distilled alcohol group versus a placebo group. In this instance, we would most likely calculate two $d$ indexes, one comparing brewed alcohol to the placebo and another comparing distilled alcohol to the placebo (we could also consider comparing brewed and distilled alcohol, if this were the focus of our review). These two $d$ indexes are not statistically independent because both rely on the means and standard deviations of the same placebo group. This complicating factor, however, is preferable to the alternative strategy of using an effect size metric associated with multiple-group inference tests.

One such effect size is called PV. PV tells us the percentage of variance in the dependent variable explained by group membership. PV has the initially appealing characteristic that it can be used regardless of the number of groups in the study (indeed, it can be used with two continuous measures as well). It has the unappealing characteristic, however, that the resulting effect size tells us nothing about which of the multiple conditions has the highest mean. Identical PVs can result from any rank ordering of the group means. Thus, PV is an unfocused effect size metric that is rarely, if ever, used by meta-analysts.

Because of this ambiguity, all effect sizes should be expressed (a) as comparisons between two groups (or as other single degree of freedom contrasts if multiple groups are involved), (b) as measures of correlation between two continuous variables, or (c) as the ratio of odds. In primary research, it is recommended that multiple degree of freedom significance tests be followed by single degree of freedom comparisons. The same would be true for the effect sizes associated with these tests. If primary researchers and research synthesists defined the problem precisely, they should be able to identify single degree of freedom inference tests and associated effect sizes for each comparison of interest.

*Estimating Effect Sizes From Analyses With Multiple Factors.* Another research design influence on effect sizes involves the number of factors employed in the data analysis procedures. For example, a primary researcher testing the effect of homework versus no homework on achievement might also include individual difference factors, such as the age or sex of the students, in a multifactored analysis of variance or multiple regression. The primary researcher also might not report the means and standard deviations for the two experimental groups. Meta-analysts then are faced with two choices. First, they can calculate an effect size estimate based on an $F$ test using an error term that has been reduced by the inclusion of the extra factors. Second, they can attempt to retrieve the standard deviation that would have occurred had all the extraneous factors been ignored (i.e., been included in the error estimate). Whenever possible, the latter strategy should be employed—that is, an attempt should be made to calculate the effect size as though the comparison of interest was the sole comparison in the analysis.

Practically speaking, it is often difficult for a meta-analyst to retrieve this overall standard deviation estimate. In such cases, when meta-analysts look for influences on study outcomes they should examine whether or not the number of factors involved in the experiment is associated with the size of the effect.

*Removing Bias From Small-Sample Estimates of Population Values.* A sample statistic—be it an effect size, a mean, or a standard deviation—is based on measurements taken on a small number of people drawn from a larger population. These sample statistics will differ in known ways from the values obtained if we could measure every person in the population. Meta-analysts have devised ways to adjust for the known biases that occur because effect size estimates based on samples are not always true reflections of their underlying population values.

Hedges (1980) showed that the $d$ index may slightly overestimate the size of an effect in the entire population. The bias is minimal, however, if the sample size is more than 20. If a meta-analyst is calculating $d$ indexes from primary research based on samples smaller than 20, Hedges's correction factor should be applied. Some ways of calculating odds ratios also can lead to over- or underestimates (see Fleiss, 1994).

In addition to the small sample bias in the effect size estimates, the meta-analyst should always be cautious in interpreting any effect size based on a small number of data points. When samples are small, a single extreme value (for the *d* index) or pair of values (for the *r* index) can create an exceptionally large effect size estimate.

*Normalizing the Distribution of r Indexes.* When *r* indexes are large— that is, when they estimate population values very different from zero— they will exhibit nonnormal sampling distributions. This occurs because *r* indexes are limited to values between 1.00 and –1.00. Therefore, as a population value approaches either of these limits, the range of possible values for a sample estimate will be restricted toward the approached limit. The distribution of sampled values will become skewed away from normal.

To adjust for this, some meta-analysts convert *r* indexes to their associated *z* scores before the effect size estimates are combined or tested for moderators. The *z* scores have no limiting value and are normally distributed. In essence, the transformation "stretches" the affected tail and restores the bell shape. Once an average *z* score has been calculated, it can be converted back to an *r* index.

If the *r* index is close to zero, there is really no need to do the transformation. Indeed, some meta-analysts eschew this transform regardless of the *r* index value. An examination of the *r*-to-*z* transformation table (see Table 5.5) reveals that the two values are nearly identical until *r* = .25. When the *r* index equals .50, however, the associated *z* score equals .55, and when the *r* index equals .8 the associated *z* score equals 1.1.

*Adjusting for the Impact of Methodological Artifacts.* The magnitude of an effect size will also be influenced by the presence of methodological artifacts in the primary data collection procedures. Hunter and Schmidt (1990, 1994) described many of these artifacts, including restrictions in the range of sampled values and lack of reliability in measurements. In the latter case, measures with more error are less sensitive for detecting relations involving the measures' conceptual variable. For example, assume two personality dimensions have equal "true" relationships with expectancy effects. If one variable is measured with more error than the other, however, this less reliable measure will produce a smaller correlation with expectancy effects.

The meta-analyst might estimate the impact of the reliability of measures on effect sizes by obtaining the reliabilities (e.g., internal consistencies) of the various measures. These can then be used to see if effect sizes correlate with the reliability of the measures. Also, using procedures described by

Hunter and Schmidt (1990, 1994), the meta-analyst could estimate effect sizes if all measures were perfectly reliable.

## COMBINING EFFECT
## SIZES ACROSS STUDIES

Once each effect size has been calculated, the meta-analyst averages the effects that estimate the same comparison or relationship. It is generally accepted that these averages should weight the individual effect sizes based on the number of participants in their respective samples. This is because larger samples give more precise population estimates. For example, a $d$ index or $r$ index based on 500 participants will give a more precise and reliable estimate of the population effect size than will an estimate based on 50 subjects. The average effect size should reflect this fact.

One way to take account of sample size when calculating an average effect size is to multiply each estimate by its sample size and then divide the sum of these products by the sum of the sample sizes. There is a more precise procedure, however, described in detail by Hedges and Olkin (1985), that has many advantages but also involves more complicated calculations.

### The $d$ Index

For the $d$ index, this procedure first requires the meta-analyst to calculate a weighting factor, $w_i$, which is the inverse of the variance associated with each $d$ index estimate:

[5.11]
$$w_i = \frac{2(n_{i1} + n_{i2})n_{i1}n_{i2}}{2(n_{i1} + n_{i2})^2 + n_{i1}n_{i2}d_i^2}$$

where

$n_{i1}$ and $n_{i2}$ = the number of data points in Group 1 and Group 2 of the comparison; and

$d_i$ = the $d$ index of the comparison under consideration.

**TABLE 5.4**
An Example of $d$ Index Estimation and Tests of Homogeneity

| Finding | $n_{i1}$ | $n_{i2}$ | $d_i$ | $w_i$ | $d_i^2 w_i$ | $d_i w_i$ | $Q_b$ Grouping |
|---|---|---|---|---|---|---|---|
| 1 | 259 | 265 | .02 | 130.98 | .052 | 2.619 | A |
| 2 | 57 | 62 | .07 | 29.68 | .145 | 2.078 | A |
| 3 | 43 | 50 | .24 | 22.95 | 1.322 | 5.509 | A |
| 4 | 230 | 228 | .11 | 114.32 | 1.383 | 12.576 | A |
| 5 | 296 | 291 | .09 | 146.59 | 1.187 | 13.193 | B |
| 6 | 129 | 131 | .32 | 64.17 | 6.571 | 20.536 | B |
| 7 | 69 | 74 | .17 | 35.58 | 1.028 | 6.048 | B |
| $\Sigma$ | 1083 | 1101 | 1.02 | 544.27 | 11.69 | 62.56 | |

$$d = \frac{62.56}{544.27} = .115$$

$$CI_{d.95\%} = .115 \pm 1.96 \sqrt{\frac{1}{544.27}} = .115 \pm .084$$

$$Q_t = 11.69 - \frac{62.56^2}{544.27} = 4.5$$
$$Q_w = 1.16 + 2.36 = 3.52$$

Although the formula for $w_i$ looks imposing, it is really a simple arithmetic manipulation of three numbers available whenever we calculate a $d$ index. It is also easy to program a computer statistical package to perform the necessary calculation, and programs designed to perform meta-analysis will do it for you.

Table 5.4 presents the group sample sizes, $d$ indexes, and $w_i$'s associated with seven comparison results. The example is drawn from actual data collected as part of the synthesis of homework research. The seven studies compared the effects on achievement of homework assignments that presented material only on the day the topic was covered in class with assignments that dispersed material over several days. All seven of the experiments produced results favoring dispersed homework assignments.

To further demystify the weighting factor, note in Table 5.4 that its values equal approximately half the average sample size in a group. It should not be surprising, then, that the next step in obtaining a weighted-average effect size involves multiplying each $d$ index by its associated weight and dividing the sum of these products by the sum of the weights. The formula is

$$d. = \frac{\sum\limits_{i=1}^{N} d_i w_i}{\sum\limits_{i=1}^{N} w_i} \qquad\qquad [5.12]$$

where all terms are defined as before.

Table 5.4 shows that the average weighted $d$ index for the seven comparisons was found to be $d = .115$.

The advantage of using the $w_i$'s as weights, rather than sample sizes, is that the $w_i$'s can be used to generate a precise confidence interval around the average effect size estimate. To do this, an estimated variance for the average effect size must be calculated. First, the inverse of the sum of the $w_i$'s is found. Then, the square root of this variance is multiplied by the $z$ score associated with the confidence interval of interest. Thus, the formula for a 95% confidence interval would be

$$CI_{d.95\%} = d. \pm 1.96 \sqrt{\frac{1}{\sum\limits_{i=1}^{N} w_i}} \qquad\qquad [5.13]$$

where all terms are defined as before.

Table 5.4 reveals that the 95% confidence interval for the seven comparisons includes values of the $d$ index .084 above and below the average $d$ index. Thus, we expect 95% of estimates of this effect to fall between $d = .031$ and $d = .199$. Note that this interval does not contain the value $d = 0$. It is this information that can be taken as a test of the null hypothesis that no relation exists in the population, in place of the combined significance levels procedures discussed earlier. In this example, we would reject the null hypothesis that there was no difference in achievement between students who did current-lesson-only versus distributed homework.

**The $r$ Index**

The procedure is simpler for finding the average weighted $r$ index and its associated confidence interval. Here, each $r$ index is first transformed to its corresponding $z$ score, $z_i$, and the following formula is applied:

$$z_{\bullet} = \frac{\displaystyle\sum_{i=1}^{N}(n_i - 3)z_i}{\displaystyle\sum_{i=1}^{N}(n_i - 3)} \qquad [5.14]$$

where
 $n_i$ = the total sample size for the $i$th comparison; and
all other terms are defined as before.

For the confidence interval, the formula is

$$CI_{z\bullet\,95\%} = z_{\bullet} \pm \frac{1.96}{\sqrt{\displaystyle\sum_{i=1}^{N}(n_i - 3)}} \qquad [5.15]$$

where all terms are defined as before.

Table 5.5 presents the $r$-to-$z$ transformations needed to carry out the procedures. Once the confidence interval has been established, the meta-analyst can refer back to Table 5.5 to retrieve the corresponding $r$ indexes (the average $r$ index and the limits of the confidence interval).

Table 5.6 presents an example of how average $r$ indexes are calculated. The data are given for six correlations relating the amount of time a student reports spending on homework and the student's achievement level. These data are also a modification of an actual data set. The average $z_i$ was .207, with the 95% confidence interval ranging from .195 to .219. Note that this confidence interval is quite narrow. This is because the effect size estimates are based on large samples. Note also that the $r$-to-$z$ transforms result in only minor changes in two of the $r$ index values. This would not be the case

## TABLE 5.5
### Transformation of $r$ to $z$

| r | z | r | z | r | z | r | z | r | z |
|---|---|---|---|---|---|---|---|---|---|
| .000 | .000 | .200 | .203 | .400 | .424 | .600 | .693 | .800 | 1.099 |
| .005 | .005 | .205 | .208 | .405 | .430 | .605 | .701 | .805 | 1.113 |
| .010 | .010 | .210 | .213 | .410 | .436 | .610 | .709 | .810 | 1.127 |
| .015 | .015 | .215 | .218 | .415 | .442 | .615 | .717 | .815 | 1.142 |
| .020 | .020 | .220 | .224 | .420 | .448 | .620 | .725 | .820 | 1.157 |
| .025 | .025 | .225 | .229 | .425 | .454 | .625 | .733 | .825 | 1.172 |
| .030 | .030 | .230 | .234 | .430 | .460 | .630 | .741 | .830 | 1.188 |
| .035 | .035 | .235 | .239 | .435 | .466 | .635 | .750 | .835 | 1.204 |
| .040 | .040 | .240 | .245 | .440 | .472 | .640 | .758 | .840 | 1.221 |
| .045 | .045 | .245 | .250 | .445 | .478 | .645 | .767 | .845 | 1.238 |
| .050 | .050 | .250 | .255 | .450 | .485 | .650 | .775 | .850 | 1.256 |
| .055 | .055 | .255 | .261 | .455 | .491 | .655 | .784 | .855 | 1.274 |
| .060 | .060 | .260 | .266 | .460 | .497 | .660 | .793 | .860 | 1.293 |
| .065 | .065 | .265 | .271 | .465 | .504 | .665 | .802 | .865 | 1.313 |
| .070 | .070 | .270 | .277 | .470 | .510 | .670 | .811 | .870 | 1.333 |
| .075 | .075 | .275 | .282 | .475 | .517 | .675 | .820 | .875 | 1.354 |
| .080 | .080 | .280 | .288 | .480 | .523 | .680 | .829 | .880 | 1.376 |
| .085 | .085 | .285 | .293 | .485 | .530 | .685 | .838 | .885 | 1.398 |
| .090 | .090 | .290 | .299 | .490 | .536 | .690 | .848 | .890 | 1.422 |
| .095 | .095 | .295 | .304 | .495 | .543 | .695 | .858 | .895 | 1.447 |
| .100 | .100 | .300 | .310 | .500 | .549 | .700 | .867 | .900 | 1.472 |
| .105 | .105 | .305 | .315 | .505 | .556 | .705 | .877 | .905 | 1.499 |
| .110 | .110 | .310 | .321 | .510 | .563 | .710 | .887 | .910 | 1.528 |
| .115 | .116 | .315 | .326 | .515 | .570 | .715 | .897 | .915 | 1.557 |
| .120 | .121 | .320 | .332 | .520 | .576 | .720 | .908 | .920 | 1.589 |
| .125 | .126 | .325 | .337 | .525 | .583 | .725 | .918 | .925 | 1.623 |
| .130 | .131 | .330 | .343 | .530 | .590 | .730 | .929 | .930 | 1.658 |
| .135 | .136 | .335 | .348 | .535 | .597 | .735 | .940 | .935 | 1.697 |
| .140 | .141 | .340 | .354 | .540 | .604 | .740 | .950 | .940 | 1.738 |
| .145 | .146 | .345 | .360 | .545 | .611 | .745 | .962 | .945 | 1.783 |
| .150 | .151 | .350 | .365 | .550 | .618 | .750 | .973 | .950 | 1.832 |
| .155 | .156 | .355 | .371 | .555 | .626 | .755 | .984 | .955 | 1.886 |
| .160 | .161 | .360 | .377 | .560 | .633 | .760 | .996 | .960 | 1.946 |
| .165 | .167 | .365 | .383 | .565 | .640 | .765 | 1.008 | .965 | 2.014 |
| .170 | .172 | .370 | .388 | .570 | .648 | .770 | 1.020 | .970 | 2.092 |
| .175 | .177 | .375 | .394 | .575 | .655 | .775 | 1.033 | .975 | 2.185 |
| .180 | .182 | .380 | .400 | .580 | .662 | .785 | 1.045 | .980 | 2.298 |
| .185 | .187 | .385 | .406 | .585 | .670 | .790 | 1.058 | .985 | 2.443 |
| .190 | .192 | .390 | .412 | .590 | .678 | .780 | 1.071 | .990 | 2.647 |
| .195 | .198 | .395 | .418 | .595 | .685 | .795 | 1.085 | .995 | 2.994 |

SOURCE: Edwards (1967). Copyright (1967) by Holt, Rinehart & Winston. Reprinted with permission.

**TABLE 5.6**

Example of $r$ Index Estimation and Tests of Homogeneity

| Finding | $n_i$ | $r_i$ | $z_i$ | $n_i - 3$ | $(n_i - 3)z_i$ | $(n_i - 3)z_i^2$ | $Q_b$ Grouping |
|---|---|---|---|---|---|---|---|
| 1 | 1,021 | .08 | .08 | 1,018 | 81.44 | 6.52 | A |
| 2 | 1,955 | .27 | .28 | 1,952 | 546.56 | 153.04 | A |
| 3 | 12,146 | .26 | .27 | 12,143 | 3278.61 | 885.22 | A |
| 4 | 3,505 | .06 | .06 | 3,502 | 210.12 | 12.61 | B |
| 5 | 3,606 | .12 | .12 | 3,603 | 432.36 | 51.88 | B |
| 6 | 4,157 | .22 | .22 | 4,154 | 913.88 | 201.05 | B |
| $\Sigma$ | 26,390 | .85 | .87 | 26,372 | 5464.97 | 1310.32 | |

$$z = \frac{5462.97}{26,372} = .207$$

$$CI_{z.95\%} = .207 \pm 1.96/\sqrt{26,372} = .207 \pm .012$$

$$Q_t = 1310.32 - \frac{(5462.97)^2}{26,372} = 178.66$$

$$Q_w = 34.95 + 50.40 = 85.35$$

$$Q_b = 178.66 = 85.35 = 93.31$$

had the $r$ indexes been larger (e.g., an $r$ index of .60 is transformed to a $z$ of .69; see Table 5.5). As with the earlier example, $z_i = 0$ is not contained in the confidence interval. Therefore, we can reject the null hypothesis that there is no relation between the amount of time students report spending on homework and their level of achievement.

## Synthesis Examples

Both the $d$ index and the $r$ index were used in the synthesis examples. The meta-analysis of studies on alcohol effects on aggression presented several overall $d$ indexes, depending on how the control group was treated. For comparisons between participants who received alcohol and those who received no treatment whatsoever, the mean $d$ index equaled .25. A $d$ index of this magnitude indicates that the average person in the alcohol group was more aggressive than approximately 60% of the people receiving no treatment. The average $d$ index for comparisons of alcohol versus placebo controls was $d = .61$, or $U_3 = 72.6\%$. For the placebo versus no treatment comparisons, the average $d$ index was .10 and $U_3$ was 54%. Finally, when people receiving alcohol were compared on aggressiveness to people in an "antiplacebo" condition—one in which they were told not to expect alcohol but then received it—the average $d$ index was .06.

The $r$ index was used to measure effect sizes in the meta-analysis of the relation between personality and interpersonal expectancy effects in photo-rating experiments. The largest average correlation, $r = .15$, was found between an experimenter's need for social influence and the generation of interpersonal expectancy effects.

## ANALYZING VARIANCE IN EFFECT
## SIZES ACROSS FINDINGS

The analytic procedures described thus far have illustrated how to test the null hypothesis using significance levels from separate studies and how to generate estimates of the strength of relations. Another set of statistical techniques helps us discover why effect sizes vary from one study to another. In these analyses, the effect sizes found in the separate studies are the "dependent" or predicted variables, and the characteristics of the studies are the predictor variables. The synthesist asks whether the magnitude of relation between two variables in a study is affected by the way the study was designed or carried out.

One obvious feature of the effect sizes in Tables 5.4 and 5.6 is that they vary from comparison to comparison. An explanation for this variability is not only important but also represents the most unique contribution of research synthesis. By performing an analysis of differences in effect sizes, the synthesist can gain insight into the factors that affect relationship strengths, even though these factors may have never been studied in a single experiment. For instance, assume that the first four studies listed in Table 5.4 were conducted in elementary schools, whereas the last three studies were conducted in high schools. Is the difference between types of home-work assignments different for students at different grades? This question could be tentatively answered through the use of the analytic techniques described next, even though no single study employed both elementary and high school samples.

The techniques that follow are a few examples of procedures for analyz-ing variance in effects. I do not cover some of the more complex synthesis techniques. In particular, I have omitted the Confidence Profile Method (Eddy, Hasselblad, & Schachter, 1992) and the Bayesian approach (Louis & Zelterman, 1994). These require knowledge of more advanced statistical concepts and operations. The descriptions I present are conceptual and brief. If you are interested in applying them, you are advised first to examine more detailed treatments, especially those contained in the references given in the text.

## Traditional Inferential Statistics

One way to analyze the variance in effect sizes is to apply the traditional inference procedures that are employed by primary researchers. A meta-analyst interested in whether alcohol's effects on aggression were stronger for males than for females might do a $t$ test on the difference between effect sizes found in comparisons using exclusively males versus comparisons using exclusively females. If the meta-analyst was interested in whether the alcohol effect size was influenced by the length of delay between consumption and the measurement of aggression, the meta-analyst might correlate the length of delay in each comparison with its effect size. In this instance, the predictor and dependent variables are continuous, so the significance test associated with the correlation coefficient is the appropriate inferential statistic. For more complex questions, a synthesist might categorize effect sizes into multifactor groupings—for instance, according to the gender and age of participants—and perform an analysis of variance or multiple regression on effect sizes. For Table 5.4, if a one-way analysis of variance were conducted comparing the first four $d$ indexes with the last three $d$ indexes, the result would be nonsignificant.

Standard inference procedures were the techniques initially used by meta-analysts for examining variance in effects. Glass, McGaw, and Smith (1981) detailed how this approach is carried out. At least two problems arise with the use of traditional inference procedures in research synthesis, however. The first is that traditional inference procedures do not test the hypothesis that the variability in effect sizes is due solely to sampling error (see the discussion of variability in main effects earlier in this chapter). Therefore, the traditional inference procedures can reveal associations between design characteristics and effect sizes without determining first whether the overall variance in effects is greater than that expected by chance.

Also, because effect sizes can be based on different numbers of data points (sample sizes), they can have different sampling variances associated with them—that is, they are measured with different amounts of error. If this is the case (and it often is), then the effect sizes violate the assumption of homogeneity of variance that underlies traditional inference tests. For these two reasons, traditional inferential statistics are no longer used when performing a meta-analysis.

## Comparing Observed to Expected Variance

In place of traditional procedures, several approaches have gained acceptance. One approach was proposed by Hunter and Schmidt (1990). It compares the variation in the observed effect sizes with the variation expected if only sampling error were causing differences in effect size estimates. This approach involves calculating (a) the observed variance in the effect sizes from the known findings and (b) the expected variance in these effect sizes given that all are estimating the same underlying population value. Sampling theory allows us to calculate precise estimates of how much sampling variation to expect in a group of effect sizes. This expected value is a function of the average effect size estimate, the number of estimates, and their sample sizes.

The meta-analyst then compares the observed with the expected variance. Hunter and Schmidt (1990) suggest that the meta-analyst refrain from formal tests to judge whether a significant difference exists between the observed and expected variances. Instead, they suggest that if the observed variance is twice as large as the expected sampling variance then one should assume the two are reliably different. Whatever the criteria, if the variance estimates are deemed not to differ, then sampling error is the simplest explanation for the variance in effect sizes. If they are deemed different—that is, if the observed variance is much greater than that expected due to sampling error—then the meta-analyst begins the search for systematic influences on effect sizes.

Hunter and Schmidt (1990) also suggest that the meta-analyst adjust effect size estimates to account for methodological artifacts. Earlier, I gave some examples of these when I discussed factors that influence effect size estimates.

### Homogeneity Analyses

A homogeneity analysis also compares the observed variance to that expected from sampling error. Unlike the first approach, however, it includes a calculation of how probable it is that the variance exhibited by the effect sizes would be observed if only sampling error was making them different. This is the approach used most often by meta-analysts, so I will provide a few more of its details.

Homogeneity analysis first asks the question, "Is the observed variance in effect sizes significantly different from that expected by sampling error alone?" If the answer is no, then some statisticians advise the meta-analyst to stop the analysis there. After all, chance or sampling error is the simplest and most parsimonious explanation for why the effect sizes differ. If the answer is yes—that is, if the effect sizes display significantly greater variability than expected by chance—the meta-analyst then begins to examine whether study characteristics are systematically associated with variance in effect sizes. Some meta-analysts feel that the search for moderators should proceed regardless of whether sampling error is rejected as the plausible sole cause of variability in effect sizes—if the meta-analyst has good theoretical or practical reasons for choosing moderators.

Suppose a meta-analysis reveals a homogeneity statistic, typically called $Q$, that has an associated $p$ value of .05. This means that only 5 times in 100 would sampling error create this amount of variance in effect sizes. Thus, we would reject the null hypothesis that sampling error alone explains the variance in effect sizes and begin the search for additional influences. We would then test whether study characteristics explain variation in effect sizes. Studies would be grouped by common features, and the average effect sizes for groups would be tested for homogeneity in the same way as the overall, average effect size.

An approach to homogeneity analysis will be described that was introduced simultaneously by Rosenthal and Rubin (1982) and Hedges (1982). The formula presented by Hedges and Olkin (1985; also see Hedges, 1994) will be given here, and the procedures using $d$ indexes will be described first.

*The d Index.* To test whether a set of $d$ indexes is homogeneous, the synthesist must calculate a statistic that Hedges and Olkin (1985) called $Q_t$:

$$Q_t = \sum_{i=1}^{N} w_i d_i^2 - \frac{\left( \sum_{i=1}^{N} w_i d_i \right)^2}{\sum_{i=1}^{N} w_i} \qquad [5.16]$$

where all terms are defined as before.

The $Q$ statistic has a chi-square distribution with $N - 1$ degrees of freedom, or one less than the number of comparisons. The meta-analyst refers the obtained value of $Q_t$ to a table of (upper-tail) chi-square values. If the obtained value is greater than the critical value for the upper tail of a chi-square at the chosen level of significance, the meta-analyst rejects the

**TABLE 5.7**

Critical Values of Chi-Square for Given Probability Levels

| df | Upper Tail Probabilities | | | | | |
|---|---|---|---|---|---|---|
| | *.500* | *.250* | *.100* | *.050* | *.025* | *.010* |
| 1 | .455 | 1.32 | 2.71 | 3.84 | 5.02 | 6.63 |
| 2 | 1.39 | 2.77 | 4.61 | 5.99 | 7.38 | 9.21 |
| 3 | 2.37 | 4.11 | 6.25 | 7.81 | 9.35 | 11.3 |
| 4 | 3.36 | 5.39 | 7.78 | 9.49 | 11.1 | 13.3 |
| 5 | 4.35 | 6.63 | 9.24 | 11.1 | 12.8 | 15.1 |
| 6 | 5.35 | 7.84 | 10.6 | 12.6 | 14.4 | 16.8 |
| 7 | 6.35 | 9.04 | 12.0 | 14.1 | 16.0 | 18.5 |
| 8 | 7.34 | 10.2 | 13.4 | 15.5 | 17.5 | 20.1 |
| 9 | 8.34 | 11.4 | 14.7 | 16.9 | 19.0 | 21.7 |
| 10 | 9.34 | 12.5 | 16.0 | 18.3 | 20.5 | 23.2 |
| 11 | 10.3 | 13.7 | 17.3 | 19.7 | 21.9 | 24.7 |
| 12 | 11.3 | 14.8 | 18.5 | 21.0 | 23.3 | 26.2 |
| 13 | 12.3 | 16.0 | 19.8 | 22.4 | 24.7 | 27.7 |
| 14 | 13.3 | 17.1 | 21.1 | 23.7 | 26.1 | 29.1 |
| 15 | 14.3 | 18.2 | 22.3 | 25.0 | 27.5 | 30.6 |
| 16 | 15.3 | 19.4 | 23.5 | 26.3 | 28.8 | 32.0 |
| 17 | 16.3 | 20.5 | 24.8 | 27.6 | 30.2 | 33.4 |
| 18 | 17.3 | 21.6 | 26.0 | 28.9 | 31.5 | 34.8 |
| 19 | 18.3 | 22.7 | 27.2 | 30.1 | 32.9 | 36.2 |
| 20 | 19.3 | 23.8 | 28.4 | 31.4 | 34.2 | 37.6 |
| 21 | 20.3 | 24.9 | 29.6 | 32.7 | 35.5 | 33.9 |
| 22 | 21.3 | 26.0 | 30.8 | 33.9 | 36.8 | 40.3 |
| 23 | 22.3 | 27.1 | 32.0 | 35.2 | 38.1 | 41.6 |
| 24 | 23.3 | 28.2 | 33.2 | 36.4 | 39.4 | 43.0 |
| 25 | 24.3 | 29.3 | 34.4 | 37.7 | 40.6 | 44.3 |
| 26 | 25.3 | 30.4 | 35.6 | 38.9 | 41.9 | 45.6 |
| 27 | 26.3 | 31.5 | 36.7 | 40.1 | 43.2 | 47.0 |
| 28 | 27.3 | 32.6 | 37.9 | 41.3 | 44.5 | 48.3 |
| 29 | 28.3 | 33.7 | 39.1 | 42.6 | 45.7 | 49.6 |
| 30 | 29.3 | 34.8 | 40.3 | 43.8 | 47.0 | 50.9 |
| 40 | 49.3 | 45.6 | 51.8 | 55.8 | 59.3 | 63.7 |
| 60 | 59.3 | 67.0 | 74.4 | 79.1 | 83.3 | 88.4 |
| | *.500* | *.750* | *.900* | *.950* | *.975* | *.990* |
| | Lower Tail Probabilities | | | | | |

SOURCE: Pearson and Hartley (1966). Copyright Cambridge University Press (1966). Reprinted with permission.

hypothesis that the variance in effect sizes was produced by sampling error alone. Table 5.7 presents the distribution of chi-square for selected probability levels.

For the set of comparisons given in Table 5.4, the value of $Q_t$ equals 4.5. The critical value for chi-square at $p < .05$ based on 6 degrees of freedom is 12.59. Therefore, the hypothesis that sampling error explains the differences in these $d$ indexes cannot be rejected.

The procedure to test whether a methodological or conceptual distinction between comparisons explains variance in effect sizes involves three steps. First, a $Q$ statistic is calculated separately for each subgroup of comparisons. For instance, to compare the first four $d$ indexes in Table 5.4 with the last three, a separate $Q$ statistic is calculated for each grouping. Then, the values of these $Q$ statistics are summed to form a value called $Q_w$. This value is then subtracted from $Q_t$ to obtain $Q_b$:

$$Q_b = Q_t - Q_w \qquad [5.17]$$

where all terms are defined as before.

The statistic $Q_b$ is used to test whether the average effects from the two groupings are homogeneous. It is referred to a chi-square table using as degrees of freedom one less than the number of groupings. If the average $d$ indexes are homogeneous, then the grouping factor does not explain variance in effects beyond that associated with sampling error. If $Q_b$ exceeds the critical value, then the grouping factor is a significant contributor to variance in effect sizes.

In Table 5.4, the $Q_b$ comparing the first four and last three $d$ indexes is .98. This result is not significant with 1 degree of freedom.

*The r Index.* The analogous procedures for performing a homogeneity analysis on $r$ indexes involves the following formula:

$$Q_t = \sum_{i=1}^{N}(n_i - 3)z_i^{\,2} - \frac{\left[\sum_{i=1}^{N}(n_i - 3)z_i\right]^2}{\sum_{i=1}^{N}(n_i - 3)} \qquad [5.18]$$

where all terms are defined as before.

To compare groups of $r$ indexes, Equation 5.18 is applied to each grouping separately, and the sum of these results, $Q_w$, is subtracted from $Q_t$ to obtain $Q_b$.

The results of a homogeneity analysis using the $r$ index are presented in Table 5.6. The $Q_t$ value of 178.66 is highly significant based on a chi-square test with 5 degrees of freedom. Although it seems that a range of $r$ indexes from .08 to .27 is not terribly large, $Q_t$ tells us that, given the sizes of the samples on which these estimates are based, the range is too great to be explained by sampling error alone. Something other than sampling error likely is contributing to the variance in $r$ indexes.

Suppose we know that the first three correlations in Table 5.6 are from samples of high school students and the last three are from elementary school students. A homogeneity analysis testing the effect of grade level on the magnitude of $r$ indexes reveals a $Q_b$ of 93.31. This value is highly significant based on a chi-square test with 1 degree of freedom. For high school students, the average weighted $r$ index is .253, whereas for elementary school students it is $r = .136$. Thus, the grade level of the student is one potential explanation for the variation in $r$ indexes.

### Practical Issues in Homogeneity Analysis

*Using Computer Statistical Packages.* Calculating average weighted effect sizes and homogeneity statistics by hand is time-consuming and open to error. Conveniently, the major computer statistics packages, such as SAS (1992) and SPSS (1990), can be used to do the calculations.

The weighting factors for the $d$ index ($w_i$) and the $r$ index ($n_i - 3$) can be generated by having the packages carry out the needed arithmetic calculations and defining these as new variables. The intermediate values for calculating average effect sizes and confidence intervals can be obtained by arithmetic definition of new variables and then by summing these variables. The sums can then be (a) used to create new data sets for further manipulation or (b) plugged into the final formulae by hand.

With regard to homogeneity analyses, Hedges and Olkin (1985) note that homogeneity analyses can be calculated using weighted least squares regression programs. For instance, to calculate a $Q$ statistic using the GLM procedure available in the SAS (1992) statistical package, the meta-analyst would write a set of commands to conduct a multiple regression analysis using (a) the $d$ indexes or $z$ transforms of $r$ indexes as the dependent variable, (b) the moderating variable of interest as the predictor variable, and (c) the appropriate weight ($w_i$ or $n_i - 3$) as a weighting factor.

The output of this SAS regression analysis is interpreted as follows: The $F$ test associated with the model mean square is ignored. The total corrected sums of squares is $Q_t$. As shown previously, the significance of $Q_t$ can be found by referring this value to a table of chi-square values (Table 5.7). The model sums of squares is $Q_b$. It also must be referred to a chi-square table to establish its significance.

For synthesists with a greater knowledge of computers and computer programming, Wang and Bushman (in press) present a complete set of computer macrocommands that permit the user to program the SAS system for meta-analysis. The corresponding programs in SPSS result in the same output.

There are also smaller computer software packages with programs devoted to meta-analysis. These include DSTAT, True Epistat, and Fast*Pro (Normand, 1995). Generally speaking, these programs are not as flexible as the large software packages. They are often limited in their capacity, the effect size metrics they handle, whether they allow input of raw data only or also permit entry of effect sizes, how many moderating variables can be included in the same analysis, whether databases can be manipulated after they are entered, and whether they can conduct both fixed and random effects models. If one of these programs fits the purposes of the meta-analyst, however, it may be easier to use then the larger statistical packages. The content and flexibility of the devoted programs is always being upgraded, so a potential user should find the most recent documentation to discover the exact capabilities of each.

*Choosing a Fixed or Random Effects Model.* In the homogeneity analysis examples I provided, I assumed that the effect sizes coming from the separate studies were estimating a fixed population value rather than one that is random. The distinction between fixed and random effects is a sophisticated data analysis problem (see Kalaian & Raudenbush, 1996; Raudenbush, 1994).

In essence, an effect size is said to be fixed when the only random influence on it is sampling error. Sometimes, however, other features of studies can be viewed as random influences. For example, in studies of the effects of homework on achievement, teachers and their styles for using homework will differ from class to class, and they will affect the impact of homework. Because they will do so in unsystematic ways, it might also be appropriate to consider teachers to be randomly sampled from a population of teachers.

The question we must ask is whether the effect sizes in a data set are affected by a large number of these uncontrollable influences, such as differences in teachers, schools, family structures, and so on. If the answer is "yes, they probably are," then the meta-analyst chooses a statistical model that takes these additional sources of random variance in effect sizes into account. If the answer is "no, probably not," then random variance in effect sizes is ignored (or more accurately, set to zero) and a fixed-effects statistical model is used.

It is rarely clear-cut which assumption, fixed or random, is most appropriate for a particular set of effect sizes. In practice, most meta-analysts opt for the fixed-effects assumption because it is analytically easier to manage. Some meta-analysts argue that fixed-effects statistical models are used too often when random-effects models are more appropriate (and conservative). Others counterargue that a fixed-effect statistical model can be applied if a thorough, appropriate search for influences on effect sizes is part of the analytic strategy—that is, if the meta-analyst looks at the systematic effects of influences such as teachers, schools, and family structures.

*Coping With Missing Data.* Another important practical issue associated with the use of homogeneity statistics involves missing data. In many instances, the synthesist will be confronted with incomplete data reports, particularly when nonsignificant effects are found. It was previously suggested that a conservative procedure should set these effect sizes at zero. If the proportion of assumed zero effects is large but an effect actually exists in the population, however, greater variance in effect sizes may be estimated using this convention than would be the case if complete information on effect sizes were available. Thus, although the assumption that researchers reporting null findings without statistics found effect sizes exactly equal to zero will have a conservative impact on combined significance levels and estimates of average effect size, this assumption may lead to too large an estimate of observed variance in effects.

Related to missing data, homogeneity statistics appear to be low in power. If so, important relations may be missed when homogeneity statistics are used along with conventional levels of statistical significance.

*Examining Multiple Moderators.* Homogeneity statistics can become unreliable and difficult to interpret when the synthesist wishes to test more than one moderator of effect sizes at a time. Hedges and Olkin (1985) present a rigorous model for testing multiple moderators. The model uses sequential or hierarchical tests for homogeneity. It removes the variance in effects due to one moderator and then removes from the remaining variance additional variance due to the next moderator.

This procedure is often difficult to apply because characteristics of studies are often correlated with one another. For example, suppose I wanted to test whether the effect of homework on achievement is influenced by both the grade level of the student and the level of standardization of the dependent measure. In the comparisons to be analyzed, I found that these two study characteristics are often confounded—more studies of high school students used standardized tests, whereas more studies of elementary school students used class grades. Just like traditional regression analyses, these intercorrelations make interpretation difficult. In particular, they make the order in which variables are entered into the analysis critical—different orders can result in dramatically different results.

One solution to intercorrelated study characteristics is to generate homogeneity statistics for each characteristic separately by repeating the calculation of $Q$ statistics as described previously. Then, when the results concerning moderators of effect are interpreted, the meta-analyst also examines a matrix of intercorrelations among the moderators. This way, the meta-analyst can alert readers to study characteristics that may be confounded and draw inferences with these relations in mind.

*Getting Different Results Depending on the Effect Size Metric.* A final practical issue is that the results of homogeneity statistics depend somewhat on the choice of the effect size metric. For instance, the same set of data can yield different results depending on whether $d$ indexes or $r$ indexes are used to express relations. This is because $d$ indexes and $r$ indexes are not related by a linear transform. The problem of nonequivalent results also appears in primary data analysis—that is, the same data analyzed with parametric and nonparametric statistics can yield different results. In primary statistical analyses, however, the differences between one technique and another are well established, and the relative appropriateness of one technique or another is fairly easy to evaluate. With the homogeneity statistics, these ground rules are not yet clear.

In summary, practical issues in interpretation as well as the precise statistical properties of meta-analysis formulas are still being discovered. Although it is clear that a formal analysis of variance in effect sizes is an essential part of any research synthesis containing large numbers of comparisons, it is also clear that meta-analysts must take great care in the application of these statistics and in the description of how they were applied. Whenever possible, they should also carry out sensitivity analyses, examining whether different procedures lead to the same or different results.

## Raw Data Analysis

The most desirable technique for combining results of independent studies is to integrate the raw data from each relevant comparison or estimate of a relationship. The separate data points can be placed into an analysis of variance or multiple regression that employs the comparison that generated the data as a blocking variable. Obviously, instances in which the integration of raw data can be achieved are rare. Raw data are seldom included in research reports, and attempts to obtain raw data from researchers often end in failure (see Chapter 4).

The benefits of integrating raw data, however, can also be achieved if the synthesist has access to the means and standard deviations associated with each comparison. A problem with the use of means and standard deviations is that the dependent-variable measurements in the separate comparisons are often not commensurate with one another—that is, they use different instruments with different ranges of values. Of course, the synthesist can standardize the measurements in each comparison to make them commensurate. Again, however, the reporting of individual group means and standard deviations in primary research reports is infrequent, though certainly not as rare as the reporting of raw data.

In instances in which raw data from comparisons are available, the moderating hypotheses examined by the homogeneity statistics can be tested by the presence or absence of statistical interactions. That is, the meta-analyst can perform a mixed-model analysis of variance on the accumulated raw data using comparison characteristics as between-groups factors and the within-study comparisons as the within-groups factor. If the influence of any within-comparison effect is dependent on the moderator, it will appear as a significant interaction in the analysis. A significant main effect attributable to research characteristics (the between-groups factor) would indicate that the overall mean on the dependent variable varied from one group of studies to the other.

Suppose 12 studies of alcohol effects on aggression were found, and the raw data from each were available. In addition, assume that 6 of these studies were conducted on men only and 6 conducted on women only. The meta-analyst could conduct an analysis so that the alcohol versus control comparison was the within-groups factor and the men versus women comparison was the between-groups factor. A main effect for the alcohol versus control comparison would indicate study-generated evidence for a drug effect. A main effect for sex would indicate that comparisons using one sex revealed greater aggression (the dependent variable) than comparisons using the other sex. Finally, significant interaction between sex and treatment would indicate that the effect of alcohol depended on whether or not the participants were men or women.

As mentioned previously, this type of analysis in research synthesis is limited both by the infrequency with which raw data can be obtained and by the use of different measurement scales by different researchers. Analyzing raw data from separate comparisons is the optimum strategy for accumulating results. It is the level of analysis to which the synthesist should aspire, and its feasibility should be assessed before other less adequate means for combining results are undertaken. In practice, however, the use of this technique is rare.

## Complex Data Analysis

The statistical procedures for meta-analysis described previously apply to synthesizing two-variable relationships from experimental and descriptive research. Meta-analysis methodologists are working to extend statistical synthesis procedures to accommodate more complex ways to express the relations between variables. These efforts include techniques for the synthesis of factor analyses (Bushman, Cooper, & Lemke, 1991) and correlation matrices so as to examine multivariate, explanatory models (Becker & Schramm, 1994).

## Variance in Effect Sizes and Synthesis-Generated Evidence

The evidence uncovered through an examination of variance in effect sizes is synthesis-generated evidence. That is, relations between study characteristics and effect sizes cannot be interpreted by the synthesist as uncovering causal relations. As discussed in detail previously, in many instances different characteristics of studies will be correlated with one another and it will be impossible to tell which of the correlated characteristics is the true causal agent. Therefore, although synthesis-generated evidence is unique to the research synthesis and represents an important addition to our understanding of research topics, statements of causality based on synthesis-generated evidence are very risky. Typically, when synthesis-generated evidence indicates a relation exists, it is used by the synthesist to point out future fruitful directions for primary researchers.

## VALIDITY ISSUES IN DATA ANALYSIS

The first threat to validity arising during the analysis stage is that the rules of inference a synthesist employs may be inappropriate. In nonquantitative syntheses, the appropriateness of inference rules is difficult to assess because the synthesist rarely makes them explicit. In quantitative syntheses, the suppositions underlying statistical tests are generally known, and some statistical biases in syntheses can be removed. A complete testing of inference rules may never be possible, but the users of meta-analyses can decide at least informally whether the statistical assumptions have been met. Regardless of the strategy used, the possibility always exists that the synthesist has used an invalid rule for inferring a characteristic of the target population.

The second threat to validity introduced during analysis is that synthesis-generated evidence may be misinterpreted as supporting statements of causality. I have noted several times in this text that any variable or relation within a synthesis can be examined through either study-generated or synthesis-generated evidence. The scientific status of conclusions based on the different types of evidence, however, can be quite different. Study-generated evidence is capable of establishing causal precedence among variables, whereas synthesis-generated evidence is always purely associational.

### Protecting Validity

Recommendations concerning what assumptions are appropriate for synthesists to make about their data will depend on the purposes of a synthesis and the peculiarities of a problem area. This is as true of quantitative procedures as it is of nonquantitative ones. The only sound general advice is that synthesists should open their rules of inference to public inspection. The following are recommended:

1. Synthesists should be as explicit as possible about their guiding assumptions when they convey their conclusions and inferences to readers.
2. If there is any evidence bearing on the validity of the interpretation rules, it should be presented. Without this information, the reader cannot evaluate the validity of conclusions. Synthesis reports that do not address this issue should be considered incomplete.
3. Whenever possible, synthesists should analyze their data using multiple procedures that require different assumptions. Much greater confidence can be placed in results that do not vary across different methods.

4. Synthesists should be careful to distinguish study-generated and synthesis-generated evidence. Even if the number of studies using each design characteristic is large, the possibility exists that some other unknown methodological feature is correlated with the one involved in an uncovered relation. The more equivocal nature of synthesis-generated inferences means that if this type of evidence indicates that a relation exists, the synthesist should call for the relation to be tested within a single study.

## EXERCISES

| Finding | $n_i$ | z Score (One-Tailed) | $d_i$ |
|---------|-------|----------------------|-------|
| 1 | 366 | −0.84 | −.08 |
| 2 | 96 | 1.55 | .35 |
| 3 | 280 | 3.29 | .47 |
| 4 | 122 | 0 | .00 |
| 5 | 154 | 1.96 | .33 |
| 6 | 120 | 2.05 | .41 |
| 7 | 144 | −1.64 | −.28 |

1. What is the combined z score and probability level of the seven studies listed using the Adding Z's method? Using the Adding Weighted Z's method? What is the Fail-safe N?
2. What is the average weighted d index?
3. Are the effect sizes of the seven studies homogeneous? Calculate your answer both by hand and by using a computer statistical package.

# 6

# *The Interpretation and Presentation Stage*

This chapter presents a format for research syntheses reports similar to that used for primary research reports, including sections for introduction of the problem, methods of synthesis, results, and interpretation and discussion. Special attention is given to how to present tabulated data in syntheses and how to interpret effect sizes. Finally, the chapter describes threats to validity that arise from poor reporting and how to protect against them.

> *Research is complete only when the results*
> *are shared with the scientific community.*
> —American Psychological Association (1994, p. 1)

The transformation of an investigator's notes, printouts, and remembrances into a public document describing the project is a task with profound implications for the accumulation of knowledge. Without careful attention by the researcher to how the investigation is interpreted and described, all efforts to conduct a trustworthy and convincing scientific study leading up to this point are for naught.

## REPORT WRITING IN SOCIAL SCIENCE RESEARCH

The codified guidelines used by many social science disciplines for reporting primary research are contained in The American Psychological Association's (APA) *Publication Manual* (1994). The *Manual* is quite specific about the style and format of reports, and it even gives some guidance concerning grammar and the clear expression of ideas. Much less detailed assistance is provided to researchers for evaluating the importance of specific aspects and conclusions of a study. The *Manual* tells researchers how to report statistical data and where to do so. Of necessity, it is much less explicit in guiding judgments about what makes a finding important to readers. For example, most researchers perform more statistical tests than they think will interest readers. Statistical significance cannot be offered as a general guideline because a null result may be of great interest in some topic areas.

Obviously, the *Manual* should not be faulted for this omission. It would be impossible to explicate general and accurate guidelines for defining the scientific importance of results. In fact, this question is itself the subject of much research within the subdiscipline of the sociology of science and embodies the creative essence of the scientific enterprise. It cannot be reduced to a formula.

The research synthesist's dilemma is similar in kind to that of the primary researcher, but it is more dramatic in degree. The synthesist has no consensual guidelines similar to the *Publication Manual* (APA, 1994) that describe how to structure the final report. The *Manual* itself makes reference to review articles in three places. It defines a review article, including meta-analysis, as "critical evaluations of material that has already been published" (p. 5) and states that "the components of review articles, unlike the sections of reports of empirical studies, are arranged by relationship rather than chronology" (p. 5). As shall be shown, the format for reporting meta-analyses has evolved to look not unlike that of reports of primary research. In many cases, however, the synthesist chooses a format convenient for the particular synthesis problem.

Recently, some efforts have appeared that help synthesists construct final reports. The relative lack of reporting guidelines for synthesists, however, is a problem because different editorial judgments create variation in how readers interpret synthesis outcomes. This variation is not found in the direction or magnitude of conclusions but in whether particular aspects and results of syntheses are included in the report. One synthesist may believe that a methodological characteristic or result would only clutter the manuscript. A second synthesist might think the same piece of information would be of interest to some readers and decide that the "clutter" was worthwhile.


## A FORMAT FOR RESEARCH
## SYNTHESIS REPORTS


Throughout this book, I have tried to extend the rules for conducting primary research to conducting research synthesis. It should not be surprising, then, to find that my suggestions concerning the format of synthesis reports draw heavily on how we report primary research. The basic division of primary research reports into four sections—introduction, methods, results, and discussion—should serve nicely as a structure for research syntheses. The division of reports into these four sections serves to highlight the types of information that need to be presented in order for readers to evaluate adequately the validity and utility of the synthesis. In the sections that follow, I suggest some types of information that should be included in each section. Also, I assume that the final report is describing the results of a synthesis that employed meta-analytic techniques. The reader is also referred to Halvorsen (1994), Light, Singer, and Willett (1994), and Rosenthal (1995) for additional suggestions.

**Introduction Section**

The introduction to a research synthesis sets the stage for the empirical results that follow. It should contain a conceptual presentation of the research problem and a statement of the problem's significance. Introductions are typically short in primary research reports. Citations are restricted to only a few works closely related to the topic of primary interest.

In research syntheses, introductions should be considerably more detailed. Synthesists should attempt to present a complete overview of the research question, including its theoretical, practical, and methodological history. Where do the concepts involved in the research come from? Are they grounded in theory, as is the notion of interpersonal expectancy effects, or in practical circumstance, as is the notion of homework? Are there theoretical debates surrounding the meaning or utility of the concepts? How do theories predict the concepts will be related to one another? Are there conflicting predictions associated with different theories?

The introduction to a research synthesis must contextualize the problem under consideration. Especially when the synthesist intends to report a meta-analysis, it is crucial that ample attention be paid to the qualitative and historical debates surrounding the research question. Otherwise, the synthesist will be open to the criticism that numbers have been crunched together without ample appreciation for the conceptual and theoretical underpinnings that give empirical data their meaning.

As mentioned in Chapter 2, the introduction to a research synthesis is also where the synthesist should discuss previous syntheses of the research topic. This review of syntheses should highlight what has been learned from past synthesis efforts as well as point out their inconsistencies and methodological strengths and weaknesses. The contribution of the new effort should be emphasized by clearly stating the unresolved empirical questions and controversies addressed by the new synthesis.

In summary, the introduction to a research synthesis should present a complete overview of the theoretical, conceptual, or practical issues, or all three, surrounding the research problem. It should present a general description of prior syntheses, the controversies these syntheses have created or left unresolved, and which of these will be the focus of the new synthesis effort.

## Methods Section

The purpose of a methods section is to describe operationally how the research was conducted. The methods section of a research synthesis will be considerably different from that of a primary research report. Most synthesis methods sections will need to address six separate sets of questions.

### Details of the Literature Search

First, the research synthesist should present the details of the literature search. This should include a listing and description of every channel used to retrieve studies. It is also good to include a rationale for the choice of sources, especially with regard to how different sources were used to complement one another to reduce bias in the sample of studies. For abstract and indexing services and bibliographies, the synthesist needs to report the years they covered and the key words that guided the search. If personal research is included in the synthesis, this should be noted as well.

Information on the sources, key words, and years covered by the literature search is perhaps the most crucial aspect of the methods section. It gives the reader the best indication of the rigor of the search and therefore how much credibility to place in the conclusions of the synthesis. In terms of attempted replication, it is the description of the literature search that would be most closely examined when other scholars attempt to understand why different syntheses on the same topic area have come to similar or conflicting conclusions.

### Criteria for Including Studies

The second topic that should be addressed in the methods section is the criteria for relevance that were applied to the studies uncovered by the literature search. What characteristics of studies were used to determine whether a particular effort was relevant to the topic of interest? How many relevance decisions were based on a reading of report titles? On abstracts?

On full reports? What characteristics of studies led to exclusion? How many studies were excluded for any given reason? For instance, if a synthesis included only studies that appeared in published journals, how many potentially relevant but unpublished studies known to the synthesist were excluded?

Of equal importance to a description of excluded studies is a general, qualitative description of the studies that were deemed relevant. For example, in the synthesis of research on the effects of alcohol on aggression, two criteria had to be met by every study included in the synthesis: (a) Because the synthesists were interested in testing a causal relationship, the study had to experimentally manipulate whether or not participants received alcohol; and (b) the study had to use behavioral measures of aggression, not just aggressive thoughts, emotions, or behavior tendencies.

When readers examine the relevance criteria employed in a synthesis, they will be critically evaluating the synthesist's notions about how concepts and operations fit together. Considerable debate about the outcome of a particular synthesis may focus on these decisions. Some readers may find that the relevance criteria were too broad—operational definitions of concepts were included that they feel were irrelevant. The synthesist can anticipate these concerns and employ the distinctions when analyzing potential moderators of study results. Other readers may find the operational definitions were too narrow. This may lead them to examine excluded studies to determine if including their findings would affect the synthesis outcome.

In general, the relevance criteria describe how the synthesist chose to leap from concepts to operations. A detailed description of this procedure will be central to constructive theoretical and conceptual debate concerning the outcome of the synthesis.

### Methods Used in Primary Research

In addition to this general description of the included evidence, the methods section is a good place for synthesists to describe methodologies often found in primary research. The presentation of prototype studies is necessary in research syntheses that cover too many studies to examine each one individually. The synthesist should choose several studies that exemplify the methods used by many studies and present the specific details of these investigations. In instances in which only a few studies are found to be relevant, this process may not be necessary—the description of the methods used in a study can be combined with the description of the study's results.

*Determination of Independent Findings*

A fourth important topic to be covered under methods involves how the synthesist identified independent findings. An explanation of the criteria used to determine whether multiple hypothesis tests from the same laboratory, report, or study were treated as independent or dependent data points should be carefully spelled out.

*Details of Study Coding*

A fifth subsection of methods should describe the characteristics of primary research studies that were retrieved and retained for examination as potential moderators of study outcomes. In other words, the synthesist should fully describe the information about each study that was collected on the coding sheets. All characteristics should be mentioned here, even if some of these characteristics are not formally tested and are not discussed later in the paper. This will alert the reader to characteristics the synthesist might be asked to test at a later date. Also, information on coding reliability should be included in this section.

It is not necessary in the methods section to describe the frequency with which each retrieved characteristic occurred in the literature. This is best presented in the results section.

*Statistical Procedures and Conventions*

The final topics described in the methods section are the procedures and conventions the synthesist used to carry out any quantitative analysis of results. Why was a particular effect size metric chosen? Was an adjustment to effect sizes used to remove bias? How were missing outcomes handled? What analyses techniques were chosen to combine results of separate testings and to examine the variability in findings across testings? This section should contain a rationale for each procedural choice and convention and consider what the impact of each choice might be on the outcomes of the research synthesis.

**Results Section**

The results section should present the summary description of the literature, the synthesis of independent findings, and the evidence that substantiates any inferences about the literature as a whole. Although the results sections of syntheses will vary considerably depending on the nature of the research topic and evidence, a general strategy for presenting results might divide this section into five subsections.

## Descriptive Statistics

In the first subsection, the synthesist should tell readers the total number of research reports, studies, and independent samples that contributed tests of the comparison or relationship. The subsection should also give a breakdown of the communication channels that led to these tests. For instance, the number of tests found in published versus unpublished reports is sometimes important, as is a description of the particular journals that provided large numbers of tests.

Often, a synthesist will present a table that lists the studies included in the synthesis. The table will also describe a few of the more critical characteristics of each study. For example, the results of the homework synthesis were first reported in a book (Cooper, 1989). In one chapter, I examined studies that compared the achievement of students who were given homework with students given no alternative treatment. The chapter began with narrative descriptions of 11 homework versus no-treatment studies conducted before 1962. Effect size estimates were calculated if these early studies contained the necessary data, but the effect sizes were not combined statistically. A table was then presented that gave the first author name, year of publication, and 13 characteristics of each study conducted after 1962. The text gave a summary of the characteristics of this set of studies. These studies were the ones used in the meta-analysis. The text also described one study not used in the meta-analysis because its results could not be transformed into a metric commensurate with the other studies. This table is reproduced here as Table 6.1.

Certain aggregate descriptive statistics about the literature should be reported as well. These include the range, average, median, or modal date of report appearances or all three; the range, average, and median number of participants in each sample; the frequency of representation in samples of other important participant characteristics, such as gender, age, or status differences, that might bear on the generality of findings; and the geographic locations for samples, if relevant.

These are but a few of the potential descriptive statistics that might appear at the beginning of a results section. In general, the first subsection should give the reader a broad quantitative overview of the literature that complements the qualitative overviews contained in the introduction and methods sections. In addition, it should give the reader a sense of the

**TABLE 6.1**

Studies Included in the Homework Versus No-Homework Meta-Analysis

| Author (Year) | Type of Document | Location of Study (State) | Research Design | Counterbalancing/ Repeated Measures (Used or Not Used) | No. Schools/ Classes/ Students | Grade Level | Subject Matter | Treatment Duration (Weeks) | No. Assignments per Week | Teacher as Experimenter | Outcome Measure |
|---|---|---|---|---|---|---|---|---|---|---|---|
| Allison and Gray (1970) | Journal article | CA | Random assign. of students | Yes/yes | 1/2/60 | 6 | General math | 4 | 3 | No | Class test |
| Ames (1983) | Paper | OH | Computer assign. of students | No/no | 1/2/54 | 7 | Science | 9 | 2 | Yes | Class test |
| Doane (1972) | Dissertation | NY | NEC without matching | No/no | 1/8/186 | 4 | Computation | 2 | 5 | No | Class test |
| Foyle (1984) | Dissertation | KS | Random assign. of classes | No/no | 1/6/131 | 10 | Social studies and history | 6 | 5 | Yes | Class test |
| Grant (1971) | Dissertation | CA | Random assign. of classes | No/no | 8/17/386 | 5 | Computation, concepts, and problem solving | 10 | 3 | No | Standard Test |
| Gray and Allison (1971) | Journal article | CA | Random assign. of students | Yes/yes | 1/2/60 | 6 | Computation | 4 | 3 | No | Class test |

| | | | | | | | | | | | |
|---|---|---|---|---|---|---|---|---|---|---|---|
| Hines (1982) | Paper | OH | Computer assign. of students | No/no | 1/2/44 | 8 | Social studies and history | 10 | NA | Yes | Class test |
| Hume-Cummings (1985) | Paper | OH | NEC with matching | Yes/yes | 1/2/39 | 7 | General math | 12 | NA | Yes | Class test |
| Koch (1965) | Journal article | MN | Random assign. of classes | No/no | 1/3/85 | 6 | Concepts and problem solving | 10 | 5 | No | Standard test |
| Maertens and Johnston (1972) | Journal article | OR | Random assign. of students | No/no | 8/NA/387 | 4-6 | Computation and concepts | 6 | 4 | Yes | Class test |
| Nadis (1965) | Dissertation | MI | NEC with matching | Yes/yes | 1/2/80 | 9 | Social studies and history | 6 | 3 | Yes | Class test |
| Parrish (1976) | Dissertation | TX | NEC without matching | No/no | 1/8/120 | 9 | General math | 2 | 3 | No | Class test |
| Rosenthal (1974) | Dissertation | MI | NEC without matching | No/no | 1/2/175 | 6,8 | Language and vocabulary | NA | NA | No | Class test |

*(continued)*

**TABLE 6.1**
*Continued*

| Author (Year) | Type of Document | Location of Study (State) | Research Design | Counterbalancing/ Repeated Measures (Used or Not Used) | No. Schools/ Classes/ Students | Grade Level | Subject Matter | Treatment Duration (Weeks) | No. Assignments per Week | Teacher as Experimenter | Outcome Measure |
|---|---|---|---|---|---|---|---|---|---|---|---|
| Singh (1969) | Dissertation | AZ | NEC without matching | No/no | 2/5/123 | 4-6 | Computation, concepts, problem solving, reading, language and vocabulary, spelling, science, social studies, and history | 16 | 3 | No | Standard test |
| Whelan (1965) | Dissertation | RI | NEC with matching | No/no | NA/20/400 | 6 | Concepts, problem solving, language, and vocabulary | 30 | 3 | No | Standard test |
| Ziebell (1968) | Paper | WI | NEC with matching | Yes/yes | 1/4/40 | 10 | Science | 10 | 5 | Yes | Class test |

SOURCE: Cooper (1989). Copyright held by author.
NOTE: NEC, nonequivalnet control group; NA, not available.

representativeness of the people, procedures, and circumstances contained in the studies. As mentioned in Chapter 3, there is reason to believe that research syntheses will pertain more directly to the population of individuals and circumstances that interest a topic area than will the separate research efforts. Whatever the outcome of this analysis, this subsection of results allows the reader to assess the representativeness of the sampled people and circumstances and therefore the specificity of the synthesis conclusions.

## Vote Counts and
## Combined Significance Levels

The second subsection describing results should present the outcomes of vote counts and combined significance tests. The synthesist should give the total number of effect sizes that were positive and statistically significant, positive but nonsignificant, negative and significant, and negative but nonsignificant. These tallies should be given using the independent sample as the unit of analysis. It might also be informative to present the same numbers using the effect size or finding as the unit.

If meta-analysts have conducted sign tests associated with vote counts, their results should be reported here. If a combined significance level test was conducted, it should follow the vote-count results.

A good way to present graphically the effect sizes that form a meta-analysis database is in the form of a stem-and-leaf display. In a simple stem-and-leaf display, the first decimal place of each effect size acts as the stem, which is placed on the left side of a vertical line. The second decimal place acts as the leaf, placed on the right side of the vertical line. Leaves of effect sizes sharing the same stems are placed on the same line.

Figure 6.1 reproduces a somewhat more complex stem-and-leaf display. I used this graphic to present the results of 50 studies that correlated the amount of homework students reported doing each night with a measure of their achievement. Here, the stems are short intervals of effect size values (2/100ths) and the leaves are used to distinguish effect sizes according to the grade level of the students in the sample. Each letter to the right of the horizontal line represents a correlation. This figure makes it easy for the reader to see the shape and dispersion of the 50 correlations, to note that the correlations are most often positive, and to detect a relationship between the magnitude of correlations and the grade level of students.

### Overall Effect Size

A third subsection of results should present the overall effect size analysis. It should begin with a description of the range, average, and

| | |
|---|---|
| .39, .40 | |
| .37, .38 | S |
| .35, .36 | |
| .33, .34 | J |
| .31, .32 | |
| .29, .30 | J |
| .27, .28 | SS |
| .25, .26 | JJSSS |
| .23, .24 | JSS |
| .21, .22 | JJS |
| .19, .20 | JSSSS |
| .17, .18 | SS |
| .15, .16 | SS |
| .13, .14 | JSS |
| .11, .12 | J |
| .09, .10 | EJJJ |
| .07, .08 | EEJ |
| .05, .06 | EEEJS |
| .03, .04 | |
| .01, .02 | SS |
| .00 —————————————————————————————— | |
| −.01, −.02 | E |
| −.03, −.04 | |
| −.05, −.06 | EE |
| −.07, −.08 | J |
| −.09, −.10 | |
| −.11, −.12 | E |
| −.13, −.14 | |
| −.15, −.16 | J |
| −.17, −.18 | J |
| −.19, −.20 | |

**Figure 6.1.** Distribution of correlations between time on homework and achievement. Correlations are distinguished by grade level: E, Grades 3 through 5; J, Grades 6 through 9; S, Grades 10 through 12.

## TABLE 6.2
Average Effect Size, Cumulative z Score, and Combined Probability for Each
Personality Subgroup

| Personality Dimension | n | r | Z | p |
|---|---|---|---|---|
| Experimenters | | | | |
| Need for social influence | 8 | .15 | 2.94 | .0032 |
| Expressiveness | 3 | .07 | 1.79 | .0734 |
| Likability | 4 | .09 | 1.71 | .0872 |
| Other | 7 | .07 | 1.29 | .1976 |
| All dimensions combined | 22 | .11 | 3.90 | .0001 |
| Subjects | | | | |
| Influenceability | 11 | .05 | 2.21 | .0300 |
| Decoding skill | 7 | .11 | 2.60 | .0094 |
| Other | 8 | −.05 | 1.37 | .1706 |
| All dimensions combined | 26 | .03 | 3.58 | .0004 |

SOURCE: Cooper and Hazelrigg (1988). Copyright 1990 by the American Psychological Association. Reprinted by permission.
NOTE: Correlations are weighted by sample size, with each study contributing only one correlation for each personality dimension. Probability levels are two-tailed. Direction of effect for miscellaneous *other* dimension is based on the prediction of the researcher.

median effect size, and the 95% confidence interval around the estimate of central tendency. The result of the overall test for homogeneity of the entire set of related effects should also be presented here.

My homework text reported that when the achievement of students doing homework was compared to that of students receiving no homework, the average d index was .21, or alternatively, the average student doing homework had a higher achievement score than 54.7% of students not doing homework. The 95% confidence interval around this estimate ranged from $d = .13$ to $d = .30$. On the basis of the confidence interval, rather than on a combined significance test, I concluded that the difference between the homework and no-treatment conditions permitted a rejection of the null hypothesis. The homogeneity analysis revealed that there was more variability in the d indexes than would be expected due to sampling error alone ($Q_t(19) = 57.41, p < .001$).

The report of the meta-analysis of personality moderators of interpersonal expectancy effects presented a table that incorporated the average r

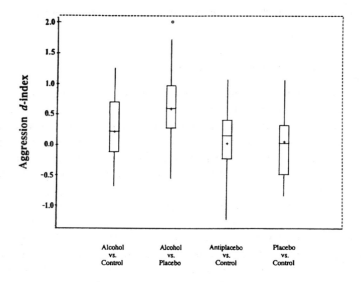

**Figure 6.2.** Box plot for the four types of comparisons.
SOURCE: Bushman and Cooper (1990). Copyright 1990 by the American Psychological Association. Reproduced with permission.
NOTE: +, sample means; o, mild outlier.

indexes for five personality dimensions and two miscellaneous categories with the results of the corresponding Adding $Z$'s method for combining significance levels. This table is reproduced here as Table 6.2. This analysis revealed that the experimenter's need for social influence ($r = .15$) and the subject's influenceability ($r = .05$) and decoding skill ($r = .11$) were significantly positively related to the magnitude of the interpersonal expectancy effect.

The report of the alcohol and aggression meta-analysis used a box plot to visually display average $d$ indexes and their degree of dispersion. Figure 6.2 reproduces this graphic. The boxes encompass values falling within an upper and lower quartile of the median value. The horizontal line running through the boxes indicates the median value. The vertical lines originating from the boxes (called "whiskers") run to the maximum and minimum values. The text of the report informed readers that the average $d$ indexes associated with the four overall comparisons—alcohol versus control, alcohol versus placebo, antiplacebo versus control, and placebo versus control—were .25, .61, .06, and .10, respectively. The $d$ indexes comparing alcohol groups to control and placebo groups had confidence intervals that did not include 0, indicating more aggression in the alcohol condition.

*Analyses of Influences on Effect Size*

A fourth subsection should describe the results of analyses meant to uncover study characteristics that moderated the size of the effect. For each moderator tested, the meta-analyst should present results on whether the study characteristic was significantly associated with variance in effect sizes. If the moderator proved significant, the meta-analyst should present an average effect size and confidence interval for each grouping of studies.

I used a table to summarize the significant results from my search for moderators of the magnitude of the effect of homework. This table is reproduced here as Table 6.3. Note that the findings for each moderator variable I tested were based on a slightly different number of study results due to the use of a shifting unit of analysis. In the text, these results were accompanied by a description of the intercorrelations among the moderator variables.

The text also contained descriptions of other analyses related to moderators of this effect size. These included sections describing the results of tests of the effect of homework with third variables controlled and the results of studies examining the effect of homework on attitudes.

*Description of Interactions*

Finally, the synthesist should devote a subsection to interaction effects found in single studies. For instance, the alcohol and aggression synthesis contained a table listing 14 studies that included third manipulated variables that the primary researchers thought might influence the effect of alcohol. The third variables included situation manipulations such as exposure to aggressive and nonaggressive films, sleep deprivation, and negative mood inductions. The outcome of the statistical test for interaction with the alcohol manipulation was given for each variable tested. This table is reproduced here as Table 6.4.

In summary, the results section should contain the synthesist's overall quantitative description of the covered literature, a description of the overall relationship strength, and the outcomes of the search for moderators of relationships. This lays the groundwork for the substantive discussion that follows.

**TABLE 6.3**

Effect Sizes for Comparisons of Homework Versus
No Homework on Measures of Academic Achievement

| | n | 95% Confidence Interval | | |
| | | Low Estimate | Mean | High Estimate |
|---|---|---|---|---|
| Overall ($\chi^2[19] = 57.41, p < .001$) | 20 | .13 | .21 | .30 |
| Year ($\chi^2[1] = 8.00, p < .01$) | | | | |
| 1960s | 6 | .01 | .16 | .32 |
| 1970s | 10 | .06 | .18 | .30 |
| 1980s | 4 | .23 | .48 | .73 |
| Counterbalancing and repeated measures ($\chi^2[1] = 4.68, p < .05$) | | | | |
| Present | 4 | −.35 | −.08 | .19 |
| Absent | 16 | .14 | .24 | .34 |
| Experimenter ($\chi^2[1] = 9.52, p < .01$) | | | | |
| Teacher | 8 | .25 | .41 | .57 |
| Not teacher | 12 | .02 | .12 | .22 |
| Duration of treatment ($\chi^2[1] = 3.89, p < .05$) | | | | |
| 10 weeks | 12 | .20 | .32 | .44 |
| More than 10 weeks | 8 | −.03 | .09 | .21 |
| Number of assignments ($\chi^2[1] = 15.43, p < .001$) | | | | |
| 1-3 per week | 14 | −.01 | .09 | .19 |
| 4 or 5 per week | 6 | .30 | .44 | .58 |
| Grade ($\chi^2[1] = 3.75, p < .06$) | | | | |
| 4-6 | 13 | .05 | .15 | .25 |
| 7-9 | 5 | .09 | .31 | .53 |
| 10-12 | 2 | .33 | .64 | .95 |
| Subject matter ($\chi^2[2] = 19.13, p < .001$) | | | | |
| Math | 25 | .10 | .16 | .22 |
| Reading and English | 13 | .18 | .32 | .46 |
| Science and social studies | 10 | .38 | .56 | .74 |
| Math areas ($\chi^2[3] = 6.79, p < .01$) | | | | |
| Computation | 9 | .12 | .24 | .36 |
| Concepts | 8 | .07 | .19 | .31 |
| Problem solving | 5 | −.12 | .02 | .16 |
| General or unspecified | 3 | −.01 | .26 | .53 |
| Outcome measure ($\chi^2[1] = 6.49, p < .02$) | | | | |
| Class tests or grades | 15 | .18 | .30 | .42 |
| Standardized tests | 5 | −.07 | .07 | .21 |

SOURCE: Cooper (1989). Copyright held by author.

## Discussion Section

The discussion section of a research synthesis serves the same functions as discussions in primary research. Discussions typically contain at least five components.

First, the synthesist should present a summary of the major results of the synthesis. This should not be lengthy but should extract the major findings that will be discussed in the text that follows. Second, the synthesist should describe the magnitude of the important effect sizes found in the synthesis and interpret their substantive meaning. An attempt should be made to assess whether the size of uncovered effects are small or large and important or trivial.

Third, the synthesist should examine the results in relation to the predictions and other prior assertions made about relationships. Often, a discussion of how the results of the present synthesis differ from past syntheses and why these differences may have occurred is necessary. The synthesist also needs to examine the results for what they tell about the theories and theoretical debates presented in the introduction.

Fourth, the discussion should include an assessment of the generality of any findings, especially with regard to limiting conditions. For instance, if a positive correlation were found between homework and achievement, the synthesist should state whether the evidence permits an assessment of whether the relationship holds for all grade levels and subject matters.

Finally, the synthesist should include a discussion of topics that should be examined in future research (see Eagley & Wood, 1994). These should include new questions raised by the outcomes of the synthesis and old questions left unresolved because of ambiguous synthesis results or a lack of prior primary research.

In general, the discussion section in both primary research and research synthesis is used to make suggestions about the substantive interpretation of findings, the resolution of past controversies, and fruitful directions for future research.

## THE SUBSTANTIVE INTERPRETATION
## OF EFFECT SIZE

In quantitative syntheses, one function of a discussion section is the interpretation of the size of group differences or relationships. Once synthesists

**TABLE 6.4**

Moderator Variables Not Included in the Meta-Analysis

| Study | Variable | Interaction With Alcohol |
|---|---|---|
| Bailey, Leonard, Cranston, and Taylor (1983) | Aggression task performed under self-aware or non-self-aware conditions | NS (alcohol *vs.* placebo) |
| Gustafson (1985) | Aggressive or nonaggressive film segment shown | NS (alcohol *vs.* placebo) |
| Gustafson (1986) | Subjects told or not told that the confederate planned to retaliate with high shock levels | No difference between alcohol and placebo subjects in the threat condition. In the standard condition, alcohol subjects were more aggressive than placebo subjects. |
| Gustafson (in press) | Positive versus negative mood induction | NS (alcohol *vs.* placebo) |
| Heermans (1980) | Misattribution of arousal: tranquilizer versus no drug, energizer versus no drug | NS (alcohol *vs.* control), NS (alcohol vs. control) |
| Jeavons & Taylor (1985) | The presence or absence of a low-aggression norm | Within the no-norm condition, alcohol subjects were more aggressive ($d = 0.93$) than placebo subjects. In the norm condition, there was no difference between alcohol and placebo subjects. |
| Myerscough (1984) | Sleep deprivation versus no sleep deprivation | NS (alcohol *vs.* placebo) |
| Pihl and Zacchia (1986) | Positive versus negative mood induction | NS (alcohol *vs.* control), NS (alcohol *vs.* placebo), NS (placebo *vs.* control) |
| Schmutte and Taylor (1980) | High or low pain feedback from provocative confederate | Pain feedback enhanced aggression in subjects with high blood alcohol levels and reduced aggression in placebo subjects. |

| Taylor and Gammon (1976) | Pressure or no pressure to reduce aggression | NS (alcohol vs. control), NS (alcohol vs. placebo) |
| Taylor, Gammon, and Capasso (1976) | Subjects told or not told that the confederate planned to use low shock levels | No difference between alcohol and placebo subjects in the no-threat condition. In the standard condition, alcohol subjects were more aggressive than placebo subjects. |
| Taylor and Sears (1988) | No pressure, mild pressure, or strong pressure to increase aggression | No difference between alcohol and placebo subjects in the no-pressure situation ($d = 0.00$). Alcohol subjects were more aggressive than placebo subjects in the mild pressure ($d = 0.12$) and strong pressure ($d = 0.31$) situations. |
| White (1987) | Attractive versus unattractive confederate | NS (alcohol vs. control), NS (alcohol vs. placebo), NS (antiplacebo vs. control), NS (placebo vs. control) |
| Zeichner, Pihl, Niaura, and Zacchia (1982) | Subjects were forced to attend to, distracted from attending to, or received no instruction about the noise level set by the confederate | In all conditions, alcohol subjects were more aggressive than placebo subjects. Regarding shock intensity, effects were highest for no-instruction ($d = 0.67$), followed by forced attention ($d = 0.24$) and distraction ($d = 0.08$). For shock duration, effects were highest for forced attention ($d = 1.15$), followed by no-instruction ($d = 0.65$) and distraction ($d = 0.07$). |

SOURCE: Bushman and Cooper (1990). Copyright 1990 by the American Psychological Association. Reprinted by Permission.
NOTE: NS, statistically nonsignificant result.

have generated effect sizes, how are they to know if they are large or small or meaningful or trivial? Because statistical significance cannot be used as a benchmark—small effects can be statistically significant and large effects nonsignificant—a set of rules must be established for determining the explanatory or practical value of a given effect magnitude.

Cohen (1988) attempted to address the issue of interpreting effect size estimates. He suggested some general definitions for small, medium, and large effect sizes in the social sciences. Cohen, however, chose these quantities to reflect the typical effect sizes encountered in the behavioral sciences as a whole—he warned against using his labels to interpret relationship magnitudes within particular social science disciplines or topic areas. His general labels, however, illustrate how to go about interpreting effects.

Cohen (1988) labeled an effect size small if $d = .20$ or $r = .10$. He wrote, "Many effects sought in personality, social, and clinical-psychological research are likely to be small . . . because of the attenuation in validity of the measures employed and the subtlety of the issue frequently involved" (p. 13). Large effects, according to Cohen, are frequently "at issue in such fields as sociology, economics, and experimental and physiological psychology, fields characterized by the study of potent variables or the presence of good experimental control or both" (p. 13). Cohen suggested large magnitudes of effect were $d = .80$ or $r = .50$. Medium-sized effects were placed between these two extremes—that is, $d = .50$ or $r = .30$.

Cohen's (1988) reasoning can be used to demonstrate the relative nature of comparing effect sizes. Suppose the synthesis of personality moderators of interpersonal expectancy effects revealed an average $r$ index of .30. How should the relation's magnitude be interpreted? Clearly, the interpretation depends on the other relations chosen as contrasting elements. According to Cohen, this is a medium-sized behavioral science effect. Thus, compared to other relations in the behavioral sciences in general, this would be an average effect size, not surprisingly large or small. Compared to other personality effects, however, this effect size may best be described as large, if we accept Cohen's suggestion that personality relations are predominantly smaller than $r = .30$.

Comparing a specific effect size to effect sizes found in other disciplines or a discipline in general may be interesting, but in most instances it is not very informative. The most informative interpretation occurs when the effect size is compared to other effects involving the same or similar variables. At the time Cohen (1988) offered his guidelines, comparing an effect size in a specialized topic area against a criteria as broad as "all behavioral science" might have been the best contrasting element available. Estimates of average effects for disciplines, subdisciplines, topic areas, or even single variables or operations were difficult to find. Today, these calculations are plentiful. Therefore, an effect size should be labeled "small" or "large" depending on its magnitude relative to a variety of related estimates. At least some of the contrasting effect sizes should be closely tied conceptually to the effect found in the specific topic area, involving the same variables contained in the relation of interest.

In addition to multiple and related choices of contrasting estimates, two other guides for effect size interpretation may be useful. First, synthesists can assess how much any relation might be valued by consumers of research. This assessment involves the difficult problem of making practical judgments about significance. A hypothetical example will illustrate the point. Suppose a study done in 1970 showed that motorists who regularly checked their tire pressure got 22 miles per gallon of gasoline, whereas motorists who did not check their tires got 20 miles per gallon. In each group, the standard deviation of the mean was 4 miles per gallon. This indicates that the average motorist driving 10,000 miles a year and buying gas at .30¢ a gallon saved 45 gallons of gas and $13.50 annually by checking tire pressure. In terms of the $d$ index, the pressure checkers and noncheckers were separated by one half a standard deviation ($d = .50$), or the average tire checker got better mileage than approximately 69% of the noncheckers. This effect might have been ignored in 1970. Practically speaking, it might have been considered inconsequential. The same results, however, produced in 1997 with gas costing $1.30 a gallon might elicit a much different reaction. Using 45 gallons less of a scarce resource and saving $58.50 annually would be appreciated by most motorists. Thus, the researcher might argue convincingly that the result of the experiment had great practical significance.

If the pressure-checking effect is contrasted with other effects on automobile fuel economy (e.g., tune-ups and observing the speed limit), the comparison might still lead to a conclusion that the effect is small. The researcher, however, can argue that although the effect is of relatively small explanatory value, it may still have great practical significance. This judgment could be justified by arguing that small intervals on the gas usage scale represent large intervals on other, societally-valued indicators—for example, the amount of oil that needs to be imported or damage to the environment. Also, it might be argued that the cost of implementing a pressure-checking program is relatively inexpensive compared to other interventions. Levin and colleagues (Levin, 1987; Levin, Glass, & Meister, 1987) have laid out some ground rules for establishing the relative cost-effectiveness of social programs.

A final guide to effect size interpretation that involves research methodology has been alluded to several times in the text. When contrasting effect
sizes are chosen, the relative size of effects will reflect not only the
explanatory power of the relations but also differences in how data were
collected. All else being equal, effect sizes based on studies with strict
control over extraneous influences should produce larger effects than less
controlled studies (i.e., have smaller deviations around the mean). For
example, a tire pressure-checking effect on gas mileage of $d = .50$ found in
lab tests may be less impressive than a similar finding obtained under normal
driving conditions. Effect sizes will also be a function of the strength of the
manipulation (e.g., the degree of tire underinflation in unchecked cars), the
sensitivity of the measures (e.g., counting the number of fill-ups vs. the
number of gallons used), and any restrictions on participant populations
(e.g., all cars vs. only new cars). These illustrations point out only a few
methodological considerations that can influence effect size interpretation.

Finally, it should be kept in mind that effect size estimates reported in
research syntheses are influenced not only by the methodology of the
studies synthesized but also by the methodology of the synthesis itself. It
is safe to say that other synthesists using similar retrieval, relevance, and
statistical procedures should expect to uncover similar effect sizes. Researchers and policymakers who are interpreting the outcomes of a synthesis need to adjust effect size estimates to account for whatever biases they
feel may be operating on the results.

In summary, Cohen's (1988) labels give only the broadest interpretive
yardstick for effect sizes. The most meaningful interpretation of an effect
size comes from comparisons to other magnitudes of relation chosen
because of their substantive relevance to the topic under study. Comple-
menting this interpretation should be an assessment of the practical value
of any explanation and the role of methodology in shaping the conclusion.

### Synthesis Examples

The two best examples of how relationship strengths can be interpreted
come from the syntheses on homework and on attitudes toward rape. For
homework, it will be recalled that the average $d$ index of the difference in
achievement between students doing homework and students doing no
homework was $d = .21$. Is this a small or large effect? To help answer this
question, I examined the results of other related meta-analyses. These were
listed in a table, reproduced here as Table 6.5. The 11 meta-analyses
contained in the table all examined the effect of instructional strategies or
teaching skills on measures of achievement. They were taken from a

## TABLE 6.5
Selected Effect Sizes From Meta-Analyses
Examining Influences on Achievement[a]

| Authors (Year) | Independent Variable | Effect Size[b] |
|---|---|---|
| Bangert et al. (1981) | Individualized versus conventional teaching | .10 |
| Carlberg and Kavale (1980) | Special- versus regular-class placement | −.12 |
| Johnson et al. (1981) | Cooperative versus competitive learning | .78 |
| Kulik and Kulik (1981) | Ability grouping | .10 |
| Kulik et al. (1982) | Programmed instruction | .08 |
| Luiten, Ames, and Aerson (1980) | Advance organizers | .23 |
| Pflaum et al. (1980) | Direct instruction | .60 |
| Redfield and Rousseau (1981) | Higher cognitive questions | .73 |
| Wilkinson (1980) | Praise | .08 |
| Williams et al. (1982) | Amount of television watching | .10 |
| Willson and Putnam (1982) | Pretests | .17 |

SOURCE: Cooper (1989). Copyright held by author.
NOTES: a. Topics are those listed by Walberg (1986) as involving achievement as the dependent variable.
b. Effect sizes are expressed in d indexes.

chapter on research synthesis appearing in the *Handbook of Research on Teaching* (Walberg, 1986).

On the basis of a comparison with the entries in the table, it was concluded that the effect of homework on achievement can best be described as "above average." The median effect size in the table is $d = .10$, half the size of the homework effect. The relative quality of methods in the different topic areas was also considered. It was assumed that the trustworthiness of the measures of achievement used in the different areas and the soundness of the research designs were approximately equivalent. Some of the assumptions on which effect size estimates were based, however, were probably more conservative in the homework synthesis than in other syntheses. Finally, the practical value of homework was assessed by comparing the relative costs of implementing the different instructional and teaching treatments. Homework can be regarded as a low-cost treatment, especially in comparison with special-class placement and individualized and programmed instruction.

In the synthesis of attitudes toward rape, the relative effects of individual difference predictors were evaluated in comparison to one another. Thus, the contrasting elements were contained in the synthesis itself. For instance, four demographic differences were used to predict attitudes toward rape: the sex of the attitude holders, their age, ethnicity, and socioeconomic status. As predicted, men expressed more accepting attitudes toward rape than women ($r = .33$). Compared to this effect, the remaining three effects were labeled small. They ranged in value from $r = .12$ to $r = .06$. A similar strategy was used to compare the magnitude of correlations revealed by eight different scales that measured rape attitude. These correlations ranged from $r = .54$ to $r = .14$.

## VALIDITY ISSUES IN REPORT WRITING

The two threats to validity accompanying report writing relate to the different target populations of the synthesis. First, the omission of details about how the synthesis was conducted is a potential threat to validity. As with primary research, an incomplete report reduces the replicability of the synthesis conclusion. The second validity threat in report writing involves the omission of evidence about moderators of relations that other inquirers may find important. Matheson, Bruce, and Beauchamp (1978) observed that "as research on a specific behavior progresses, more details concerning the experimental conditions are found to be relevant" (p. 265). Thus, a synthesis will lose its timeliness if the synthesist is not astute enough to identify the variables and moderators that are (or will be) important to an area. More complete syntheses will take longer to be replaced by newer syntheses and will therefore have greater temporal generality.

### Protecting Validity

This chapter provides numerous suggestions for how synthesists can protect against these threats to validity arising during report preparation. Synthesists, however, will never be able to perfectly predict which omitted characteristic or result of their syntheses will eventually render their conclusion invalid or obsolete. On the positive side, synthesists certainly want their documents to have long lives. We can anticipate that synthesists who give considerable thought to how to present the most exhaustive report in the most readable manner will produce the most enduring documents.

## EXERCISES

1. Read two research syntheses. Outline what the authors tell about each of the following: (a) how the literature search was conducted, (b) what rules were used to decide if studies were relevant to the hypothesis, and (c) what rules were used to decide if cumulative relations existed.

2. Find two primary research reports on the same topic that vary in method. Calculate the effect size reported in each. Compare the effect sizes to one another, taking into account the influence of the different methods. Using other criteria, decide whether you consider each effect size large, medium, or small. Justify your decision.

# 7

# *General Issues*

**This chapter presents some general issues pertaining to rigorous research synthesis. It also considers the feasibility of conducting syntheses that meet rigorous criteria. Several issues concerning research synthesis and the philosophy of science are also discussed.**

There are several issues related to research synthesis that cannot be placed easily into the events represented by the five-stage model. These more general and philosophical considerations deal with problems and promises in applying the guidelines set forth in the previous chapters.

## VALIDITY ISSUES REVISITED

First, I mentioned 11 threats to validity in the five stages of synthesis. Many other threats exist that were not discussed in this treatment. Recall that Campbell and Stanley's (1963) list of validity threats to primary research was expanded by Bracht and Glass (1968), Campbell (1969), and Cook and Campbell (1979). This same expansion and respecification of threats to validity has also occurred in the area of research synthesis (Matt & Cook, 1994). This is not a bad sign but a good one. It shows progress in the systematization of issues surrounding legitimate scientific inference.

Several of the threats to validity arising in the course of research synthesis are simply holdovers that represent pervasive problems in primary research. For instance, I asserted that when data are being collected a threat to the validity of a synthesis was that the people sampled in the covered studies might not be representative of the target population. This suggests that any threat associated with a particular primary research design is applicable to a synthesis if the design characteristic appears in a substantial portion of the covered research. In the examination of synthesis-generated evidence, research designs should be carefully examined as potential moderators of study results. The creation of these "nomological nets" (Cronbach & Meehl, 1955) can be one of the research synthesist's most valuable contributions. If an assortment of research designs is not contained in a synthesis, however, then threats associated with the dominant designs also threaten the synthesis' conclusions.

## FEASIBILITY AND COST

It is considerably more expensive for synthesists to undertake a project using the guidelines set forth in this book than to conduct syntheses in the traditional manner. More people are involved who need to be compensated for their time. More time is needed to search the literature, develop coding frames, run analyses, and prepare reports.

Given these costs, should a potential synthesist with limited resources be discouraged from undertaking a project? Certainly not. Just as the perfect, irrefutable primary study has never been conducted, so too the perfect synthesis remains an ideal. My guidelines represent yardsticks for evaluating syntheses more then a set of absolute requirements. In fact, the reader should be aware of several instances in which the syntheses I used as examples fell short of complete adherence to the guidelines. Sacks, Berrier, Reitman, Ancona-Berk, and Chalmers (1987) surveyed 86 meta-analyses and concluded that there was an urgent need for improved methods. A potential synthesist should not hold the guidelines as absolute criteria that must be met but rather as targets that help refine procedures until a good balance between rigor and feasibility is struck.

## THE SCIENTIFIC METHOD
## AND DISCONFIRMATION

Although the practical aspects of conducting research syntheses may mean the investigator must settle for a less-than-perfect product, the ideals of science still must be strictly applied to the research synthesis process. The crucial scientific element that has been missing from traditional synthesis procedures has been the potential for the disconfirmation of the synthesist's prior beliefs. In most instances, primary researchers undertake their work with some recognition that the results of their study may alter their belief system: Not so for the traditional synthesist. By extending the scientific method to research syntheses, the potential for disconfirmation is also expanded. Ross and Lepper (1980) have stated this position well:

> We know all too well that the scientific method is not immune to the diseases of biased assimilation, causal explanation, and a host of other nagging afflictions; scientists can be blind, sometimes deliberately so, to unanticipated or uncongenial interpretations of their data and recalcitrant in their theoretical allegiances. . . . Nevertheless, it is the scientific method . . . that has often been responsible for increasing human understanding of the natural and social world. Despite its flaws, it remains the best means of delivering us from the errors of intuitive beliefs and intuitive methods for testing those beliefs. (p. 33)

## CREATIVITY IN
## RESEARCH SYNTHESIS

One objection to the use of scientific guidelines for research syntheses is that this system stifles creativity. Critics who raise this issue think the rules for conducting and reporting primary research are a "straitjacket" on innovative thinking. I cannot disagree more. Rigorous criteria will not produce syntheses that are mechanical and uncreative. The expertise and intuition of the synthesist will be challenged to capitalize on or create opportunities to obtain, evaluate, and analyze information unique to each problem area. I hope the syntheses examples have demonstrated the diversity and complexity of issues that confront synthesists who adopt the scientific method. These challenges are created by scientific rules.

## CONCLUSION

I began this book with the supposition that research synthesis was a data-gathering exercise that needed to be evaluated against scientific criteria. Because of the growth in empirical research and the increased access to information, the conclusions of research syntheses will become less and less trustworthy unless we systematize the process and make it more rigorous. I hope that the concepts and techniques presented here have convinced readers that it is feasible and desirable for social scientists to require more rigorous syntheses. Such rules bring with them greater potential for creating consensus among scholars and for focusing discussion on specific and testable areas of disagreement when conflict does exist. Because of the increasing role that research syntheses play in the definition of knowledge, these adjustments in procedures are inevitable if social scientists hope to retain their claim to objectivity as well as their credibility with those who turn to scientists to help solve social problems and increase understanding of the social world.

# References

American Psychological Association. (1994). *Publication manual* (4th ed.). Washington, DC: Author.

Anderson, K. B., Cooper, H., & Okamura, L. (1997). Individual differences and attitudes toward rape: A meta-analytic review. *Personality and Social Psychology Bulletin, 23,* 295-315.

Association of Research Libraries. (1997). *Directory of electronic journals, newsletters and academic discussion groups.* Washington, DC: Author.

Atkinson, D. R., Furlong, M. J., & Wampold, B. E. (1982). Statistical significance, reviewer evaluations, and the scientific process: Is there a (statistically) significant relationship? *Journal of Counseling Psychology, 29,* 189-194.

Barber, T. X. (1978). Expecting expectancy effects: Biased data analyses and failure to exclude alternative interpretations in experimenter expectancy research. *Behavioral and Brain Sciences, 3,* 388-390.

Barnett, V., & Lewis, T. (1984). *Outliers in statistical data* (2nd ed.). New York: John Wiley.

Becker, B. J. (1994). Combining significance levels. In H. Cooper & L. V. Hedges (Eds.), *The handbook of research synthesis.* New York: Russell Sage Foundation.

Becker, B. J., & Schramm, C. M. (1994). Examining explanatory models through research synthesis. In H. Cooper & L. V. Hedges (Eds.), *The handbook of research synthesis.* New York: Russell Sage Foundation.

Begg, C. B., & Berlin, J. A. (1988). Publication bias: A problem in interpreting medical research. *Journal of the Royal Statistical Society Series A, 151,* 419-463.

Bem, D. J. (1967). Self-perception: An alternative interpretation of cognitive dissonance phenomena. *Psychological Review, 74,* 183-200.

Bourque, L. B., & Clark, V. A. (1992). *Processing data.* Newbury Park, CA: Sage.

Boyce, B., & Banning, C. (1979). Data accuracy in citation studies. *RQ, 18,* 349-350.

Bracht, G. H., & Glass, G. V. (1968). The external validity of experiments. *American Educational Research Journal, 5,* 437-474.

Bradley, J. V. (1981). Pernicious publication practices. *Bulletin of Psychonomic Society, 18,* 31-34.

Brown, S. P. (1996). A meta-analysis and review of organizational research on job involvement. *Psychological Bulletin, 120,* 235-255.

Bushman, B. J., & Cooper, H. (1990). Effects of alcohol on human aggression: An integrative research review. *Psychological Bulletin, 107,* 341-354.

Bushman, B. J., Cooper, H., & Lemke, K. M. (1991). Meta-analysis of factor analysis: An illustration using the Buss-Durkee Hostility Inventory. *Personality and Social Psychology Bulletin, 17,* 344-349.

Bushman, B. J., & Wang, M. C. (1995). A procedure for combining sample correlations and vote counts to obtain an estimate and a confidence interval for the population correlation coefficient. *Psychological Bulletin, 117,* 530-546.

Campbell, D. T. (1969). Reforms as experiments. *American Psychologist, 24,* 409-429.

Campbell, D. T., & Stanley, J. C. (1963). *Experimental and quasi-experimental designs for research.* Chicago: Rand McNally.

Carlson, M., & Miller, N. (1987). Explanation of the relation between negative mood and helping. *Psychological Bulletin, 102,* 91-108.

Cohen, J. (1988). *Statistical power analysis for the behavior sciences* (2nd ed.). Hillsdale, NJ: Erlbaum.

Cohen, J. (1994). The earth is round ($p < .05$). *American Psychologist, 49,* 997-1003.

Cook, T. D., & Campbell, D. T. (1979). *Quasi-experimentation.* Chicago: Rand McNally.

Cook, T. D., Cooper, H., Cordray, D. S., Hartmann, H., Hedges, L. V., Light, R. J., Louis, T. A., & Mosteller, F. (1992). *Meta-analysis for explanation: A casebook.* New York: Russell Sage Foundation.

Cooper, H. (1979). Statistically combining independent studies: A meta-analysis of sex differences in conformity research. *Journal of Personality and Social Psychology, 37,* 131-146.

Cooper, H. (1982). Scientific guidelines for conducting integrative research reviews. *Review of Educational Research, 52,* 291-302.

Cooper, H. (1986). On the social psychology of using research reviews: The case of desegregation and black achievement. In R. Feldman (Ed.), *The social psychology of education.* Cambridge, UK: Cambridge University Press.

Cooper, H. (1988). The structure of knowledge synthesis: A taxonomy of literature reviews. *Knowledge in Society, 1,* 104-126.

Cooper, H. (1989). *Homework.* New York: Longman.

Cooper, H., & Arkin, R. M. (1981). On quantitative reviewing. *Journal of Personality, 49,* 225-230.

Cooper, H., DeNeve, K., & Charlton, K. (1997). Finding the missing science: The fate of studies submitted for review by a human subjects committee. *Psychological Methods, 2,* 447-452.

Cooper, H., & Dorr, N. (1995). Race comparisons on need for achievement: A meta-analytic alternative to Graham's narrative review. *Review of Educational Research, 65,* 483-508.

Cooper, H., & Hazelrigg, P. (1988). Personality moderators of interpersonal expectancy effects. *Journal of Personality and Social Psychology, 55,* 937-949.

Cooper, H., & Hedges, L. V. (1994). *The handbook of research synthesis.* New York: Russell Sage Foundation.

Cooper, H., & Ribble, R. G. (1989). Influences on the outcome of literature searches for integrative research reviews. *Knowledge: Creation, Diffusion, Utilization, 10,* 179-201.

Cooper, H., & Rosenthal, R. (1980). Statistical versus traditional procedures for summarizing research findings. *Psychological Bulletin, 87,* 442-449.

Crane, D. (1969). Social structure in a group of scientists: A test of the "invisible college" hypothesis. *American Sociological Review, 34,* 335-352.

Cronbach, L. J., & Meehl, P. E. (1955). Construct validity in psychological tests. *Psychological Bulletin, 52,* 281-302.

Cuadra, C. A., & Katter, R. V. (1967). Opening the black box of relevance. *Journal of Documentation, 23,* 291-303.

Davidson, D. (1977). The effects of individual differences of cognitive style on judgements of document relevance. *Journal of the American Society for Information Science, 8,* 273-284.

Dickerson, K. (1994). Research registers. In H. Cooper & L. V. Hedges (Eds.), *The handbook of research synthesis*. New York: Russell Sage Foundation.

Eagley, A. H., & Wood, W. (1994). Using research synthesis to plan future research. In H. Cooper & L. V. Hedges (Eds.), *The handbook of research synthesis*. New York: Russell Sage Foundation.

Eddy, D. M., Hasselblad, V., & Schachter, R. (1992). *Meta-analysis by the confidence profile approach*. Boston: Academic Press.

Edwards, A. L. (1967). *Statistical methods* (2nd ed.). New York: Holt, Rinehart & Winston.

Elmes, D. G., Kantowitz, B. H., & Roediger, H. L. (1995). *Research methods in psychology*. St. Paul, MN: West.

Eysenck, H. J. (1978). An exercise in mega-silliness. *American Psychologist, 33*, 517.

Festinger, L., & Carlsmith, J. M. (1959). Cognitive consequences of forced compliance. *Journal of Abnormal and Social Psychology, 58*, 203-210.

Fisher, R. A. (1932). *Statistical methods for research workers*. London: Oliver & Boyd.

Fiske, D. W., & Fogg, L. (1990). But the reviewers are making different criticisms of my paper! *American Psychologist, 45*, 591-598.

Fleiss, J. L. (1994). Measures of effect size for categorical data. In H. Cooper & L. V. Hedges (Eds.), *The handbook of research synthesis*. New York: Russell Sage Foundation.

Fowler, F. J. (1993). *Survey research methods* (2nd ed.). Newbury Park, CA: Sage.

Garvey, W. D., & Griffith, B. C. (1971). Scientific communication: Its role in the conduct of research and creation of knowledge. *American Psychologist, 26*, 349-361.

Glass, G. V. (1976). Primary, secondary, and meta-analysis of research. *Educational Researcher, 5*, 3-8.

Glass, G. V. (1977). Integrating findings: The meta-analysis of research. In *Review of research in education* (Vol. 5). Itasca, IL: F. E. Peacock.

Glass, G. V., McGaw, B., & Smith, M. L. (1981). *Meta-analysis in social research*. Beverly Hills, CA: Sage.

Glass, G. V., & Smith, M. L. (1978a). Reply to Eysenck. *American Psychologist, 33*, 517-518.

Glass, G. V., & Smith, M. L. (1978b). Meta-analysis of research on the relationship of class size and achievement. *Educational Evaluation and Policy Analysis, 1*, 2-16.

Gleser, L. J., & Olkin, I. (1994). Stochastically dependent effect sizes. In H. Cooper & L. V. Hedges (Eds.), *The handbook of research synthesis*. New York: Russell Sage Foundation.

Gottfredson, S. D. (1978). Evaluating psychological research reports. *American Psychologist, 33*, 920-934.

Graham, S. (1994). Motivation in African Americans. *Review of Educational Research, 64*, 55-117.

Greenberg, J., & Folger, R. (1988). *Controversial issues in social research methods*. New York: Springer-Verlag.

Greenwald, A. G. (1975). Consequences of prejudices against the null hypothesis. *Psychological Bulletin, 82*, 1-20.

Hahn, H. (1996). *The Internet complete reference* (2nd ed.). Berkeley, CA: Osborne.

Halvorsen, K. T. (1994). The reporting format. In H. Cooper & L. V. Hedges (Eds.), *The handbook of research synthesis*. New York: Russell Sage Foundation.

Harris, M. J., & Rosenthal, R. (1985). Mediation of interpersonal expectancy effects: 31 meta-analyses. *Psychological Bulletin, 97*, 363-386.

Hedges, L. V. (1980). Unbiased estimation of effect size. *Evaluation in Education: An International Review Series, 4,* 25-27.

Hedges, L. V. (1982). Fitting categorical models to effect sizes from a series of experiments. *Journal of Educational Statistics, 7*(2), 119-137.

Hedges, L. V. (1994). Fixed effects models. In H. Cooper & L. V. Hedges (Eds.), *The handbook of research synthesis.* New York: Russell Sage Foundation.

Hedges, L. V., & Olkin, I. (1980). Vote-counting methods in research synthesis. *Psychological Bulletin, 88,* 359-369.

Hedges, L. V., & Olkin, I. (1985). *Statistical methods for meta-analysis.* Orlando, FL: Academic Press.

Hunter, J. E., & Schmidt, F. L. (1990). *Methods of meta-analysis: Correcting for sources of error and bias in research findings.* Newbury Park, CA: Sage.

Hunter, J. E., & Schmidt, F. L. (1994). Correcting for sources of artifactual variance across studies. In H. Cooper & L. V. Hedges (Eds.), *The handbook of research synthesis.* New York: Russell Sage Foundation.

Hunter, J. E., Schmidt, F. L., & Hunter, R. (1979). Differential validity of employment tests by race: A comprehensive review and analysis. *Psychological Bulletin, 86,* 721-735.

Judd, C. M., Smith, E. R., & Kidder, L. H. (1991). *Research methods in social relations.* Fort Worth, TX: Holt, Rinehart & Winston.

Justice, A. C., Berlin, J. A., Fletcher, S. W., & Fletcher, R. A. (1994). Do readers and peer reviewers agree on manuscript quality? *Journal of the American Medical Association, 272,* 117-119.

Kalaian, H. A., & Raudenbush, S. W. (1996). A multivariate mixed linear model for meta-analysis. *Psychological Methods, 1,* 227-235.

Katz, W. A. (1997). *Introduction to reference work: Volume I.* New York: McGraw-Hill.

Kazdin, A., Durac, J., & Agteros, T. (1979). Meta-meta analysis: A new method for evaluating therapy outcome. *Behavioral Research and Therapy, 17,* 397-399.

King, D. W., McDonald, D. D., & Roderer, N. K. (1981). *Scientific journals in the United States: Their production, use, and economics.* Stroudsburg, PA: Hutchinson Ross.

Levin, H. M. (1987). Cost-benefit and cost-effectiveness analysis. *New Directions for Program Evaluation, 34,* 83-99.

Levin, H. M., Glass, G. V., & Meister, G. R. (1987). Cost-effectiveness and computer-assisted instruction. *Evaluation Review, 11,* 50-72.

Light, R. J., & Pillemer, D. B. (1984). *Summing up: The science of reviewing research.* Cambridge, MA: Harvard University Press.

Light, R. J., Singer, J. D., & Willett, J. B. (1994). The visual presentation and interpretation of meta-analysis. In H. Cooper & L. V. Hedges (Eds.), *The handbook of research synthesis.* New York: Russell Sage Foundation.

Lipsey, M. W. (1990). *Design sensitivity: Statistical power for detecting the effects of interventions.* Newbury Park, CA: Sage.

Lipsey, M. W., & Wilson, D. B. (1993). The efficacy of psychological, educational, and behavioral treatment: Confirmation from meta-analysis. *American Psychologist, 48,* 1181-1209.

Lord, C. G., Ross, L., & Lepper, M. R. (1979). Biased assimilation and attitude polarization: The effects of prior theories on subsequently considered evidence. *Journal of Personality and Social Psychology, 37,* 2098-2109.

Louis, T. A., & Zelterman, D. (1994). Bayesian approaches to research synthesis. In H. Cooper & L. V. Hedges (Eds.), *The handbook of research synthesis.* New York: Russell Sage Foundation.

Mahoney, M. J. (1977). Publication prejudices: An experimental study of confirmatory bias in the peer review system. *Cognitive Therapy and Research, 1,* 161-175.

Mann, C. (1990). Meta-analysis into the breech. *Science, 249,* 476-480.

Mansfield, R. S., & Bussey, T. V. (1977). Meta-analysis of research: A rejoinder to Glass. *Educational Researcher, 6,* 3.

Marsh, H. W., & Ball, S. (1989). The peer review process used to evaluate manuscripts submitted to academic journals: Interjudgmental reliability. *Journal of Experimental Education, 57,* 151-170.

Matheson, D., Bruce, R., & Beauchamp, K. (1978). *Experimental psychology.* New York: Holt, Rinehart & Winston.

Matt, G. E., & Cook, T. D. (1994). Threats to the validity of research synthesis. In H. Cooper & L. V. Hedges (Eds.), *The handbook of research synthesis.* New York: Russell Sage Foundation.

Menzel, H. (1966). Scientific communication: Five themes from sociology. *American Psychologist, 21,* 999-1004.

Miller, N., Lee, J. Y., & Carlson, M. (1991). The validity of inferential judgements when used in theory-testing meta-analysis. *Personality and Social Psychology Bulletin, 17,* 335-343.

Noether, G. (1971). *Introduction to statistics: A fresh approach.* Boston: Houghton Mifflin.

Normand, S. T. (1995). Meta-analysis software: A comparative review. *The American Statistician, 49,* 298-309.

Nunnally, J. (1960). The place of statistics in psychology. *Education and Psychological Measurement, 20,* 641-650.

Oakes, M. (1986). *Statistical inference: A commentary for the social and behavioural sciences.* Chichester, UK: Wiley.

Olkin, I. (1990). History and goals. In K. Wachter & M. Straf (Eds.), *The future of meta-analysis.* New York: Russell Sage Foundation.

Orwin, R. G. (1994). Evaluating coding decisions. In H. Cooper & L. V. Hedges (Eds.), *The handbook of research synthesis.* New York: Russell Sage Foundation.

Pearson, E., & Hartley, H. (1966). *Biometrika tables for statisticans, Vol. 1* (3rd ed.). Cambridge: Cambridge University Press.

Pearson, K. (1904). Report on certain enteric fever inoculation statistics. *British Medical Journal, 3,* 1243-1246.

Pearson, K. (1933). On a method of determining whether a sample of size $n$ supposed to have been drawn from a parent population having a known probability integral has probably been drawn at random. *Biometrika, 25,* 379-410.

Peters, D. P., & Ceci, S. J. (1982). Peer-review practices of psychological journals: The fate of published articles, submitted again. *Behavioral and Brain Sciences, 5,* 187-255.

Pigott, T. D. (1994). Methods for handling missing data in research synthesis. In H. Cooper & L. V. Hedges (Eds.), *The handbook of research synthesis.* New York: Russell Sage Foundation.

Price, D. (1965). Networks of scientific papers. *Science, 149,* 510-515.

Raudenbush, S. W. (1994). Random effects models. In H. Cooper & L. V. Hedges (Eds.), *The handbook of research synthesis*. New York: Russell Sage Foundation.

Raudenbush, S. W., Becker, B. J., & Kalaian, H. (1988). Modeling multivariate effect sizes. *Psychological Bulletin, 103*, 111-120.

Raudenbush, S. W., & Bryk, A. S. (1985). Empirical Bayes meta-analysis. *Journal of Educational Statistics, 10*, 75-98.

Reed, J. G., & Baxter, P. M. (1992). *Library use: A handbook for psychology* (2nd ed.). Washington, DC: American Psychological Association.

*Report of the National Enquiry Into Scholarly Communication*. (1979). Baltimore: Johns Hopkins University Press.

Rosenthal, R. (1978). How often are our numbers wrong? *American Psychologist, 33*, 1005-1008.

Rosenthal, R. (1979a). The "file drawer problem" and tolerance for null results. *Psychological Bulletin, 86*, 638-641.

Rosenthal, R. (1979b). Replications and their relative utility. *Replications in Social Psychology, 1*, 15-23.

Rosenthal, R. (1991). *Meta-analytic procedures for social research* (rev. edition). Newbury Park, CA: Sage.

Rosenthal, R. (1994). Parametric measures of effect. In H. Cooper & L. V. Hedges (Eds.), *The handbook of research synthesis*. New York: Russell Sage Foundation.

Rosenthal, R. (1995). Writing meta-analytic reviews. *Psychological Bulletin, 118*, 183-192.

Rosenthal, R., & Rubin, D. B. (1978). Interpersonal expectancy effects: The first 345 studies. *Behavioral and Brain Sciences, 3*, 377-386.

Rosenthal, R., & Rubin, D. (1982). Comparing effect sizes of independent studies. *Psychological Bulletin, 92*, 500-504.

Ross, L., & Lepper, M. R. (1980). The perseverance of beliefs: Empirical and normative considerations. *New Directions for Methodology of Social and Behavioral Science, 4*, 17-36.

Sacks, H. S., Berrier, J., Reitman, D., Ancona-Berk, V. A., & Chalmers, T. C. (1987). Meta-analysis of randomized controlled trials. *New England Journal of Medicine, 316*, 450-455.

SAS Institute. (1992). *SAS user's guide: Statistics* (Version 6). Cary, NC: Author.

Scarr, S., & Weber, B. L. R. (1978). The reliability of reviews for the *American Psychologist*. *American Psychologist, 33*, 935.

Schauder, D. (1994). Electronic publishing of professional articles: Attitudes of academics and implication for the scholarly communication industry. *Journal of the American Society for Information Science, 45*, 73-100.

Schramm, C. M. (1989, March). *An examination of differential-photocopying*. Paper presented at the annual meeting of the American Educational Research Association, San Francisco.

Smith, M. L., & Glass, G. V. (1977). Meta-analysis of psychotherapy outcome studies. *American Psychologist, 32*, 752-760.

SPSS, Inc. (1990). *SPSS*. Chicago: Author.

Stoan, S. (1982). Computer searching: A primer for uninformed scholars. *Academe, 68*, 10-15.

Stock, W. A. (1994). Systematic coding for research synthesis. In H. Cooper & L.V. Hedges (Eds.), *The handbook of research synthesis.* New York: Russell Sage Foundation.

Stock, W. A., Okun, M. A., Haring, M. J., Miller, W., & Kinney, C. (1982). Rigor and data synthesis: A case study of reliability in meta-analysis. *Educational Researcher, 11*(6), 10-14.

Stouffer, S. A., Suchman, E. A., DeVinney, L. C., Star, S. A., & Williams, R. M., Jr. (1949). *The American soldier, Vol. 1: Adjustment during army life.* Princeton, NJ: Princeton University Press.

Taveggia, T. C. (1974). Resolving research controversy through empirical cumulation. *Sociological Methods and Research, 2,* 395-407.

Walberg, H. J. (1986). Synthesis of research on teaching. In M. C. Wittrock (Ed.), *Handbook of research on teaching* (3rd ed.). New York: Macmillan.

Wang, M. C., & Bushman, B. J. (in press). *A step-by-step approach to using the SAS system for meta-analysis.* Cary, NC: SAS Institute.

Webb, E. J., Campbell, D. T., Schwartz, R. D., Sechrest, L., & Grove, J. B. (1981). *Nonreactive measures in the social sciences.* Boston: Houghton Mifflin.

Wehmeyer, L. B. (1995). *The educator's information highway.* Lancaster, PA: Technomics.

Whitehurst, G. J. (1984). Interrater agreement for journal manuscript reviews. *American Psychologist, 39,* 22-28.

Wortman, P. M. (1994). Judging research quality. In H. Cooper & L. V. Hedges (Eds.), *The handbook of research synthesis.* New York: Russell Sage Foundation.

Xhignesse, L. V., & Osgood, C. (1967). Bibliographical citation characteristics of the psychological journal network in 1950 and 1960. *American Psychologist, 22,* 779-791.

# Author Index

# Subject Index

# *About the Author*

**Harris Cooper** is Professor of Psychology and Director of the Program in Social Psychology at the University of Missouri—Columbia. He has also taught at Colgate University, been a postdoctoral fellow at Harvard University, a visiting professor at the University of Oregon, and a visiting scholar at Stanford University and the Russell Sage Foundation. He is a fellow of the American Psychological Association and the American Psychological Society. He is or has been an advising editor for seven journals in psychology and education. He was the first recipient of the American Educational Research Association's Raymond B. Cattell Early Career Award for Programmatic Research and has also received AERA's Interpretive Scholarship Award.

# APPLIED SOCIAL RESEARCH